HMH Math

Standards • Actions • Processes

4

Updated 2019 Edition
Copyright © 2019 by Houghton Mifflin Harcourt Publishing Company

Printed in the U.S.A.

ISBN 978-1-328-96596-7

7 8 9 10 0928 28 27 26 25 24 23 22 21 20

4500796906   C D E F G

Table of Contents

Chapter 4
Algebra • Use Addition, Subtraction, Multiplication, and Division

Chapter 5
Geometry and Patterns

© Houghton Mifflin Harcourt Publishing Company

Chapter 12
Three-Dimensional Figures and Volume

Chapter 13
Divide by 1-Digit Numbers

Chapter 1

Understand Decimals and Place Value

Math in the Real World

Shade the grid models below to show three different ways to represent $\frac{16}{100}$.

What skills do I know that will help me solve this problem?

_____

_____

_____

What do I need to know that can help me solve this problem?

_____

_____

_____

My solution to the problem:

Building Your Math Abilities

Before you begin to explore decimals and place value, fill in the chart with what you know about decimals and place value, and then, what you would like to learn. As you go through the chapter, add to the chart the things you have learned.

What I know . . .	What I want to know . . .	What I have learned . . .

Go Deeper

What additional questions do you have about decimals and place value? Write your questions in the space below.

_____

_____

_____

Name _____

Lesson **1.1**

Lesson Objective: Compare and order whole numbers based on the values of the digits in each number.

Compare and Order Whole Numbers

Compare 31,072 and 34,318. Write <, >, or =.

Step 1 Align the numbers by place value using grid paper.

Step 2 Compare the digits in each place value. Start at the greatest place.

Are the digits in the ten thousands place the same? **Yes**

Move to the thousands place.

Are the digits in the thousands place the same? **No**

1 thousand is less than 4 thousands.

start here

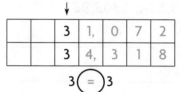

3 ⃝= 3   1 ⃝< 4

Think:
< means *is less than.*
> means *is greater than.*
= means *is equal to.*

Step 3 Use the symbols <, >, or = to compare the numbers.
There are two ways to write the comparison.

31,072 ⃝< 34,318   or   34,318 ⃝> 31,072

You can order three numbers by deciding which number is the greatest or least.
Then compare the remaining two numbers.
Order 1,237; 1,054; and 1,145 from least to greatest.
__1,054__ , __1,145__ , __1,237__

---

1. Use the grid paper to compare 21,409 and 20,891. Write <, >, or =.

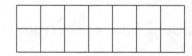

21,409 ◯ 20,891

Order from greatest to least.

2. 16,451; 16,250; 17,014

3. 561,028; 582,073; 549,006

_____   _____

Compare. Write <, >, or =.

4. 3,273 ◯< 3,279

5. $1,323 ◯ $1,400

6. 52,692 ◯ 52,692

7. $413,005 ◯ $62,910

8. 382,144 ◯ 382,144

9. 157,932 ◯ 200,013

10. 401,322 ◯ 410,322

11. 989,063 ◯ 980,639

12. 258,766 ◯ 258,596

Order from least to greatest.

13. 23,710; 23,751; 23,715

_____

14. 52,701; 54,025; 5,206

_____

15. 465,321; 456,321; 456,231

_____

_____

16. $330,820; $329,854; $303,962

_____

_____

Problem Solving  REAL WORLD

17. An online newspaper had 350,080 visitors in October, 350,489 visitors in November, and 305,939 visitors in December. What is the order of the months from greatest to least number of visitors?

_____

_____

18. The total land area in square miles of each of three states is shown below.
    Colorado: 103,718
    New Mexico: 121,356
    Arizona: 113,635
    What is the order of the states from least to greatest total land area?

_____

_____

Name _____

Lesson Objective: Record tenths as fractions and as decimals.

Relate Tenths and Decimals

A **decimal** names part of a whole. The **decimal point** separates the whole-number part from the part of a whole.

A decimal such as 0.1 is read as one tenth. It shares the same name as the fraction $\frac{1}{10}$.

Write the fraction and the decimal that are shown by the point on the number line.

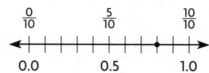

Step 1 Count the number of equal parts of the whole shown on the number line. There are ten equal parts.

This tells you that the number line shows tenths.

Step 2 Label the number line with the missing fractions. What fraction is shown by the point on the number line?

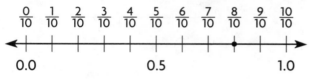

The fraction shown by the point on the number line is $\frac{8}{10}$.

Step 3 Label the number line with the missing decimals. What decimal is shown by the point on the number line?

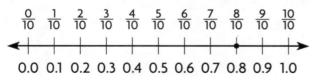

The decimal shown by the point on the number line is 0.8.

So, the fraction and decimal shown by the point on the number line are $\frac{8}{10}$ and 0.8.

Write the fraction and the decimal shown by the model.

1.
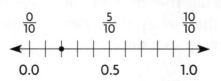

_____

2.
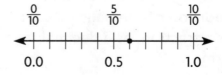

_____

© Houghton Mifflin Harcourt Publishing Company

Write the fraction and the decimal shown by the model.

3. 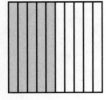   **Think:** The model is divided into 10 equal parts. Each part represents one tenth.

4.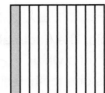

$\dfrac{5}{10}$; 0.5

_____

5.

_____

6.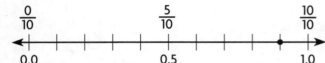

_____

Write the fraction as a decimal.

7. $\dfrac{4}{10}$ 8. $\dfrac{1}{10}$ 9. $\dfrac{7}{10}$ 10. $\dfrac{2}{10}$ 11. $\dfrac{9}{10}$

_____   _____   _____   _____   _____

Problem Solving

12. There are 10 sports balls in the equipment closet. Four are kickballs. Write the portion of the balls that are kickballs as a fraction, as a decimal, and in word form.

13. Peyton's pizza is cut into 10 equal slices. She and her friends eat 6 slices. What part of the pizza did they eat? Write your answer as a decimal.

_____   _____

Relate Hundredths and Decimals

Write the fraction and the decimal shown by the model.

Step 1 Count the number of shaded squares in the model and the total number of squares in the whole model.

Number of shaded squares: **53**

Total number of squares: **100**

Step 2 Write a fraction to represent the part of the model that is shaded.

$\dfrac{\text{Number of Shaded Squares}}{\text{Total Number of Squares}} = \dfrac{53}{100}$

The fraction shown by the model is $\dfrac{53}{100}$.

Step 3 Write the fraction in decimal form.

Think: The fraction shown by the model is $\dfrac{53}{100}$.

0.53 names the same amount as $\dfrac{53}{100}$.

The decimal shown by the model is **0.53**.

The fraction and decimal shown by the model are $\dfrac{53}{100}$ and **0.53**.

Write the fraction and the decimal shown by the model.

1.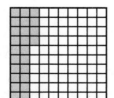

_____

2.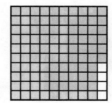

_____

Write the fraction and the decimal shown by the model.

3. 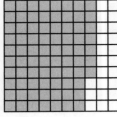 **Think:** The whole is divided into one hundred equal parts, so each part is one hundredth.

$\frac{77}{100}$; 0.77

4.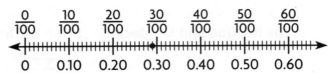

_____

5.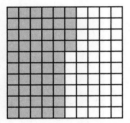

_____

6.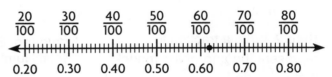

_____

Write the fraction as a decimal.

7. $\frac{37}{100}$

8. $\frac{11}{100}$

9. $\frac{98}{100}$

10. $\frac{50}{100}$

11. $\frac{6}{100}$

_____ _____ _____ _____ _____

Problem Solving REAL WORLD

12. There are 100 pennies in a dollar. What fraction of a dollar is 61 pennies? Write it as a fraction, as a decimal, and in word form.

_____

_____

13. Kylee has collected 100 souvenir thimbles from different places she has visited with her family. Twenty of the thimbles are carved from wood. Write the fraction of thimbles that are wooden as a decimal.

_____

Lesson **1.4**

Lesson Objective: Use decimal models and place-value charts to explore decimal place value.

Explore Decimal Place Value

Use a decimal model and a place-value chart to show decimals.

Shade the model to show $\frac{64}{100}$.

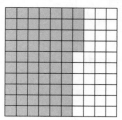

Complete the place-value chart.

Ones	.	Tenths	Hundredths
0	.	6	4

Write: _____0.64_____

Read: __sixty-four hundredths__

Write: _____0.64_____

Read: __sixty-four hundredths__

Write the decimal that is shown by the decimal model in the place-value chart.

1.

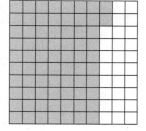

Ones	.	Tenths	Hundredths

2.

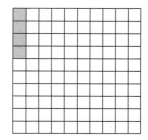

Ones	.	Tenths	Hundredths

3.

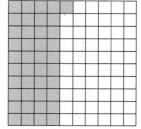

Ones	.	Tenths	Hundredths

Shade the decimal model to show the decimal.

4. 0.7

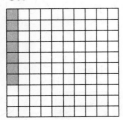

5. 0.29

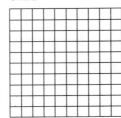

6. forty two hundredths

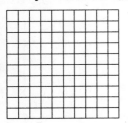

7. seventy-six hundredths

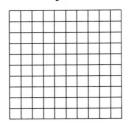

8. Complete the following for 0.17.

Fraction: _____

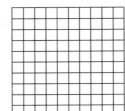

Ones	.	Tenths	Hundredths

Read: _____

Problem Solving REAL WORLD

9. Ben lives 0.8 mile from school. He shades 8 parts of this decimal model to show the distance. Is Ben's model correct? Explain why or why not.

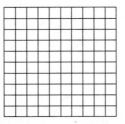

10. Eli and Amelia are reading the same book. So far, Eli has read 0.75 of the book. Amelia has read seventy-five hundredths of the book. Who has read more of the book? Tell how you know.

_____

_____

_____

_____

_____

_____

_____

_____

1. Blake answered 92 of 100 questions correctly on his science test. Which number shows the portion of the science test Blake answered correctly?

   A 92

   B 9.2

   C 9.02

   D 0.92

2. Carrie looked at three houses for sale. The least expensive house was priced at $239,450. The most expensive house was priced at $250,980. Which could be the price of the house that is in between?

   A $247,230

   B $239,199

   C $252,680

   D $260,740

3. Lynne has mowed 7/10 of her lawn. Which decimal shows what portion of the lawn has been mowed?

   A 7.10

   B 0.71

   C 0.7

   D 0.07

4. Which of the following numbers is the same as forty-three hundredths?

   A 0.43

   B 4.3

   C 43

   D 4300

5. On Monday, 12,845 people visited the Statue of Liberty. On Tuesday, there were 12,491 visitors. On Wednesday, there were more visitors than Tuesday, but less than Monday. Which number could be the number of visitors on Wednesday?

   A 12,932

   B 12,849

   C 12,587

   D 12,399

6. Jeremy is putting in a square patio. The model shows the part of the patio he has completed.

   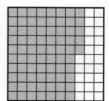

   What portion of the patio has Jeremy completed?

   A 0.25

   B 0.75

   C 0.7

   D 7.5

GO ON

7. Malik ate $\frac{5}{10}$ of his vegetables at dinner. He had the following model to represent how much he ate.

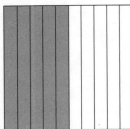

What decimal represents the part of Malik's vegetables that were eaten?

A 5.10   B 0.51

C 0.5   D 0.05

8. Three hundred honey bees have a mass of about $\frac{3}{100}$ kilogram. What is the mass, in kilograms, as a decimal?

A 0.03

B 0.3

C 3.0

D 300

9. In 2010, the population of Ponca City, OK was 25,387. The population of Shawnee, OK was 29,897 and the population of Owasso, OK was 28,915. What is the order of the cities from greatest to least by population? Explain your answer.

_____

_____

_____

10. Joyce is doing the lettering for 100 invitations. The model show how many invitations she has already done. Write this number in decimal, fraction and word form. Explain your answers.

_____

_____

Apply Your Understanding

STOP

Compare Decimals Using Benchmarks

A **benchmark** is a known size or amount that helps you understand a different size or amount. The number line below shows the decimal benchmarks 0, 0.5, and 1.0.

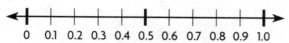

Penny hiked 0.64 miles through a wildlife preserve. Henry hiked 0.47 miles. Who hiked the greater distance?

Compare 0.64 **and** 0.47.

Step 1 Locate 0.64 and 0.47 on the number line.

Think: 0.64 is to the right of 0.5 on the number line. So, 0.64 > 0.5

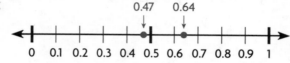

Think: 0.47 is to the left of 0.5 on the number line So, 0.47 < 0.5.

Step 2 Compare the decimals to the benchmark 0.5.

0.64 is greater than 0.5

0.47 is less than 0.5.

Step 3 Compare the decimals.

0.64 is greater than 0.47.

0.64 $\bigcirc>$ 0.47

So, Penny hiked the greater distance.

**Use the number line and the benchmarks
0, 0.5, and 1.0 to compare the decimals.
Write <, >, or =.**

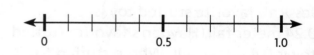

1. 0.89 $\bigcirc$ 0.35

2. 0.42 $\bigcirc$ 0.7

3. 0.1 $\bigcirc$ 1.0

4. 0.9 $\bigcirc$ 0.26

5. 0.65 $\bigcirc$ 0.65

6. 0.15 $\bigcirc$ 0.4

Use the number line and the benchmarks 0, 0.25, 0.5, 0.75, and 1.0 to compare the decimals. Write <, >, or =.

```
←┤──┤─┤┤┤─┤──┤─┤──┤┤┤─┤──┤→
  0    0.25    0.5   0.75   1.0
```

7. 0.18 $<$ 0.3

Think: 0.18 is
less than 0.25.
0.3 is more than 0.25.

8. 0.78 ◯ 0.61

9. 0.45 ◯ 0.45

10. 0.91 ◯ 0.72

11. 0.05 ◯ 0.22

12. 0.57 ◯ 0.8

13. 0.3 ◯ 0.4

14. 0.29 ◯ 0.92

15. 0.81 ◯ 0.74

16. 0.24 ◯ 0.24

17. 0.6 ◯ 0.51

18. 0.03 ◯ 0.19

Problem Solving 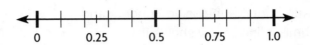 REAL WORLD

19. Jessica's favorite stuffed toy is 0.24 meter tall. Hayden's favorite stuffed toy is 0.4 meter tall. Whose stuffed toy is taller?

20. Gabrielle mixed 0.8 liter of yellow paint and 0.76 liter of blue paint to make green paint. Did she use more yellow paint or blue paint?

_____

_____

Lesson 1.6

Lesson Objective: Compare decimals to
hundredths by reasoning about their size.

Compare Decimals

Alfie found 0.20 of a dollar, and Gemma found 0.23 of a dollar.
Who found more money?

To compare decimals, you can use a number line.

Step 1   Locate each decimal on a number line.

0.0   0.10   0.20   0.30

Step 2   The number farther to the right is greater.

Since ___0.23___ (>) ___0.20___, ___Gemma___ found more money.

To compare decimals, you can use a place-value chart.

Ones	.	Tenths	Hundredths
0	.	2	0
0	.	2	3

Since ___0.23___ (>) ___0.20___, ___Gemma___ found more money.

To compare decimals, you can use a decimal model.

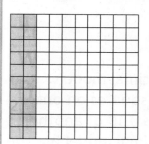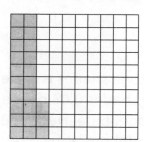

Since ___0.23___ (>) ___0.20___, ___Gemma___ found more money.

Compare. Write <, >, or =.

1. 0.17 ◯ 0.13   2. 0.80 ◯ 0.08   3. 0.36 ◯ 0.63   4. 0.40 ◯ 0.40

5. 0.75 ◯ 0.69   6. 0.3 ◯ 0.7   7. 0.45 ◯ 0.37   8. 0.96 ◯ 0.78

Compare. Write <, >, or =.

9. 0.35 ⬤< 0.53

   Think: 3 tenths is less than 5 tenths.
   So, 0.35 < 0.53.

10. 0.60 ◯ 0.60

11. 0.24 ◯ 0.31

12. 0.94 ◯ 0.92

13. 0.3 ◯ 0.4

14. 0.45 ◯ 0.28

15. 0.39 ◯ 0.93

Use the number line to compare. Write *true* or *false*.

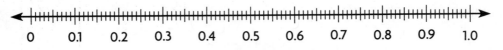

16. 0.81 > 0.78

    _____

17. 0.4 > 0.8

    _____

18. 0.72 < 0.70

    _____

19. 0.40 > 0.04

    _____

Compare. Write *true* or *false*.

20. 0.09 > 0.10

    _____

21. 0.24 = 0.42

    _____

22. 0.17 < 0.32

    _____

23. 0.85 > 0.82

    _____

Problem Solving REAL WORLD

24. Kelly walks 0.71 mile to school. Mary walks 0.49 mile to school. Write a statement using <, >, or = to compare the distances they walk to school.

    _____

25. Tyrone shades two decimal models. He shades 0.03 of the squares on one model blue. He shades 0.13 of another model red. Which decimal model has the greater part shaded? Explain.

    _____

    _____

    _____

Name _____

Lesson 1.7

Lesson Objective: Use number lines, place-value models, and decimal models to compare and order decimals to hundredths.

Order Decimals

There are different ways to order the decimals 0.48, 0.42, and 0.5 from least to greatest.

Use a number line.

Step 1 Locate and label each decimal on the number line.

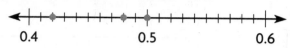

0.4   0.5   0.6

Step 2 A number to the left is less than a number to the right.

The order from least to greatest is ___0.42, 0.48, 0.5___ .

Use a place-value chart.

Step 1 Write the decimals in the chart.

Step 2 Compare the tenths.
Since 5 > 4, the greatest decimal is ___0.5___ .

Step 3 Compare the hundredths.
Since 2 < 8, the least decimal is ___0.42___ .

Ones	•	Tenths	Hundredths
0	•	4	8
0	•	4	2
0	•	5	0

So, the order from least to greatest is ___0.42, 0.48, 0.5___ .

Use a decimal model.

Step 1 Shade a decimal model to show each decimal.

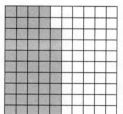 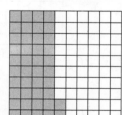 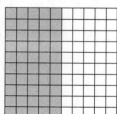

Step 2 Write the decimals in order from least to greatest. ___0.42, 0.48, 0.5___

Use the number line to order the decimals from greatest to least.

0.1 0.2 0.3 0.4 0.5 0.6 0.7 0.8

1. 0.67, 0.72, 0.59

2. 0.3, 0.34, 0.29

3. 0.18, 0.12, 0.21

_____ _____ _____

Use a place-value chart to order the decimals from greatest to least.

4. 0.84, 0.87, 0.9

Ones	.	Tenths	Hundredths
0	.	8	4
0	.	8	7
0	.	9	

_____0.9, 0.87, 0.84_____

5. 0.07, 0.1, 0.12

Ones	.	Tenths	Hundredths

_____

6. 0.64, 0.71, 0.66

Ones	.	Tenths	Hundredths

_____

Shade the decimal model to order the decimals from least to greatest.

7. 0.28, 0.03, 0.32 _____

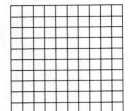 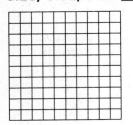 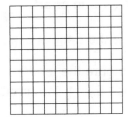

8. 0.6, 0.58, 0.5 _____

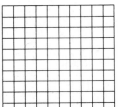 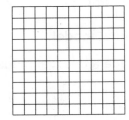

Problem Solving REAL WORLD

9. Jodi ran 0.62 mile, Marisa ran 0.58 mile, and Jordyn ran 0.67 mile. Amy ran less than 0.6 mile, but did not run the least distance. What decimal tells the part of a mile Amy ran?

_____

10. Grace painted a ten-by-ten grid different colors. She painted 0.2 of the grid green, 0.37 of the grid red, 0.19 of the grid yellow, and 0.24 of the grid blue. Order colors of the grid from greatest to least amounts.

_____

Name _____

Naming and Using Arrays in Multiplication

Write one addition sentence and one multiplication sentence to describe each array.

1. • • • • •
   • • • • •
   • • • • •

   _____ = _____

   _____ = _____

2. • • • • • • •
   • • • • • • •

   _____ = _____

   _____ = _____

Solve.

3. 2 + 2 = _____

   2 × 2 = _____

4. 2 + 2 + 2 = _____

   3 × 2 = _____

5. 2 + 2 + 2 + 2 = _____

   4 × 2 = _____

6. 2 + 2 + 2 + 2 + 2 = _____

   5 × 2 = _____

7. 9 × 2 = _____

8. 8 × 2 = _____

Draw counters to show the array. Then write the product.

9.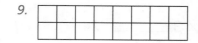

   2 × 7 = _____

10.

   6 × 2 = _____

11.

   4 × 2 = _____

Name _____

Naming and Using Arrays in Multiplication

Draw counters to show the array. Then find the product.

1.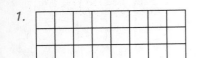

    $3 \times 6 =$ _____

2.

    $3 \times 8 =$ _____

3.

    $3 \times 5 =$ _____

Multiply. Think of doubles or the Order Property.

4. $2 \times 7 =$ _____

5. $6 \times 2 =$ _____

6. $2 \times 9 =$ _____

7. $4 \times 2 =$ _____

8. $2 \times 8 =$ _____

9. $2 \times 5 =$ _____

10. $2 \times 3 =$ _____

11. $9 \times 2 =$ _____

12. $2 \times 2 =$ _____

13. $5 \times 3 =$ _____

14. $4 \times 3 =$ _____

15. $3 \times 7 =$ _____

Use estimation. Write $<$ or $>$.

16. $4 \times 3 = 12$, so 3×3 _____ 12

17. $7 \times 2 = 14$, so 7×3 _____ 14

18. $3 \times 2 = 6$, so 4×2 _____ 6

19. $8 \times 3 = 24$, so 9×3 _____ 24

20. $3 \times 3 = 9$, so 4×3 _____ 9

21. $6 \times 3 = 18$, so 7×3 _____ 18

Read each question and choose the best answer.

1. Arnold lives $\frac{8}{10}$ miles from his friend, John. What is this distance written as a decimal?

   A 8.10

   B 0.81

   C 0.8

   D 0.08

2. Sheldon has $0.54 in his pocket. Who has more money in their pocket than Sheldon?

   A Connor: $0.61

   B Travis: $0.49

   C Elsa: $0.28

   D Rachel: $0.52

3. Which decimal is shown by the model?

   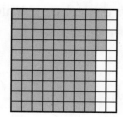

   A 8.4

   B 0.84

   C 0.084

   D 0.0084

4. Colby rearranged six tiles to make the number 516,243. Norah used the same tiles to make the number 543,612. Kelvin also used the same tiles to make a number. Kelvin's number is greater than Colby's number, but less than Norah's number. Which could be Colby's number?

   A 534,621

   B 561,423

   C 512,634

   D 546,321

5. Which number is greater than 0.7, but less than 0.82

   A 0.08

   B 0.74

   C 0.84

   D 0.9

6. Which of the following numbers is the same as fifty-one hundredths?

   A 0.51

   B 5.1

   C 51

   D 5,100

GO ON

7. On Tuesday, there was 0.32 inch of rain. Which measurement could be used as an estimate for this amount rainfall?

   A 0.75 inch

   B 0.5 inch

   C 0.25 inch

   D 0 inches

8. Krysta is writing a decimal to represent thirty hundredths. Which choice shows an equivalent decimal?

   A 0.03

   B 0.3

   C 3.0

   D 30

9. Several schools are all trying to each raise $12,500 to donate to a charity. Jefferson Elementary raised $12,679, Barclay Elementary raised $12,096, Brasser Elementary raised $12,504, and Edison Elementary raised $13,420. Which school did not meet their goal?

   A Jefferson

   B Barclay

   C Brasser

   D Edison

10. Kyra completed 0.48 of her assignment. Which student has completed more than Kyra?

    A Daniel: 0.60

    B Geoff: 0.42

    C Zirah: 0.39

    D Lolita: 0.09

11. Which lists the decimals in order from least to greatest?

    A 0.4, 0.37, 0.09, 0.61

    B 0.09, 0.37, 0.4, 0.61

    C 0.4, 0.09, 0.61, 0.37

    D 0.09, 0.4, 0.37, 0.61

12. Of the songs on Tonya's computer, eight hundredths are hip hop. Which is this number in standard form?

    A 800

    B 8.0

    C 0.8

    D 0.08

GO ON

13. Kuna used 3 of the 10 pieces of paper to draw pictures.

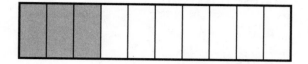

What decimal represents the portion of the paper that Kuna used?

A 3.10

B 0.31

C 0.3

D 0.03

14. Eliana is comparing numbers. Which statement is true?

A 0.67 > 0.73

B 0.22 = 0.20

C 0.49 > 0.62

D 0.38 < 0.53

15. Brad finished the race $\frac{3}{100}$ of a second faster than everyone else. What is this fraction written as a decimal?

A 0.03

B 0.3

C 3.0

D 300

16. Which decimal is closest to 0.75?

A 0.52

B 0.91

C 0.6

D 0.8

17. During a close town election, Mr. Hawthorne received 24,381 votes and Mrs. Smithson received 25,143 votes. Mr. Tindal received more votes than Mr. Hawthorne but less votes than Mrs. Smithson. Which could be the number of votes Mr. Tindal received?

A 24,297

B 25,472

C 24,106

D 25,098

GO ON

18. Joe made 9 out of 10 shots. Which decimal represents the portion of shots that Joe made?

A 9.10

B 0.910

C 0.9

D 0.09

19. Burrell lives 0.7 mile from the library and Joel lives 0.48 mile from the library. Akuna lives farther from the library than Joel, but closer than Burrell. Which could be the distance, in miles, Akuna lives from the library?

A 0.32 mile

B 0.06 mile

C 0.84 mile

D 0.5 mile

20. Tyrese has already read 67 pages of a book 100-page book. Which decimal represents the portion of the book Tyrese has read?

A 6.7

B 0.67

C 0.07

D 0.06

STOP

Chapter 2

Fraction Equivalence and Comparison

Math in the Real World

After dinner, $\frac{2}{3}$ of the corn bread is left. Suppose 4 friends want to share it equally. What fraction names how much of the whole pan of corn bread each friend will get? Use the model on the right. Explain your answer.

What skills do I know that will help me solve this problem?

_____

_____

_____

What do I need to know that can help me solve this problem?

_____

_____

_____

_____

My solution to the problem:

Building Your Math Abilities

Before you begin to explore fraction equivalence and comparisons, fill in the chart with what you know about fraction equivalence and comparisons, and then, what you would like to learn. As you go through the chapter, add to the chart the things you have learned.

What I know . . .	What I want to know . . .	What I have learned . . .

Go Deeper

What additional questions do you have about fraction equivalence and comparisons? Write your questions in the space below.

_____

_____

_____

_____

Lesson 2.1

Lesson Objective: Locate fractions on a number line using benchmark fractions.

Use Benchmarks to Locate Fractions on a Number Line

A benchmark is a known size or amount that helps you understand a different size or amount. You can use the benchmarks 0, $\frac{1}{4}$, $\frac{1}{3}$, $\frac{1}{2}$, $\frac{2}{3}$, $\frac{3}{4}$, and 1 to help you locate other fractions on a number line.

Locate and label $\frac{5}{6}$ on the number line.

Think: $\frac{1}{2}$ is the same as $\frac{2}{4}$, $\frac{3}{6}$, $\frac{4}{8}$, $\frac{5}{10}$, and $\frac{6}{12}$.

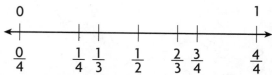

This number line is divided into thirds, or three equal lengths. If this number line were divided into sixths, there would be six equal lengths. So, each third would be divided into two smaller equal lengths.

$\frac{5}{6}$ is 5 out of 6 equal lengths. Picture 5 equal lengths from zero. Draw a point at $\frac{5}{6}$ to represent the distance from 0 to $\frac{5}{6}$. Label the point.

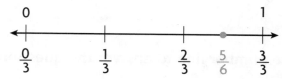

So, $\frac{5}{6}$ is located between $\frac{2}{3}$ and 1.

A **fraction greater than 1** has a numerator that is greater than the denominator.

Locate and label $\frac{7}{6}$ on the number line.

$\frac{7}{6}$ is greater than 1. So, $\frac{7}{6}$ is to the right of $\frac{3}{3}$ on this number line. Picture 7 sixth-size lengths from zero. Draw a point at $\frac{7}{6}$ to represent the distance from 0 to $\frac{7}{6}$. Label the point.

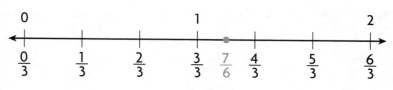

So, $\frac{7}{6}$ is located between 1 and $\frac{4}{3}$.

Use the benchmarks to locate and label the fraction on the number line. Then circle the two benchmarks the point is between.

 1. $\frac{1}{10}$
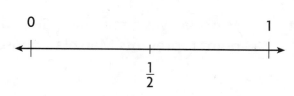

2. $\frac{3}{8}$
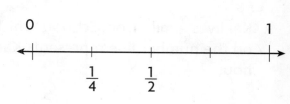

Use the benchmark fractions to locate and label the fractions on the number line.

3. $\frac{2}{8}$, $\frac{6}{10}$

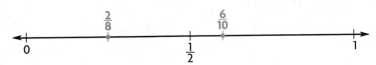

4. $\frac{1}{6}$, $\frac{12}{12}$

5. $\frac{4}{8}$, $\frac{8}{12}$

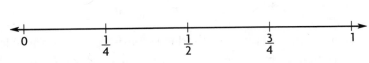

6. $\frac{9}{6}$, $\frac{10}{6}$

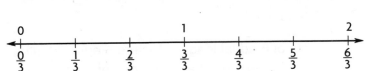

Use the number line to answer the question.

7. At which fraction is point *A*?

_____

8. At which fraction is point *R*?

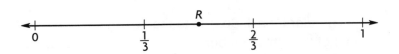

_____

Problem Solving REAL WORLD

Use the benchmark fractions on the number line for 9–10.

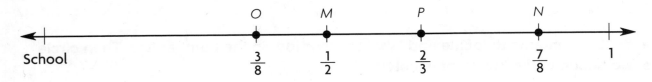

9. Kai lives $\frac{7}{8}$ mile from School. Which point on the number line represents Kai's house?

10. Marcela lives $\frac{2}{3}$ mile from School. Which point represents Marcela's house?

_____   _____

Name _____

Lesson 2.2

Lesson Objective: Model equivalent fractions by folding paper, using area models, and using number lines.

Investigate • Model Equivalent Fractions

> **Equivalent fractions** are two or more fractions that name the same amount.
>
> You can use fraction circles to model equivalent fractions.
>
> **Find a fraction that is equivalent to $\frac{1}{2}$.** $\frac{1}{2} = \frac{\blacksquare}{4}$
>
> **Step 1** Look at the first circle. It is divided into 2 equal parts. Shade one part to show $\frac{1}{2}$.
>
> **Step 2** Draw a line to divide the circle into 4 equal parts because 4 is the denominator in the second fraction.
>
> **Step 3** Count the number of parts shaded now. There are 2 parts out of 4 parts shaded.
>
> $\frac{1}{2} = \frac{2}{4}$ So, $\frac{1}{2}$ is equivalent to $\frac{2}{4}$.

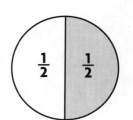

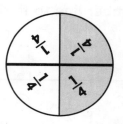

Shade the model. Then divide the pieces to find the equivalent fraction.

1.

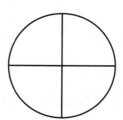

$\frac{1}{4} = \frac{\blacksquare}{8}$

2.

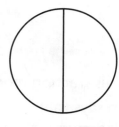

$\frac{1}{2} = \frac{\blacksquare}{8}$

3.

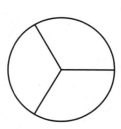

$\frac{2}{3} = \frac{\blacksquare}{6}$

4.

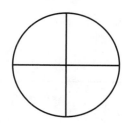

$\frac{3}{4} = \frac{\blacksquare}{8}$

Shade the model. Then divide the pieces to find the equivalent fraction.

5.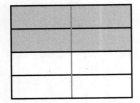

$$\frac{2}{4} = \frac{4}{8}$$

6.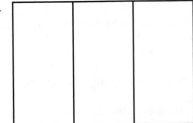

$$\frac{1}{3} = \frac{\boxed{}}{6}$$

Use the number line to find the equivalent fraction.

7.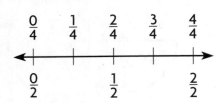

$$\frac{1}{2} = \frac{\boxed{}}{4}$$

8.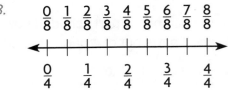

$$\frac{3}{4} = \frac{\boxed{}}{8}$$

Problem Solving REAL WORLD

9. Mike says that $\frac{3}{3}$ of his fraction model is shaded blue. Ryan says that $\frac{6}{6}$ of the same model is shaded blue. Are the two fractions equivalent? If so, what is another equivalent fraction?

_____

10. Brett shaded $\frac{4}{8}$ of a sheet of notebook paper. Aisha says he shaded $\frac{1}{2}$ of the paper. Are the two fractions equivalent? If so, what is another equivalent fraction?

_____

Lesson 2.3

Lesson Objective: Generate equivalent fractions by using area models and fraction strips.

Equivalent Fractions

Kaitlyn used $\frac{3}{4}$ of a sheet of wrapping paper.

Find a fraction that is equivalent to $\frac{3}{4}$. $\frac{3}{4} = \frac{\blacksquare}{8}$

Step 1 The top fraction strip is divided into 4 equal parts. Shade $\frac{3}{4}$ of the strip to show how much paper Kaitlyn used.

| $\frac{1}{4}$ | $\frac{1}{4}$ | $\frac{1}{4}$ | $\frac{1}{4}$ |

Step 2 The bottom strip is divided into 8 equal parts. Shade parts of the strip until the same amount is shaded as in the top strip.

6 parts of the bottom strip are shaded.

| $\frac{1}{8}$ | $\frac{1}{8}$ | $\frac{1}{8}$ | $\frac{1}{8}$ | $\frac{1}{8}$ | $\frac{1}{8}$ | $\frac{1}{8}$ | $\frac{1}{8}$ |

$$\frac{3}{4} = \frac{6}{8}$$

So, $\frac{6}{8}$ is equivalent to $\frac{3}{4}$.

Each shape is 1 whole. Shade the model to find the equivalent fraction.

1.
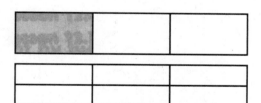

$$\frac{1}{3} = \frac{\blacksquare}{6}$$

2.
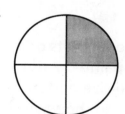

$$\frac{1}{4} = \frac{\blacksquare}{8}$$

3.
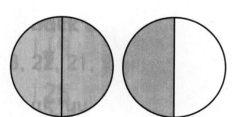

$$\frac{3}{2} = \frac{\blacksquare}{8}$$

Each shape is 1 whole. Shade the model to find the equivalent fraction.

4.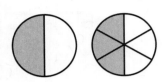

$$\frac{1}{2} = \frac{3}{6}$$

5.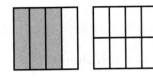

$$\frac{3}{4} = \frac{6}{\boxed{}}$$

Circle equal groups to find the equivalent fraction.

6.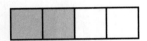

$$\frac{2}{4} = \frac{\boxed{}}{2}$$

7.

$$\frac{4}{6} = \frac{\boxed{}}{3}$$

Problem Solving REAL WORLD

8. May painted 4 out of 8 equal parts of a poster board blue. Jared painted 2 out of 4 equal parts of a same-size poster board red. Write fractions to show which part of the poster board each person painted.

_____

9. Are the fractions equivalent? Draw a model to explain.

_____

Equivalent Fractions and Set Models

Mr. Wright is ordering supplies for the school store. Two out of five of the pencils in each box he orders are yellow. What fraction of the pencils in 2 boxes are yellow?

Step 1 Draw circles to represent the pencils in each box.

1 box  Think: $\frac{2}{5}$ of the pencils are yellow.

Step 2 Shade the circles to represent the yellow pencils.

2 boxes  Think: $\frac{4}{10}$ of the pencils are yellow.

The fractions $\frac{2}{5}$ and $\frac{4}{10}$ are equivalent, $\frac{2}{5} = \frac{4}{10}$.

So, $\frac{4}{10}$ of the pencils in 2 boxes are yellow.

Shade the circles to show the equivalent fraction.

1. $\frac{3}{4} =$

_____

2. $\frac{2}{3} =$

_____

Draw a quick picture and then write the equivalent fraction.

3. $\frac{3}{12} =$

_____

4. $\frac{8}{10} =$

_____

Shade the circles to show the equivalent fraction.

5. $\frac{1}{2} = \frac{4}{8}$

_____

6. $\frac{3}{5} =$

_____

7. $\frac{1}{4} =$

_____

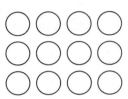

Draw a quick picture. Then write the equivalent fraction.

8. $\frac{3}{6} =$

_____

9. $\frac{8}{12} =$

_____

10. $\frac{1}{5} =$

_____

Problem Solving

11. A 12-pack of pudding has different flavors. Every third cup in the pack is vanilla. What are two equivalent fractions that represent the fraction of pudding cups in the pack that is vanilla?

_____

12. There are 6 scented markers in a pack of 9 markers. What are two equivalent fractions that represent the fraction of scented markers in the pack of markers?

_____

1. Which fraction is equivalent to the fraction shown in the model?

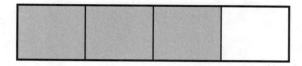

   A $\frac{6}{8}$

   B $\frac{5}{8}$

   C $\frac{4}{8}$

   D $\frac{3}{12}$

2. Between which two numbers will $\frac{7}{8}$ be located?

   A 0 and $\frac{1}{4}$

   B $\frac{1}{4}$ and $\frac{1}{2}$

   C $\frac{1}{2}$ and $\frac{3}{4}$

   D $\frac{3}{4}$ and 1

3. Two of the 8 books Lisa read were mysteries. Which fraction could also be used to describe the number of books that Lisa read that are mysteries?

   A $\frac{1}{4}$

   B $\frac{1}{3}$

   C $\frac{1}{2}$

   D $\frac{2}{3}$

4. Maya used $\frac{3}{4}$ of the carton of milk to make pudding. Which fraction is equivalent to $\frac{3}{4}$?

   A $\frac{5}{8}$

   B $\frac{8}{12}$

   C $\frac{7}{10}$

   D $\frac{9}{12}$

5. Which fraction would be located between $\frac{1}{2}$ and $\frac{3}{4}$ on the number line?

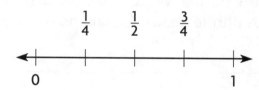

   A $\frac{5}{8}$ B $\frac{2}{8}$

   C $\frac{1}{3}$ D $\frac{5}{3}$

6. Miranda says that $\frac{2}{8}$ of the pizza has been taken. Which fraction could be used to describe the remaining pizza?

   A $\frac{1}{4}$ B $\frac{1}{2}$

   C $\frac{2}{3}$ D $\frac{3}{4}$

GO ON

Apply Your Understanding

Name _____

7. Six out of 10 of the plants Abby planted are tomatoes. Which fraction is equivalent to the fraction of the plants that are tomatoes?

A $\frac{2}{5}$

B $\frac{1}{2}$

C $\frac{3}{5}$

D $\frac{2}{3}$

8. Between which two numbers will $\frac{3}{10}$ be located?

0   1

A 0 and $\frac{1}{4}$ B $\frac{1}{4}$ and $\frac{1}{2}$

C $\frac{1}{2}$ and $\frac{3}{4}$ D $\frac{3}{4}$ and 1

9. Lydia is making a bracelet. She used a total of 20 beads and 5 of the beads were purple. Write two equivalent fractions for the part of the bracelet that has purple beads. Explain how you found the equivalent fractions.

_____

_____

_____

_____

_____

_____

10. In a group of 12 people, every third person was given a green marker to write with. What are two equivalent fractions that represent the fraction of people that have a green marker? Explain how you found the equivalent fractions.

_____

_____

_____

_____

_____

Apply Your Understanding

Compare Fractions Using Benchmarks

A **benchmark** is a known size or amount that helps you understand a different size or amount. Benchmark fractions include $0, \frac{1}{4}, \frac{1}{3}, \frac{1}{2}, \frac{2}{3}, \frac{3}{4}$, and 1.

Sara reads for $\frac{3}{6}$ hour every day after school. Connor reads for $\frac{2}{3}$ hour. Who reads for a greater amount of time?

Compare the fractions. $\frac{3}{6}$ ● $\frac{2}{3}$

Step 1 Divide one circle into 6 equal parts. Divide another circle into 3 equal parts.

Step 2 Shade $\frac{3}{6}$ of the first circle. How many parts will you shade? **3 parts**

Step 3 Shade $\frac{2}{3}$ of the second circle. How many parts will you shade? **2 parts**

Step 4 Compare the shaded parts of each circle. Half of Sara's circle is shaded. More than half of Connor's circle is shaded.

$\frac{3}{6}$ is less than $\frac{2}{3}$. $\frac{3}{6}$ ⟨<⟩ $\frac{2}{3}$

So, **Connor** reads for a greater amount of time.

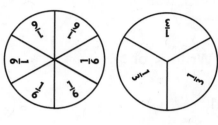

Sara   Connor

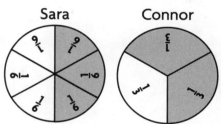

1. Compare $\frac{2}{8}$ and $\frac{3}{4}$. Write < or >.

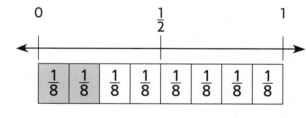
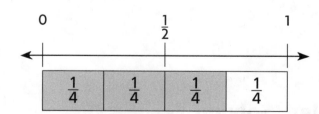

$\frac{2}{8}$ ◯ $\frac{3}{4}$

Compare. Write < or >.

2. $\frac{1}{4}$ ◯ $\frac{4}{5}$ 3. $\frac{7}{8}$ ◯ $\frac{1}{3}$ 4. $\frac{5}{12}$ ◯ $\frac{1}{2}$

5. $\frac{1}{4}$ ◯ $\frac{2}{3}$ 6. $\frac{2}{3}$ ◯ $\frac{1}{2}$ 7. $\frac{7}{12}$ ◯ $\frac{1}{2}$

Compare. Write < or >.
Shade in the models and compare the fractions.

8. $\frac{1}{8}$ $\left(<\right)$ $\frac{3}{5}$

$\frac{1}{8}$	$\frac{1}{8}$	$\frac{1}{8}$	$\frac{1}{8}$	$\frac{1}{8}$	$\frac{1}{8}$	$\frac{1}{8}$	$\frac{1}{8}$

$\frac{1}{5}$	$\frac{1}{5}$	$\frac{1}{5}$	$\frac{1}{5}$	$\frac{1}{5}$

9. $\frac{1}{3}$ $\bigcirc$ $\frac{2}{5}$

$\frac{1}{3}$	$\frac{1}{3}$	$\frac{1}{3}$

$\frac{1}{5}$	$\frac{1}{5}$	$\frac{1}{5}$	$\frac{1}{5}$	$\frac{1}{5}$

10. $\frac{3}{8}$ $\bigcirc$ $\frac{1}{2}$

$\frac{1}{8}$	$\frac{1}{8}$	$\frac{1}{8}$	$\frac{1}{8}$	$\frac{1}{8}$	$\frac{1}{8}$	$\frac{1}{8}$	$\frac{1}{8}$

$\frac{1}{2}$	$\frac{1}{2}$

Compare. Write < or >.

11. $\frac{3}{5}$ $\bigcirc$ 1

12. $\frac{7}{8}$ $\bigcirc$ $\frac{1}{2}$

13. $\frac{3}{4}$ $\bigcirc$ $\frac{1}{3}$

14. $\frac{2}{3}$ $\bigcirc$ $\frac{7}{8}$

15. $\frac{1}{5}$ $\bigcirc$ $\frac{2}{3}$

16. $\frac{3}{5}$ $\bigcirc$ $\frac{1}{4}$

17. $\frac{1}{2}$ $\bigcirc$ $\frac{2}{5}$

18. $\frac{1}{8}$ $\bigcirc$ $\frac{5}{6}$

19. $\frac{2}{3}$ $\bigcirc$ $\frac{5}{12}$

20. $\frac{1}{3}$ $\bigcirc$ $\frac{5}{6}$

21. $\frac{3}{5}$ $\bigcirc$ $\frac{3}{4}$

22. 1 $\bigcirc$ $\frac{3}{4}$

Problem Solving REAL WORLD

23. Erika ran $\frac{1}{2}$ mile. Maria ran $\frac{7}{10}$ mile. Who ran farther?

_____

24. Carlos finished $\frac{1}{3}$ of his art project on Monday. Tyler finished $\frac{1}{2}$ of his art project on Monday. Who finished more of his art project on Monday?

_____

38

Name _____

Lesson Objective: Compare fractions by first writing them as fractions with a common numerator or a common denominator.

Compare Fractions

Theo filled a beaker $\frac{2}{4}$ full with water. Angelica filled a beaker $\frac{3}{8}$ full with water. Whose beaker has more water?

Compare $\frac{2}{4}$ and $\frac{3}{8}$.

Step 1 Divide one beaker into 4 equal parts. Divide another beaker into 8 equal parts.

Step 2 Shade $\frac{2}{4}$ of the first beaker.

Step 3 Shade $\frac{3}{8}$ of the second beaker.

Step 4 Compare the shaded parts of each beaker. Half of Theo's beaker is shaded. Less than half of Angelica's beaker is shaded.

$\frac{2}{4}$ is greater than $\frac{3}{8}$.

$\frac{2}{4}$ ⊖ $\frac{3}{8}$

So, __Theo's__ beaker has more water.

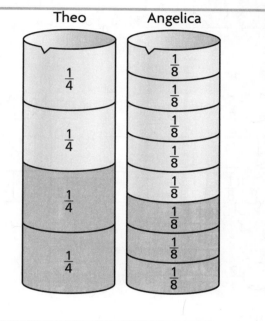

---

1. Compare $\frac{1}{2}$ and $\frac{1}{4}$.

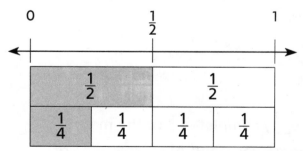

Which is greater? _____

2. Compare $\frac{2}{3}$ and $\frac{3}{6}$.

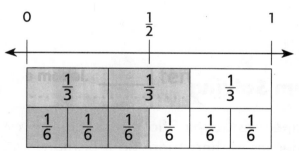

Which is less? _____

Compare. Write <, >, or =.

3. $\frac{1}{2}$ ◯ $\frac{3}{4}$ 4. $\frac{1}{2}$ ◯ $\frac{5}{8}$ 5. $\frac{2}{3}$ ◯ $\frac{4}{6}$ 6. $\frac{3}{8}$ ◯ $\frac{1}{4}$

Compare. Write <, >, or =.
Shade in the models and compare the fractions.

7. $\frac{3}{4}$ ◯< $\frac{5}{6}$

| $\frac{1}{4}$ | $\frac{1}{4}$ | $\frac{1}{4}$ | $\frac{1}{4}$ |

| $\frac{1}{6}$ | $\frac{1}{6}$ | $\frac{1}{6}$ | $\frac{1}{6}$ | $\frac{1}{6}$ | $\frac{1}{6}$ |

8. $\frac{1}{4}$ ◯ $\frac{2}{8}$

| $\frac{1}{4}$ | $\frac{1}{4}$ | $\frac{1}{4}$ | $\frac{1}{4}$ |

| $\frac{1}{8}$ | $\frac{1}{8}$ | $\frac{1}{8}$ | $\frac{1}{8}$ | $\frac{1}{8}$ | $\frac{1}{8}$ | $\frac{1}{8}$ | $\frac{1}{8}$ |

9. $\frac{2}{3}$ ◯ $\frac{1}{4}$

| $\frac{1}{3}$ | $\frac{1}{3}$ | $\frac{1}{3}$ |

| $\frac{1}{4}$ | $\frac{1}{4}$ | $\frac{1}{4}$ | $\frac{1}{4}$ |

10. $\frac{2}{3}$ ◯ $\frac{5}{8}$

| $\frac{1}{3}$ | $\frac{1}{3}$ | $\frac{1}{3}$ |

| $\frac{1}{8}$ | $\frac{1}{8}$ | $\frac{1}{8}$ | $\frac{1}{8}$ | $\frac{1}{8}$ | $\frac{1}{8}$ | $\frac{1}{8}$ | $\frac{1}{8}$ |

11. $\frac{1}{3}$ ◯ $\frac{2}{5}$

| $\frac{1}{3}$ | $\frac{1}{3}$ | $\frac{1}{3}$ |

| $\frac{1}{5}$ | $\frac{1}{5}$ | $\frac{1}{5}$ | $\frac{1}{5}$ | $\frac{1}{5}$ |

12. $\frac{2}{8}$ ◯ $\frac{1}{4}$

| $\frac{1}{8}$ | $\frac{1}{8}$ | $\frac{1}{8}$ | $\frac{1}{8}$ | $\frac{1}{8}$ | $\frac{1}{8}$ | $\frac{1}{8}$ | $\frac{1}{8}$ |

| $\frac{1}{4}$ | $\frac{1}{4}$ | $\frac{1}{4}$ | $\frac{1}{4}$ |

13. $\frac{3}{5}$ ◯ $\frac{2}{3}$

14. $\frac{1}{3}$ ◯ $\frac{1}{6}$

15. $\frac{2}{6}$ ◯ $\frac{1}{3}$

16. $\frac{1}{3}$ ◯ $\frac{1}{2}$

17. $\frac{2}{5}$ ◯ $\frac{1}{2}$

18. $\frac{4}{8}$ ◯ $\frac{2}{4}$

19. $\frac{5}{4}$ ◯ $\frac{4}{4}$

20. $\frac{1}{8}$ ◯ $\frac{3}{4}$

Problem Solving REAL WORLD

21. A recipe uses $\frac{2}{3}$ cup of flour and $\frac{1}{4}$ cup of blueberries. Is there more flour or more blueberries in the recipe?

22. Peggy completed $\frac{5}{6}$ of the math homework, and Al completed $\frac{1}{2}$ of the math homework. Did Peggy or Al complete more of the math homework?

_____

_____

Lesson 2.7

Lesson Objective: Compare and order fractions by using models and reasoning strategies.

Compare and Order Fractions

You can use a number line to compare and order fractions.

Order $\frac{5}{8}$, $\frac{2}{8}$, and $\frac{9}{8}$ from least to greatest.

Since you are comparing eighths, use a number line divided into eighths.

Step 1 Draw a point on the number line to show $\frac{5}{8}$.

Step 2 Repeat for $\frac{2}{8}$ and $\frac{9}{8}$.

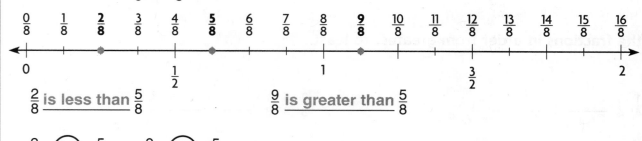

$\frac{2}{8}$ is less than $\frac{5}{8}$ $\frac{9}{8}$ is greater than $\frac{5}{8}$

$\frac{2}{8}$ $\bigcirc<$ $\frac{5}{8}$ and $\frac{9}{8}$ $\bigcirc>$ $\frac{5}{8}$

Step 3 Fractions increase in size as you move right on the number line. Write the fractions in order from left to right.

So, the order from least to greatest is $\frac{2}{8}$, $\frac{5}{8}$, $\frac{9}{8}$.

Draw points on the number lines to show fractions. Then write *is greater than* or *is less than* to compare fractions.

1.

$\frac{1}{4}$ $\frac{1}{2}$ $\frac{3}{4}$

0   1

$\frac{4}{5}$ _____ $\frac{3}{5}$

2.

$\frac{0}{4}$ $\frac{1}{4}$ $\frac{2}{4}$ $\frac{3}{4}$ $\frac{4}{4}$

0          $\frac{1}{2}$ 1

$\frac{3}{4}$ _____ $\frac{0}{4}$

Use <, >, or = to compare fractions.

3. $\frac{1}{2}$ $\bigcirc$ $\frac{1}{12}$

4. $\frac{2}{12}$ $\bigcirc$ $\frac{2}{4}$

Write *is greater than* or *is less than* to compare fractions.

5. $\frac{2}{4}$ __<__ $\frac{4}{4}$

6. $\frac{9}{8}$ _____ $\frac{5}{8}$

Use <, >, or = to compare fractions.

7. $\frac{7}{8}$ ◯ $\frac{3}{8}$

8. $\frac{3}{4}$ ◯ $\frac{3}{4}$

Write the fractions in order from greatest to least.

9. $\frac{4}{4}, \frac{1}{4}, \frac{3}{4}$ _____, _____, _____

10. $\frac{2}{8}, \frac{5}{8}, \frac{1}{8}$ _____, _____, _____

11. $\frac{1}{3}, \frac{1}{5}, \frac{1}{2}$ _____, _____, _____

12. $\frac{2}{3}, \frac{2}{10}, \frac{2}{8}$ _____, _____, _____

Problem Solving REAL WORLD

13. Mr. Jackson ran $\frac{7}{8}$ mile on Monday. He ran $\frac{3}{8}$ mile on Wednesday and $\frac{5}{8}$ mile on Friday. On which day did Mr. Jackson run the shortest distance?

_____

14. Delia has three pieces of ribbon. Her red ribbon is $\frac{2}{4}$ foot long. Her green ribbon is $\frac{2}{3}$ foot long. Her yellow ribbon is $\frac{2}{10}$ foot long. She wants to use the longest piece for a project. What color ribbon should Delia use?

_____

Fractions: Comparing and Ordering

Use the list. Write the common multiple(s) and the least common multiple.

Multiples of 3: 3, 6, 9, 12, 15, 18   Multiples of 4: 4, 8, 12, 16, 20, 24

Multiples of 5: 5, 10, 15, 20, 25, 30   Multiples of 6: 6, 12, 18, 24, 30, 36

Multiples of 10: 10, 20, 30, 40, 50, 60   Multiples of 12: 12, 24, 36, 48, 60, 72

1. 3 and 5   *2.* 3 and 6   *3.* 4 and 12

_____   _____   _____

_____   _____   _____

4. 5 and 6   *5.* 5 and 10   *6.* 6 and 10

_____   _____   _____

_____   _____   _____

Write the least common multiple.

7. 3 and 8 _____   *8.* 6 and 8 _____   *9.* 6 and 7 _____

10. 4 and 5 _____   *11.* 3 and 7 _____   *12.* 4 and 9 _____

Compare. Write whether the fraction is closest to 0, $\frac{1}{2}$, or 1.

13. $\frac{1}{12}$ _____   *14.* $\frac{2}{4}$ _____   *15.* $\frac{7}{8}$ _____

16. $\frac{1}{3}$ _____   *17.* $\frac{2}{5}$ _____   *18.* $\frac{1}{7}$ _____

Name _____

Fractions: Comparing and Ordering

Compare. Write >, <, or =.

1. $\dfrac{1}{6} \bigcirc \dfrac{5}{6}$

2. $\dfrac{2}{3} \bigcirc \dfrac{4}{6}$

3. $\dfrac{3}{4} \bigcirc \dfrac{2}{4}$

4. $\dfrac{5}{7} \bigcirc \dfrac{2}{3}$

5. $\dfrac{7}{8} \bigcirc \dfrac{4}{5}$

6. $\dfrac{5}{6} \bigcirc \dfrac{7}{9}$

7. $\dfrac{1}{4} \bigcirc \dfrac{3}{8}$

8. $\dfrac{2}{3} \bigcirc \dfrac{4}{5}$

9. $\dfrac{3}{4} \bigcirc \dfrac{7}{8}$

Order from least to greatest.

10. $\dfrac{7}{8}, \dfrac{4}{5}, \dfrac{6}{10}$

11. $\dfrac{2}{3}, \dfrac{5}{6}, \dfrac{2}{9}$

12. $\dfrac{3}{4}, \dfrac{2}{9}, \dfrac{10}{12}$

_____   _____   _____

Order from greatest to least.

13. $\dfrac{7}{10}, \dfrac{4}{5}, \dfrac{1}{2}$

14. $\dfrac{3}{8}, \dfrac{1}{4}, \dfrac{13}{16}$

15. $\dfrac{1}{2}, \dfrac{6}{8}, \dfrac{2}{3}$

_____   _____   _____

16. $\dfrac{1}{3}, \dfrac{1}{5}, \dfrac{1}{4}$

17. $\dfrac{2}{3}, \dfrac{3}{4}, \dfrac{7}{8}$

18. $\dfrac{5}{6}, \dfrac{9}{10}, \dfrac{4}{5}$

_____   _____   _____

19. $\dfrac{2}{3}, \dfrac{1}{12}, \dfrac{4}{9}$

20. $\dfrac{3}{4}, \dfrac{1}{3}, \dfrac{11}{12}$

21. $\dfrac{3}{5}, \dfrac{1}{2}, \dfrac{1}{3}, \dfrac{7}{10}$

_____   _____   _____

Read each question and choose the best answer.

1. Carina is making a smoothie. She combines $\frac{3}{8}$ cup of blueberries, $\frac{5}{6}$ cup of strawberries, and $\frac{1}{2}$ cup of bananas. Which list shows the amounts of ingredients in order from least to greatest?

   A $\frac{1}{2}, \frac{3}{8}, \frac{5}{6}$

   B $\frac{1}{2}, \frac{5}{6}, \frac{3}{8}$

   C $\frac{3}{8}, \frac{1}{2}, \frac{5}{6}$

   D $\frac{3}{8}, \frac{5}{6}, \frac{1}{2}$

2. Kyla mowed $\frac{3}{5}$ of her lawn. Which fraction is equivalent to $\frac{3}{5}$?

   A $\frac{3}{10}$

   B $\frac{4}{10}$

   C $\frac{9}{15}$

   D $\frac{9}{16}$

3. Which fraction is equivalent to the fraction shown in the model?

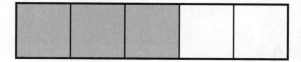

   A $\frac{3}{10}$ **B** $\frac{4}{10}$

   C $\frac{5}{10}$ **D** $\frac{6}{10}$

4. Yasmin swam $\frac{2}{3}$ mile. Abdi swam $\frac{7}{9}$ mile. Which statement is true?

   A $\frac{2}{3} > \frac{7}{9}$

   B $\frac{7}{9} > \frac{2}{3}$

   C $\frac{2}{3} = \frac{7}{9}$

   D $\frac{7}{9} < \frac{2}{3}$

5. Two of the 8 phone calls Li Na received were from her mom. Which fraction is equivalent to the fraction of the phone calls that were from Li Na's mom?

   A $\frac{2}{10}$

   B $\frac{4}{10}$

   C $\frac{1}{4}$

   D $\frac{1}{8}$

GO ON

6. Which fraction would be located between $\frac{4}{3}$ and $\frac{5}{3}$ on the number line?

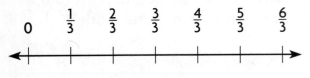

$$0 \qquad \frac{1}{3} \qquad \frac{2}{3} \qquad \frac{3}{3} \qquad \frac{4}{3} \qquad \frac{5}{3} \qquad \frac{6}{3}$$

A $\frac{4}{9}$

B $\frac{3}{6}$

C $\frac{13}{9}$

D $\frac{11}{6}$

7. Evan lives $\frac{1}{2}$ mile from the school. Omolara lives $\frac{5}{10}$ mile from the school. Which statement is true?

A $\frac{1}{2} > \frac{5}{10}$

B $\frac{5}{10} > \frac{1}{2}$

C $\frac{1}{2} = \frac{5}{10}$

D $\frac{5}{10} < \frac{1}{2}$

8. At a grocery store, 3 of the last 15 customers have bought bread. Which fraction represents the fraction of the customers that bought bread?

A $\frac{6}{18}$

B $\frac{1}{3}$

C $\frac{3}{10}$

D $\frac{1}{5}$

9. George read $\frac{3}{8}$ of a book on Monday. Soo Jin read $\frac{1}{3}$ of the same book. Which statement is true?

A $\frac{3}{8} > \frac{1}{3}$

B $\frac{1}{3} > \frac{3}{8}$

C $\frac{1}{3} = \frac{3}{8}$

D $\frac{3}{8} < \frac{1}{3}$

10. The shaded part of the model shows the part of his garden that Tom planted with spinach. Which two fractions could be used to describe the part of the garden that is spinach?

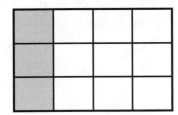

A $\frac{1}{3}$ and $\frac{1}{12}$

B $\frac{1}{4}$ and $\frac{1}{12}$

C $\frac{1}{3}$ and $\frac{3}{12}$

D $\frac{1}{4}$ and $\frac{3}{12}$

GO ON

11. Becky is making muffins. The recipe calls for $\frac{1}{2}$ cup of oil. Becky only has a $\frac{1}{8}$-cup measuring cup. Which equivalent fraction shows the amount of oil Becky needs to use for the recipe?

[table grid — 8 cells]

A $\frac{1}{8}$ cup

B $\frac{2}{8}$ cup

C $\frac{3}{8}$ cup

D $\frac{4}{8}$ cup

12. June used $\frac{7}{8}$ cup of strawberries and $\frac{3}{4}$ cup of orange juice to make ice pops. Which statement correctly compares the fractions?

A $\frac{7}{8} < \frac{3}{4}$

B $\frac{3}{4} > \frac{7}{8}$

C $\frac{7}{8} = \frac{3}{4}$

D $\frac{3}{4} < \frac{7}{8}$

13. Anika filled vases with flowers to go on each table for a wedding reception. Each vase held 8 flowers with 3 being roses. Which fraction represents the fraction of the flowers that are roses?

A $\frac{9}{24}$

B $\frac{8}{24}$

C $\frac{7}{12}$

D $\frac{6}{12}$

14. Between which two fractions will $\frac{3}{8}$ be located?

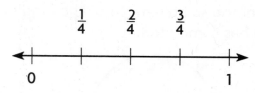

A 0 and $\frac{1}{4}$

B $\frac{1}{4}$ and $\frac{1}{2}$

C $\frac{1}{2}$ and $\frac{3}{4}$

D $\frac{3}{2}$ and 1

15. Stan spent $\frac{3}{4}$ hour cleaning his room. Beth spent $\frac{5}{6}$ hour cleaning her room. Which statement is true?

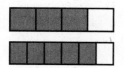

A $\frac{3}{4} > \frac{5}{6}$

B $\frac{5}{6} > \frac{3}{4}$

C $\frac{3}{4} = \frac{5}{6}$

D $\frac{5}{6} < \frac{3}{4}$

16. Erika lives $\frac{9}{8}$ miles from the bowling alley, Ashton lives $\frac{11}{12}$ mile from the bowling alley, and Tara lives $\frac{3}{4}$ mile from the bowling alley. Which list shows the distances in order from closest to farthest from the bowling alley?

A $\frac{3}{4}, \frac{11}{12}, \frac{9}{8}$

B $\frac{3}{4}, \frac{9}{8}, \frac{11}{12}$

C $\frac{11}{12}, \frac{3}{4}, \frac{9}{8}$

D $\frac{9}{8}, \frac{11}{12}, \frac{3}{4}$

GO ON

17. John is digging up the ground to build a circular pond in his backyard. The model shows how much of the digging John has completed.

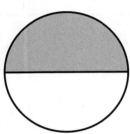

Which fraction is equivalent to the model that shows how much of the digging John has completed?

A $\frac{1}{8}$

B $\frac{1}{4}$

C $\frac{2}{4}$

D $\frac{2}{8}$

18. Jamie is graphing point *B*, which should be located at $\frac{5}{8}$. Between which two fractions should Jamie place point *B*?

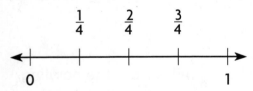

A 0 and $\frac{1}{4}$

B $\frac{1}{4}$ and $\frac{1}{2}$

C $\frac{1}{2}$ and $\frac{3}{4}$

D $\frac{3}{4}$ and 1

19. Mary is using fabric to sew a bag. She has $\frac{1}{2}$ yard of black fabric, $\frac{7}{12}$ yard of red fabric, and $\frac{3}{3}$ yard of white fabric. Which list shows the lengths of the fabrics in order from greatest to least?

A $\frac{7}{12}, \frac{3}{3}, \frac{1}{2}$

B $\frac{1}{2}, \frac{3}{3}, \frac{7}{12}$

C $\frac{3}{3}, \frac{7}{12}, \frac{1}{2}$

D $\frac{7}{12}, \frac{1}{2}, \frac{3}{3}$

20. Brennan uses the track at school to exercise. He walked the first loop and ran the next three loops. What fraction is equivalent to the amount Brennan ran?

A $\frac{1}{8}$

B $\frac{1}{6}$

C $\frac{3}{9}$

D $\frac{6}{8}$

STOP

Chapter 3

Understand Multiplication and Division

Math in the Real World

Mr. Lee divides 1 package of clay and 1 package of glitter dough equally among 4 students. How many more glitter dough sections than clay sections does each student get?

Clay Supplies	
Item	**Number in Package**
Clay	12 sections
Clay tool set	11 tools
Glitter dough	36 sections

What skills do I know that will help me solve this problem?

_____

_____

_____

What do I need to know that can help me solve this problem?

_____

_____

_____

My solution to the problem:

Building Your Math Abilities

Before you begin to explore multiplication and division, fill in the chart with what you know about multiplication and division, and then, what you would like to learn. As you go through the chapter, add to the chart the things you have learned.

What I know . . .	What I want to know . . .	What I have learned . . .

Go Deeper

What additional questions do you have about multiplication and division? Write your questions in the space below.

_____

_____

_____

_____

Lesson 3.1

Lesson Objective: Use repeated addition to show multiplication and repeated subtraction to show division.

Algebra • Relate Operations

Write the related multiplication sentence.
Draw a picture that shows the sentence.

$3 + 3 + 3 + 3 + 3 = 15$

Step 1 Start with 0 on the number line. Skip count by 3s **five** times. Stop at 15.

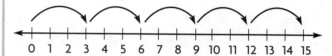

5 groups of 3 is the same as 5×3.

So, the related multiplication sentence is $5 \times 3 = 15$.

Write the related division sentence.
Draw a picture that shows the sentence.

$9 - 3 - 3 - 3 = 0$

Step 1 Start with 9 on the number line. Subtract 3 **three** times. Stop at 0.

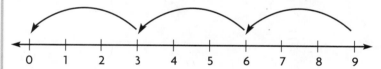

A group of 9 divided into equal groups of 3 is the same as $9 \div 3$.

So, the related division sentence is $9 \div 3 = 3$.

Write the related multiplication or division sentence.
Draw a quick picture that shows the sentence.

1. $2 + 2 + 2 + 2 + 2 = 10$

2. $15 - 3 - 3 - 3 - 3 - 3 = 0$

_____

_____

3. $5 + 5 + 5 + 5 = 20$

4. $18 - 6 - 6 - 6 = 0$

_____

_____

Write the related multiplication or division sentence.
Draw a quick picture that shows the sentence.

5. $3 + 3 + 3 + 3 = 12$

   $\underline{\quad 4 \times 3 = 12 \quad}$

6. $18 - 6 - 6 - 6 = 0$

   _____

7. 5 groups of 5 equals 25

   _____

8. 24 among 4 groups equals 6

   _____

9. $7 + 7 + 7 = 21$

   _____

10. $32 - 8 - 8 - 8 - 8 = 0$

   _____

11. $36 - 9 - 9 - 9 - 9 = 0$

   _____

12. 4 groups of 7 equals 28

   _____

13. $8 + 8 + 8 = 24$

   _____

Problem Solving REAL WORLD

14. Courtney is pouring 18 cups of lemonade into glasses. Each glass holds 2 cups of lemonade. How many glasses will Courtney fill?

   _____

15. It costs 6 tickets to ride the Ferris wheel. The ride operator collected tickets from 7 children. How many tickets did she collect in all?

   _____

Lesson 3.2

Lesson Objective: Use models to solve
multiplication and division problems.

Model Equal Groups

A cafe has 3 tables outdoors with 4 seats at each table.
Draw a picture to find the number of seats.

There are 12 seats, so 3 × 4 = 12.

A cafe has 12 seats. They have 3 tables for outdoor seating.
Draw a picture to find the number of seats at each table.

Draw 3 circles to show 3 tables. Put 1 seat at each table.

Put 1 more seat at each table until all of seats are used.

The 12 seats can be divided into 3 tables of 4 seats each. So, 12 ÷ 3 = 4.

Draw a quick picture to find the product or quotient.

1. 12 ÷ 2 = _____

2. 3 × 5 = _____

Draw a quick picture to find the product or quotient.

3. $5 \times 4 =$ __20__

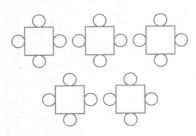

4. $21 \div 3 =$ _____

5.
$$\begin{array}{r} 2 \\ \times\ 7 \\ \hline \end{array}$$

6. $28 \div 4 =$ _____

7.
$$\begin{array}{r} 5 \\ \times\ 3 \\ \hline \end{array}$$

8. $8 \times 0 =$ _____

9. $6 \div 1 =$ _____

10. $18 \div 3 =$ _____

11. $8 \times 4 =$ _____

Problem Solving REAL WORLD

12. Isaiah has 8 goody bags for his party. He puts 5 party favors in each bag. How many party favors are there in all?

13. There are 16 swings in all at the park. Each swing set has 4 swings on it. How many swing sets are there at the park?

_____

_____

Lesson **3.3**

Lesson Objective: Use arrays and area models to model multiplication and division problems.

Model Arrays and Area Models

A booth at the State Fair has 15 pies. There are 3 rows of pies, with the same number of pies in each row. How many pies are in each row?

COMPLETE THE MODEL	THINK	RECORD
	__15__ pies in all	$15 \div 3 = 5$ or $3\overline{)15}$ with 5
	__3__ rows of pies	$\uparrow$ $\uparrow$ $\uparrow$
	__5__ pies in each row	dividend divisor quotient

So, there are 5 pies in each row.

Another booth at the fair has pies in 3 rows, with 5 pies in each row. How many pies are there in all?

COMPLETE THE MODEL	THINK	RECORD
	__3__ rows of pies	$5 \leftarrow$ factor
	__5__ pies in each row	$\underline{\times 3} \leftarrow$ factor
	__15__ pies in all	$15 \leftarrow$ product

So, the booth has 15 pies.

Draw a quick picture to find the product or quotient.

1. $4\overline{)12}$

2. 7×3

_____   _____

Draw a quick picture to find the product or quotient.

3. $24 \div 4 = $ ___6___

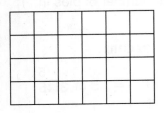

4. $9 \times 3 = $ _____

5. $5\overline{)30}$

6. $\begin{array}{r} 8 \\ \times\ 2 \\ \hline \end{array}$

7. $4 \div 4 = $ _____

8. $3 \times 2 = $ _____

9. $5\overline{)20}$

10. $\begin{array}{r} 3 \\ \times\ 0 \\ \hline \end{array}$

11. $40 \div 5 = $ _____

Problem Solving REAL WORLD

12. One page of Jenna's baseball card album holds 25 cards. There are 5 cards in each row. How many rows of cards are there?

13. Louisa knits a pattern in her scarf that is 8 stitches long and 4 rows high. How many total stitches are in the pattern?

_____

_____

1. Which number sentence is a related multiplication sentence for
$4 + 4 + 4 = 12$?

   A $4 \times 3 = 12$

   B $3 \times 3 \times 3 = 27$

   C $12 \times 3 = 36$

   D $4 \times 4 \times 4 = 64$

2. Which number sentence could be completed using the drawing?

   A $6 \times 3 = $ ▢

   B $6 + 3 = $ ▢

   C $6 \div 3 = $ ▢

   D $6 - 3 = $ ▢

3. Candice placed 48 cans of corn on the shelf at the grocery store. There are 6 cans in each row. How many rows of cans did Candice place on the shelf?

   A 6

   B 7

   C 8

   D 9

4. Which number sentence is a related division sentence for
$24 - 6 - 6 - 6 - 6 = 0$?

   A $24 \div 6 = 4$

   B $24 - 6 = 18$

   C $24 + 6 = 30$

   D $24 \times 6 = 144$

5. Ellen has 3 gardens and each garden has 6 different types of flowers. How many different types of flowers are there in all the gardens?

   A 15

   B 18

   C 21

   D 24

6. There are 8 tables in Mrs. Metcalf's classroom. She places 4 laptops on each table. The number sentence $4 + 4 + 4 + 4 + 4 + 4 + 4 + 4 = 32$ can be used to represent the total number of laptops. Which related multiplication sentence can also be used to represent the total number of laptops?

   A $7 \times 4 = 28$

   B $8 \times 4 = 32$

   C $7 \times 5 = 35$

   D $8 \times 5 = 40$

GO ON

7. Gina places trading cards in an album. Each page holds 4 rows of 3 cards. How many cards will fit on each page?

A 8

B 9

C 10

D 12

8. Renita has 28 marbles and places 4 marbles in each bag. How many bags does Renita fill with marbles?

A 6

B 7

C 8

D 9

9. Mina bought 5 packages of 8 juice boxes each. Write an addition sentence and the related multiplication sentence to show how many juice boxes Mina bought in all. Explain how your number sentences represent the problem.

_____

_____

_____

_____

10. Jane made a quilt using 54 squares. There were 9 rows of squares. Explain how you can use an array or area model to determine the number of squares in each row.

_____

_____

_____

_____

Apply Your Understanding

Lesson 3.4

Lesson Objective: Use inverse operations and related facts to solve for products and quotients.

Algebra • Relate Multiplication and Division

Multiplication and division by the same number are opposite operations, or inverse operations. One operation undoes the other.

Related facts are a set of multiplication and division statements that are related.

$2 \times 3 = 6$ 2 rows of 3 triangles each So, $2 \times 3 = 6$.	$6 \div 2 = 3$  Divide 6 triangles into 2 equal rows with 3 triangles in each row. There are 2 rows of 3 triangles. So, $6 \div 2 = 3$.
$3 \times 2 = 6$ 3 rows of 2 triangles each So, $3 \times 2 = 6$.	$6 \div 3 = 2$ Divide 6 triangles into 3 equal rows with 2 triangles in each row. There are 3 rows of 2 triangles. So, $6 \div 3 = 2$.

So, the related facts for 2, 3, 6 are $2 \times 3 = 6$, $3 \times 2 = 6$, $6 \div 2 = 3$, and $6 \div 3 = 2$.

Write the related multiplication and division sentences to complete the set of related facts.

1. $8 \div 8 = 1$

_____

_____

2. $16 \div 2 = 8$

_____

_____

3. $5 \times 8 = 40$

_____

_____

4. $8 \times 3 = 24$

_____

_____

Write the related multiplication and division sentences to complete the set of related facts.

5. $3 \times 6 = 18$

    $6 \times 3 = 18,$

    $18 \div 6 = 3,$

    $18 \div 3 = 6$

6. $28 \div 4 = 7$

    _____

    _____

    _____

7. $9 \div 9 = 1$

    _____

    _____

    _____

8. $8 \times 2 = 16$

    _____

    _____

    _____

9. $20 \div 4 = 5$

    _____

    _____

    _____

10. $3 \times 9 = 27$

    _____

    _____

    _____

Find the product or quotient.

11. $7 \times 2 = $ _____

12. $24 \div 3 = $ _____

13. _____ $= 16 \div 4$

14. $3 \times 1 = $ _____

Complete the equations.

15. $5 \times$ _____ $= 40$

    $40 \div 5 = $ _____

16. _____ $= 7 \div 7$

    $7 \times$ _____ $= 7$

17. $5 \times 6 = $ _____

    _____ $\div 6 = 5$

18. $8 \div$ _____ $= 2$

    _____ $\times 2 = 8$

Problem Solving REAL WORLD

Use the graph for 19–20

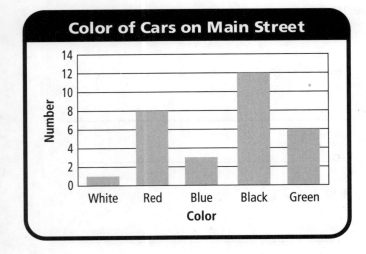

Color of Cars on Main Street

19. There are 8 times as many red cars as white cars. Write a multiplication problem to show this.

    _____

20. There are 4 times as many of which color car as there are blue cars on Main Street?

    _____

Name _____

Lesson 3.5

Lesson Objective: Use different strategies to recall multiplication and division facts.

Use Multiplication and Division Strategies

Use a multiplication table.

Divide. 16 ÷ 8

- Since the divisor is 8, find row 8.

- Move across that row to the right until you find 16, which is the dividend.

- Move up the column to find the quotient, which is 2.

So, 16 ÷ 8 = 2.

×	0	1	2	3	4	5	6	7	8	9	10
0	0	0	0	0	0	0	0	0	0	0	0
1	0	1	2	3	4	5	6	7	8	9	10
2	0	2	4	6	8	10	12	14	16	18	20
3	0	3	6	9	12	15	18	21	24	27	30
4	0	4	8	12	16	20	24	28	32	36	40
5	0	5	10	15	20	25	30	35	40	45	50
6	0	6	12	18	24	30	36	42	48	54	60
7	0	7	14	21	28	35	42	49	56	63	70
8	0	8	16	24	32	40	48	56	64	72	80
9	0	9	18	27	36	45	54	63	72	81	90
10	0	10	20	30	40	50	60	70	80	90	100

Use doubles.

Multiply. 8 × 9

Think: The factor 8 is an even number. 4 + 4 = 8

_____ × 9 = 36

_____ × 9 = 36

36 + 36 = _____

So, 8 × 9 = _____.

Use the Commutative Property of Multiplication.

Multiply. 4 × 8

If you know 8 × 4, use that fact to find 4 × 8.

8 × 4 = _____

So, 4 × 8 = _____.

Use inverse operations.

Divide. 63 ÷ 9

Think: 9 × 7 = 63

So, 63 ÷ 9 = _____.

Find the product or quotient. Write the strategy you used. Write *multiplication table, doubles, Commutative Property of Multiplication,* or *inverse operations.*

1. 6)‾48‾

_____

_____

2. 4 × 9 = _____

_____

_____

Find the product or quotient. Write the strategy you used. Write *multiplication table, doubles, Commutative Property of Multiplication,* or *inverse operations.*

3. $9 \times 6 = \underline{\ \ 54\ \ }$ 4. $56 \div 7 = \underline{\hspace{1.5cm}}$ 5. $7\overline{)42}$ 6. $\underline{\hspace{1.5cm}} = 9 \times 9$

   $6 = 3 + 3$

   $9 \times 3 = 27$

   $9 \times 3 = 27$

   $27 + 27 = 54.$

   $\underline{\ \ \text{doubles}\ \ }$ $\underline{\hspace{3cm}}$ $\underline{\hspace{3cm}}$ $\underline{\hspace{3cm}}$

7. $\underline{\hspace{1.5cm}} = 36 \div 9$ 8. $\begin{array}{r} 0 \\ \times\ 7 \\ \hline \end{array}$ 9. $40 \div 10 = \underline{\hspace{1.5cm}}$ 10. $\underline{\hspace{1.5cm}} = 3 \times 6$

$\underline{\hspace{3cm}}$ $\underline{\hspace{3cm}}$ $\underline{\hspace{3cm}}$ $\underline{\hspace{3cm}}$

Problem Solving REAL WORLD

11. Randy has a piece of rope that is 36 feet long. He wants to cut it into 6 equal pieces to make jump ropes for his friends. How long will each rope be?

12. Bailey buys 7 sheets of stickers. Each sheet has 2 rows of stickers with 3 stickers in each row. How many stickers does Bailey buy in all?

$\underline{\hspace{6cm}}$ $\underline{\hspace{6cm}}$

Lesson 3.6

Lesson Objective: Use a multiplication table to find products and quotients.

Multiplication Table Through 12

Find the product. 11 × 5

To find the product, you can complete a multiplication table for the factors.

×	0	1	2	3	4	5	6	7	8	9	10	11	12
0						0							
1						5							
2						10							
3						15							
4						20							
5						25							
6						30							
7						35							
8						40							
9						45							
10						50							
11	0	11	22	33	44	55	66	77	88	99	110	121	132
12						60							

Step 1 Count by **elevens** to complete the row for 11.	**Step 2** Count by **fives** to complete the column for 5.	**Step 3** Find the product where row 11 and column 5 meet. The product is **55**.

So, 11 × 5 = **55**.

Find the product or quotient.

1. 7 × 12 = _____

2. 9 × 6 = _____

3. 3)‾21‾

4. 108 ÷ 9 = _____

5. 7)‾42‾

6. 8 × 11 = _____

Find the product or quotient.

7. $72 \div 8 = \underline{\quad 9 \quad}$

8. $\begin{array}{r} 7 \\ \times\ 6 \\ \hline \end{array}$

9. $40 \div 10 = \underline{\quad\quad}$

10. $6 \times 12 = \underline{\quad\quad}$

11. $9\overline{)63}$

12. $\underline{\quad\quad} = 5 \times 10$

13. $144 \div 12 = \underline{\quad\quad}$

14. $\begin{array}{r} 9 \\ \times\ 4 \\ \hline \end{array}$

15. $7 \times 7 = \underline{\quad\quad}$

16. $8\overline{)56}$

17. $8 \times 10 = \underline{\quad\quad}$

18. $\underline{\quad\quad} = 54 \div 6$

19. $\begin{array}{r} 12 \\ \times\ 3 \\ \hline \end{array}$

20. $\underline{\quad\quad} = 96 \div 8$

21. $6 \times 6 = \underline{\quad\quad}$

22. $11\overline{)110}$

Problem Solving  REAL WORLD

Use the multiplication table for 23–24.

×	0	1	2	3	4	5	6	7	8	9	10	11	12
0	0	0	0	0	0	0	0	0	0	0	0	0	0
1	0	1	2	3	4	5	6	7	8	9	10	11	12
2	0	2	4	6	8	10	12	14	16	18	20	22	24
3	0	3	6	9	12	15	18	21	24	27	30	33	36
4	0	4	8	12	16	20	24	28	32	36	40	44	48
5	0	5	10	15	20	25	30	35	40	45	50	55	60
6	0	6	12	18	24	30	36	42	48	54	60	66	72
7	0	7	14	21	28	35	42	49	56	63	70	77	84
8	0	8	16	24	32	40	48	56	64	72	80	88	96
9	0	9	18	27	36	45	54	63	72	81	90	99	108
10	0	10	20	30	40	50	60	70	80	90	100	110	120
11	0	11	22	33	44	55	66	77	88	99	110	121	132
12	0	12	24	36	48	60	72	84	96	108	120	132	144

23. Jon says the products in the column for 12 are twice the products in the column for 6. Kate says the products in the column for 12 are six more than the products in the column for 6. Who is correct?

_____

24. In which two columns and rows can you find the product 63?

_____

_____

_____

Lesson 3.7

Lesson Objective: Use mental math and multiplication properties to find products.

Algebra • Multiplication Properties

Recall the properties of multiplication.

Zero Property of Multiplication

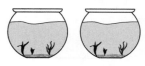

$2 \times 0 = $ **0**

Identity Property of Multiplication

$1 \times 4 = $ **4**

Commutative Property of Multiplication

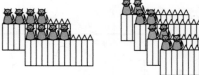

$2 \times 4 = $ **8** $4 \times 2 = $ **8**

Associative Property of Multiplication

$(3 \times 2) \times 4 = $ **24** $3 \times (2 \times 4) = $ **24**

Distributive Property of Multiplication

$4 \times 4 \quad + \quad 4 \times 3$
$16 \quad + \quad 12 \quad = 28$

Use the properties and mental math to find the product.

1. $6 \times 2 \times 4$

_____

2. 8×9

_____

3. $6 \times 0 \times 4$

_____

4. $2 \times 7 \times 1$

_____

5. 5×7

_____

6. $5 \times 2 \times 3$

_____

7. $4 \times 3 \times 3$

_____

8. $2 \times 0 \times 3$

_____

9. $8 \times 1 \times 5$

_____

Use the properties and mental math to find the product.

10. $3 \times 6 \times 2$

   $3 \times (6 \times 2) =$
   $3 \times (2 \times 6) =$
   $(3 \times 2) \times 6 =$
   $6 \times 6 = 36$.

11. $8 \times 6 \times 0$

12. $2 \times 7 \times 4$

Find the unknown number. Name the property used.

13. $6 \times \boxed{} = 6$

14. $4 \times 7 = \boxed{} \times 4$

15. $5 \times \boxed{} = 0$

16. $(6 \times 4) \times 2 = \boxed{} \times (4 \times 2)$

17. $5 \times 8 = (5 \times 4) + (\boxed{} \times 4)$

Show two ways to group by using parentheses. Find the product.

18. $7 \times 1 \times 10 = \underline{}$

19. $8 \times 2 \times 5 = \underline{}$

20. $3 \times 7 \times 0 = \underline{}$

Problem Solving REAL WORLD

21. Two teams of 9 children gather to play baseball. Each child brings 1 glove. How many gloves are there in all?

22. Cedric, Lauren, and Jay each bought 4 packs of trading cards. Each pack costs $3. How much did the three friends spend on cards all together?

Fact Families

Write two multiplication facts.

1. • • • •
    • • • •
    • • • •

    _____

    _____

2. • • • • • •
    • • • • • •
    • • • • • •

    _____

    _____

3. • • • • •
    • • • • •
    • • • • •

    _____

    _____

Use the Order Property of Multiplication. Complete.

4. $4 \times 5 =$ _____ $\times$ _____

5. $2 \times 6 =$ _____ $\times$ _____

6. $7 \times 3 =$ _____ $\times$ _____

7. $8 \times 2 =$ _____ $\times$ _____

Write a multiplication fact.

8. 3 sevens = _____

9. 5 fives = _____

Write a division number sentence.

10. • • • • • •
     • • • • • •

     _____

11. • • • • •
     • • • • •
     • • • • •

     _____

Name _____

Fact Families

Draw an array. Then multiply.

1. $\begin{array}{r} 2 \\ \times\ 3 \\ \hline \end{array}$
2. $\begin{array}{r} 4 \\ \times\ 4 \\ \hline \end{array}$
3. $\begin{array}{r} 3 \\ \times\ 6 \\ \hline \end{array}$
4. $\begin{array}{r} 2 \\ \times\ 8 \\ \hline \end{array}$

5. $\begin{array}{r} 5 \\ \times\ 3 \\ \hline \end{array}$
6. $\begin{array}{r} 4 \\ \times\ 2 \\ \hline \end{array}$
7. $\begin{array}{r} 2 \\ \times\ 7 \\ \hline \end{array}$
8. $\begin{array}{r} 3 \\ \times\ 4 \\ \hline \end{array}$

9. $\begin{array}{r} 5 \\ \times\ 2 \\ \hline \end{array}$
10. $\begin{array}{r} 2 \\ \times\ 6 \\ \hline \end{array}$
11. $\begin{array}{r} 3 \\ \times\ 3 \\ \hline \end{array}$
12. $\begin{array}{r} 5 \\ \times\ 4 \\ \hline \end{array}$

Draw an array. Then divide.

13. $8 \div 2 =$ _____
14. $15 \div 3 =$ _____
15. $6 \div 3 =$ _____

16. $18 \div 3 =$ _____
17. $6 \div 2 =$ _____
18. $18 \div 2 =$ _____

19. $10 \div 2 =$ _____
20. $12 \div 3 =$ _____
21. $16 \div 2 =$ _____

Read each question and choose the best answer.

1. Roxanne planted 16 spinach plants in her garden. There are 2 rows of plants. How many plants are in each row?

   A 6

   B 7

   C 8

   D 9

2. Jasper has 108 apples. He places 12 apples in each bag. How many bags of apples does Jasper have?

   A 8

   B 9

   C 10

   D 11

3. Which number sentence is a related sentence multiplication sentence for $5 + 5 + 5 + 5 = 20$?

   A $5 \times 5 \times 5 \times 5 = 20$

   B $4 \times 4 \times 4 \times 4 = 20$

   C $20 \times 4 = 5$

   D $4 \times 5 = 20$

4. Maxine wants to find the product of 8×6. Which expression could Maxine use to find the product?

   A $(4 \times 6) + (4 \times 6)$

   B $(4 \times 3) + (4 \times 3)$

   C $(4 + 6) \times (4 + 6)$

   D $(4 + 3) \times (4 + 3)$

5. Which is an example of the Identity Property of Multiplication?

   A $7 \times 0 = 0$

   B $8 \times 1 = 8$

   C $9 \times 2 = 2 \times 9$

   D $(10 \times 3) \times 2 = 10 \times (3 \times 2)$

6. Which number sentence could be completed using the drawing?

   A $8 \times 2 = \square$

   B $8 + 2 = \square$

   C $8 \div 2 = \square$

   D $8 - 2 = \square$

GO ON

7. Which number sentence completes the set of related facts?

   $9 \times 4 = 36$; $4 \times 9 = 36$

   $36 \div 4 = 9$

   A $6 \times 6 = 36$

   B $36 \div 6 = 6$

   C $4 \div 36 = 9$

   D $36 \div 9 = 4$

8. Carl is creating a game board. He drew 8 rows on a piece of paper, with 5 small squares in each row. How many total small squares did Carl draw?

   A 35

   B 40

   C 45

   D 48

9. Lena waited in line 4 minutes. Oscar waited 3 times as long. How long did Oscar wait in line?

   A 8 minutes

   B 9 minutes

   C 12 minutes

   D 16 minutes

10. Which number sentence is a related division sentence for $30 - 5 - 5 - 5 - 5 - 5 - 5 = 0$?

    A $30 \div 5 = 6$

    B $30 \div 5 = 7$

    C $6 \div 30 = 5$

    D $6 \div 5 = 30$

11. Mrs. Wilkins has 24 pencils. She gives 3 pencils to each student. How many students receive pencils from Mrs. Wilkins?

    A 6

    B 7

    C 8

    D 9

12. Tara's coupon book is 9 pages long and each page has 4 rows with 2 coupons in each row. How many coupons are in the book?

    A 36

    B 54

    C 63

    D 72

GO ON

13. Which correctly completes the number sentence?

$$\boxed{} \div 8 = 7$$

A 48

B 54

C 56

D 64

14. Dana shared 24 apple slices equally with 6 friends. To determine the number of slices each friend will get, Dana used the number sentence $24 - 6 - 6 - 6 - 6 = 0$. Which related division sentence shows the number of apple slices each friend was given?

A $24 \div 6 = 6$

B $24 \div 6 = 5$

C $24 \div 6 = 4$

D $24 \div 6 = 3$

15. There are 3 groups of students, with 4 students in each group working on an art project. Each student uses 2 pieces of paper. How many pieces of paper were used in all?

A 8

B 9

C 18

D 24

16. During a book sale, Mia set up 9 rows of books, with 7 books in each row. How many books did Mia set up?

A 49

B 54

C 56

D 63

17. There are 11 students taking an art class. Each student brought 12 different paints. How many paints were brought to art class?

A 110

B 121

C 132

D 144

18. Which number sentence is in the set of related facts with $5 \times 4 = 20$

A $4 \times 5 = 20$

B $2 \times 10 = 20$

C $20 \div 10 = 2$

D $5 \div 20 = 4$

GO ON

19. A cook bought 2 cases of eggs. Each case has 4 cartons and each carton has 12 eggs. How many eggs did the cook buy?

   A 48

   B 72

   C 96

   D 108

20. Henley used the break apart strategy to solve 9×7. Which could be Henley's work?

   A $9 + 2 + 5$

   B $9 \times (2 \times 5)$

   C $(9 + 2) \times (9 + 5)$

   D $(9 \times 2) + (9 \times 5)$

STOP

Chapter 4

Algebra: Use Addition, Subtraction, Multiplication, and Division

Math in the Real World

What if Tanisha needs 40 bowls for a picnic? Explain how to write an equation with a letter for an unknown factor to find the number of packs she should buy. Then find the unknown factor.

Picnic Supplies

Item	Number in 1 Pack	Cost
Bowls	6	$ 10
Cups	8	$ 3
Tablecloth	1	$ 2
Napkins	36	$ 2
Forks	50	$ 3

What skills do I know that will help me solve this problem?

_____

_____

_____

What do I need to know that can help me solve this problem?

_____

_____

_____

My solution to the problem:

Building Your Math Abilities

Before you begin to use addition, subtraction, multiplication, and division, fill in the chart with what you know about addition, subtraction, multiplication, and division and what you would like to learn. As you go through the chapter, add to the chart the things you have learned.

What I know . . .	What I want to know . . .	What I have learned . . .

Go Deeper

What additional questions do you have about addition, subtraction, multiplication, and division? Write your questions in the space below.

_____

_____

_____

_____

Lesson 4.1

Lesson Objective: Use the strategy *draw a diagram* to solve comparison problems with addition and subtraction.

Problem Solving • Comparison Problems with Addition and Subtraction

For a community recycling project, a school collects aluminum cans and plastic containers. This year the fourth grade collected 5,923 cans and 4,182 containers. This is 410 more cans and 24 more containers than the fourth grade collected last year. How many cans did the fourth grade collect last year?

Read the Problem

What do I need to find?	What information do I need to use?	How will I use the information?
I need to find the number of <u>cans the fourth grade</u> <u>collected last year.</u>	The fourth grade students collected <u>5,923</u> cans this year. They collected <u>410</u> more cans this year than the fourth grade collected last year.	I can draw a <u>bar model</u> to find the number of cans the fourth grade collected last year.

Solve the Problem

I can draw a bar model and write an equation to represent the problem.

5,923

410	

5,513

<u>5,923</u> − <u>410</u> = <u>5,513</u>

So, the fourth grade collected <u>5,513</u> aluminum cans last year.

I can use addition to check subtraction. <u>5,513</u> + <u>410</u> = <u>5,923</u>

So, the answer checks.

Use the information above for 1.

1. This year the fifth grade collected 216 fewer plastic containers than the fourth grade. How many plastic containers did the fifth grade collect?

_____

Draw a model and write a number sentence to solve. Use addition to check your answer. Use the information in the table for 2–4.

Surface Area of the Great Lakes	
Lake	**Surface Area (in square miles)**
Lake Superior	31,700
Lake Michigan	22,278
Lake Huron	22,973
Lake Erie	9,906
Lake Ontario	7,340

2. How many square miles larger is the surface area of Lake Huron than the surface area of Lake Erie?

   Think: How can a bar model help represent the problem? What equation can be written?

   Lake Huron | 22,973

   Lake Erie | 9,906 | ?

   $\underline{22,973} - \underline{9,906} = \underline{13,067}$ square miles

   I can use addition to check subtraction.

   $\underline{13,067} - \underline{9,906} = \underline{22,973}$

   So, the answer checks.

   So, the surface area of Lake Huron is 13,067 square miles larger than the surface area of Lake Erie.

3. Which lake has a surface area that is 14,938 square miles greater than the surface area of Lake Ontario? Draw a model and write a number sentence to solve the problem.

   _____

   Is your answer reasonable? Explain.

   _____

4. Lake Victoria has the largest surface area of all lakes in Africa. Its surface area is 26,828 square miles. How much larger is the surface area of Lake Victoria than the combined surface areas of Lake Erie and Lake Ontario?

   _____

   Is your answer reasonable? Explain.

   _____

Algebra • Multiplication Comparisons

Tara has 3 times as many soccer medals as Greg. Greg has
4 soccer medals. How many soccer medals does Tara have?

Step 1 Draw a model.

Greg ◯◯◯◯

Tara ◯◯◯◯　◯◯◯◯　◯◯◯◯

Step 2 Use the model to write an equation.

$n = \underline{\ 3\ } \times \underline{\ 4\ }$　**Think:** n is how many soccer medals Tara has.

Step 3 Solve the equation.

$n = \underline{\ 12\ }$　**Think:** 12 is 3 times as many as 4 since $3 \times 4 = 12$.

So, Tara has __12__ soccer medals.

Draw a model and write an equation.

1. 4 times as many as 7 is 28.

2. 16 is 8 times as many as 2.

_____

_____

3. 3 times as many as 6 is 18.

4. 10 is 2 times as many as 5.

_____

_____

Write a comparison sentence.

5. $6 \times 3 = 18$

   ___6___ times as many as ___3___ is ___18___ .

6. $63 = 7 \times 9$

   _____ is _____ times as many as _____ .

7. $5 \times 4 = 20$

   _____ times as many as _____ is _____ .

8. $48 = 8 \times 6$

   _____ is _____ times as many as _____ .

Write an equation.

9. 2 times as many as 8 is 16.

   _____

10. 42 is 6 times as many as 7.

    _____

11. 3 times as many as 5 is 15.

    _____

12. 36 is 9 times as many as 4.

    _____

13. 72 is 8 times as many as 9.

    _____

14. 5 times as many as 6 is 30.

    _____

Problem Solving 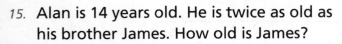 REAL WORLD

15. Alan is 14 years old. He is twice as old as his brother James. How old is James?

16. There are 27 campers. This is 9 times as many as the number of counselors. Mark says there are 3 counselors. How can you tell if he found the correct number of counselors? Explain.

    _____

    _____

    _____

_____

_____

Lesson **4.3**

Lesson Objective: Solve problems involving multiplicative comparison and additive comparison.

Algebra • Comparison Problems

Jamie has 3 times as many baseball cards as Rick. Together, they have 20 baseball cards. How many cards does Jamie have?

Step 1 Estimate. 3 times 6 is 18 and 18 + 6 is greater than than 20, so the number of cards that Jamie has must be less than 18.

Step 2 Draw a box with the letter *n* in it to show that Rick has an unknown number of cards. Jamie has 3 times as many cards as Rick, so draw three identical boxes to represent Jamie's cards.

Jamie | *n* | *n* | *n* |
Rick | *n* |
20

Step 3 Use the model to write an equation. There are a total of 20 cards. So, ___4___ × *n* = ___20___.

Think: There are 4 equal bars. The number in each bar is represented by *n*.

Step 4 Solve the equation to find the value of *n*. Since 4 × ___5___ = 20, the value of *n* is ___5___.

Rick has ___5___ cards.

Think: 4 times what number is 20?

Step 5 Find how many cards Jamie has. So, Jamie has 3 × ___5___ = ___15___ baseball cards. 15 is less than 18. The answer is reasonable.

Think: Jamie has 3 times as many cards as Rick.

Estimate. Then draw a model and write an equation to solve.

1. Maddie has 2 times as many stickers on her notebook as Meg. Together, they have 15 stickers. How many stickers are on Maddie's notebook?

   Estimate:_____

   _____

   _____

   _____

2. _____

Estimate. Then draw a model and write an equation to solve.

2. Stacey made a necklace using 4 times as many blue beads as red beads. She used a total of 40 beads. How many blue beads did Stacey use?

   Estimate: <u>4 times 9 is 36, 36 + 9 is</u>

   <u>greater than 40, so the number of blue</u>

   <u>beads that Stacey used must be less</u>

   <u>than 36.</u>

   Think: Stacey used a total of 40 beads. Let n represent the number of red beads.

   $5 \times n = 40; 5 \times 8 = 40;$

   $4 \times 8 = 32$ blue beads

3. Fred's frog jumped 7 times as far as Al's frog. The two frogs jumped a total of 56 inches. How far did Fred's frog jump?

   Estimate: _____

   _____

   _____

   _____

Problem Solving REAL WORLD

4. Rafael counted a total of 40 white cars and yellow cars. There were 9 times as many white cars as yellow cars. How many white cars did Rafael count?

© Houghton Mifflin Harcourt Publishing Company

1. There are 54 students on a field trip to the theater. This is 9 times as many as the number of adults on the field trip. How many adults are with the students?

   A 5

   B 6

   C 7

   D 8

2. This week, Mateo ran 4 times as far as Billy. Together, they ran a total of 20 miles. How many miles did Mateo run?

   A 4 miles

   B 5 miles

   C 15 miles

   D 16 miles

3. Mr. Silver drove 23,678 miles last year. This year he drove 5,493 more miles than last year. How many miles did Mr. Silver drive over the past two years?

   A 29,171 miles

   B 41,863 miles

   C 51,739 miles

   D 52,849 miles

4. Tristan saw 8 times as many birds as bunnies during his walk. If he saw 36 birds and bunnies, how many bunnies did he see?

   A 4

   B 6

   C 24

   D 32

5. Which comparison sentence best represents the number sentence?

   $$5 \times 7 = 35$$

   A 7 more than 5 is 35.

   B 5 is 7 times as many as 35.

   C 35 is 7 times as many as 5.

   D 7 is 5 times as many as 35.

6. How many square miles greater is Uganda than Uruguay and Taiwan combined?

Country Sizes	
Country	**Area in Square Miles**
Uganda	93,072
Greece	50,949
Uruguay	68,037
Iceland	39,769
Taiwan	13,972

   A 11,063 miles

   B 25,035 miles

   C 79,100 miles

   D 82,009 miles

GO ON

7. Sandy has 3 stuffed animals on her bed. Julia has 6 times as many on her bed. How many stuffed animals does Julia have on her bed?

   A 2

   B 9

   C 18

   D 21

8. Olivia made a quilt using 5 times as many blue fabric squares as white fabric squares. Olivia used a total of 60 squares. How many blue fabric squares did she use?

   A 10

   B 12

   C 50

   D 55

9. Riya has 24 comic books. This is 3 times as many as Nick. Write a comparison sentence and an equation to represent the situation. Explain how the comparison sentence and equation are related.

   _____

   _____

   _____

10. Quentin works at a pizza place. He made 7 times as many pizzas on Friday as he did on Tuesday. He made 48 pizzas over the two days. Draw a model to find the number of pizzas Quentin made on Friday. Explain your answer.

   _____

   _____

   _____

Apply Your Understanding

Name _____

Lesson 4.4

Lesson Objective: Find an unknown number to solve a problem.

Algebra • Find Unknown Numbers

Luis has 18 model cars. How many sets of 6 cars can he make?

Write a number sentence to represent the problem.

 × 6 = 18   **Think:** What number times 6 equals 18?

Way 1: Draw a model.
Draw 18 counters in rows of 6.
Count the number of rows to
find the missing factor.
There are 3 rows of 6 counters.

Way 2: Use a fact family.
Use a related division sentence to find the missing factor.
18 ÷ 6 = 3, so 3 × 6 = 18. The missing factor is 3.

So, Luis can make 3 sets of 6 cars.

Check: ■ × 6 = 18
$\qquad$ ■ = 3
$\qquad$ 3 × 6 = 18
$\qquad$ 18 = 18
The missing factor is 3.
Is this sentence true? yes

Write a number sentence with an unknown to represent each problem. Then solve.

1. There are 14 roses in a vase. Some are red, and 8 are yellow. How many of the roses are red?

2. The coach has 8 bags of soccer balls. Each bag holds 4 balls. How many soccer balls does the coach have?

_____

_____

Write a number sentence to represent each problem. Then solve.

3. Wayne has 4 homework problems left to do. He has completed 6 problems. How many problems did he have for homework?

    $\blacksquare - 4 = 6$
    $6 + 4 = 10$, so $10 - 4 = 6$
    So, Wayne had 10 problems for homework.

4. Amy has 36 beads. How many bracelets with 9 beads can she make?

Write a problem to represent each number sentence. Then solve.

5. $b + 9 = 12$

6. $\bullet - 7 = 8$

7. $\bullet \times 3 = 15$

8. $n \div 5 = 4$

Problem Solving

9. A florist has 42 flowers. She puts 6 flowers in each vase. How many flowers are in each vase?

10. A store receives a delivery of 6 boxes of candles. Each box has a dozen candles. How many candles are delivered to the store?

Name _____

Lesson **4.5**

Lesson Objective: Use a pan balance to model and solve an equation with a variable.

Algebra • Balance Equations

A pan balance weighs objects whose weights are unknown by balancing them with objects whose weights are known. When the two pans are balanced, the objects have the same weight.

You can use a pan balance to model and solve an equation. An **equation** is a mathematical sentence that shows that two amounts are equal.

Use a pan balance to model and solve $15 = 8 + n$.

Step 1 Model the equation.

$15 = 8 + n$

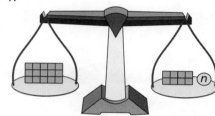

Step 2 Model the solution.

The number of squares that balance the pans is the value of n. Complete the picture by drawing squares to show how you balanced the equation.

Step 3 Solve the equation.

$15 = 8 + \underline{\hphantom{xx}7\hphantom{xx}}$

$7 = n$

1. $2 + a = 10$

$a = $ _____

2. $14 = x + 8$

_____ $= x$

Use the pan balance to solve the equation.

3. $1 + b = 11$

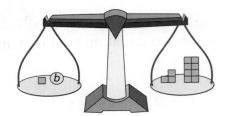

$b = \underline{\quad 10 \quad}$

4. $13 = 8 + k$

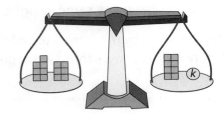

$\underline{\qquad} = k$

5. $n + 5 = 8$

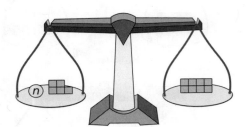

$n = \underline{\qquad}$

6. $10 = 7 + y$

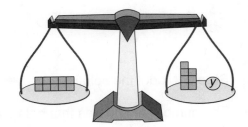

$\underline{\qquad} = y$

Problem Solving REAL WORLD

7. The mass of 6 blocks is shown on the pan balance. What is the mass of each block?

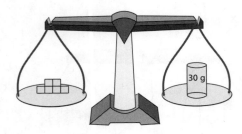

1 block = _____

8. The mass of 4 blocks is shown on the pan balance. What is the mass of the cylinder? Each block has a mass of 8 grams.

1 cylinder = _____

Lesson 4.6

Lesson Objective: Determine the solution set of an inequality involving addition or multiplication.

Algebra • Inequalities

An **inequality** is a number sentence that contains the symbols $<$, or $>$. It shows a relationship between quantities that are not equivalent.

$x < 7$ is an inequality.

A solution of an inequality with a variable is a value for the variable that makes it true.

You can use a number line to show solutions of an inequality.

Step 1 Draw a number line.

Step 2 Draw a point on the number line to show each solution for $x < 7$.

0, 1, 2, 3, 4, 5, and 6 are solutions.

A inequality may have many solutions. The group containing all of the solutions to a problem is called a **solution set**.

So, 5 is a solution of the inequality $x < 7$ because $5 < 7$.

---

1. Use the number line to circle the solutions of $3 + n > 7$.

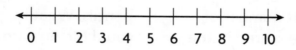

$3 + 1 > 7$ $3 + 5 > 7$ $3 + 0 > 7$

$3 + 2 > 7$ $3 + 6 > 7$ $3 + 8 > 7$

Which of the numbers 3, 4, and 5 are solutions of the inequality?

2. $x < 5$

_____3 < 5_____

_____4 < 5_____

3. $r - 3 > 1$

_____

_____

4. $j + 7 < 12$

_____

_____

Which of the numbers 6, 7, 8, 9 are solutions of the inequality?

5. $2 \times k < 20$

_____

_____

_____

6. $7 \times l > 21$

_____

_____

_____

7. $32 > m \times 8$

_____

_____

_____

Use the number line. Locate points to show the whole-number solutions from 0 to 8 for each equality.

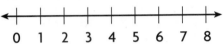

$\begin{array}{ccccccccc} 0 & 1 & 2 & 3 & 4 & 5 & 6 & 7 & 8 \end{array}$

8. $x < 6$

_____

_____

_____

9. $7 + p > 12$

_____

_____

_____

10. $q < g \times 2$

_____

_____

_____

_____

Problem Solving REAL WORLD

11. The Lions soccer team scored fewer than 4 goals in its game. They scored 1 goal in the first half. What number of goals could the Lions have scored in the second half?

_____

Write an inequality to represent the number of goals the Lions could have scored in the second half. Let g represent the number of goals scored.

_____

12. Each box comes with 8 pencils. Mr. Edwards bought more than 48 pencils. What number of boxes of pencils could Mr. Edwards have bought?

_____

Write an inequality to represent the number of boxes that Mr. Edwards could have bought. Let b represent the number of boxes of pencils.

_____

Lesson 4.7

Lesson Objective: Use, extend, and create input/output tables to solve pattern problems.

Algebra • Patterns in Tables

An **input/output** table shows the output for a given input.

Find a rule for the pattern in the table. Use an expression to write the rule. Use the rule to find the missing numbers.

Input	m	30	24	21	15	12	6
Output	n	10	8	7			

Think: The output is less than the input. The rule may involve subtraction or division.

Step 1 Try subtraction. To get the first output 10 from 30, subtract 20.

Try the rule, subtract 20.

Does your rule work for each pair of numbers?

No, because $24 - 20$ does not equal 8.

Step 2 Try division. If you divide the first input 30 by 3, you get 10.

Try the rule, divide by 3.

Does your rule work for each pair of numbers?

$30 \div 3 = 10$
$24 \div 3 = 8$
$21 \div 3 = 7$
Yes, the rule works.

Step 3 Use the rule to write an expression. Then use the rule to find the missing numbers.

Rule: The output is $m \div 3$.

Input	m	30	24	21	15	12	6
Output	n	10	8	7	5	4	2

Think:
$15 \div 3 = 5$
$12 \div 3 = 4$
$6 \div 3 = 2$

Find a rule. Use an expression to write the rule. Use the rule to find the missing numbers.

Input	x	2	5	7	9	11	12
Output	y	8	11	13			

Input	c	9	7	6	5	2	1
Output	d	36	28	24			

1. Rule: _____

2. Rule: _____

_____

Find a rule. Use an expression to write the rule.
Use the rule to find the missing numbers.

3. Rule:

The output is $p \times 7$.

Input	p	9	8	6	4	3	1
Output	q	63	56	42	28	21	7

4. Rule:

Input	b	12	10	9	7	6	3
Output	c	21	19	18			

5. Rule:

Input	w	24	18	16	12	10	8
Output	x	16	10	8			

6. Rule:

Input	k	12	9	8	6	5	2
Output	m	72	54	48			

Use the rule to make an input/output table.

7. Rule: The output, p, is $k \div 5$.

8. Rule: The output, t, is $s - 3$.

Problem Solving REAL WORLD

9. There are 3 markers in a package. How many packages would be needed for each group of 12, 18, and 27 students? Make a table and write the rule to solve.

10. Rae uses the rule $x - 12$ to start an input/output table. Complete his table.

Input	x	27	37	42	45	51
Output	y	12	25	30		

Multiplication and Division: Mental Math Strategies

Write a multiplication fact.

1. 4 + 4 + 4 + 4 + 4 = _____

2. 4 + 4 + 4 = _____

3. 4 + 4 = _____

4. 2 + 2 + 2 + 2 = _____

5. 6 fours _____

6. 9 fours _____

7. 9 twos _____

8. 4 threes _____

9. 3 twos _____

10. 7 threes _____

Use skip-counting to find the answer. Write the product only.

11. $7 \times 2 =$ ____

12. $6 \times 2 =$ ____

13. $3 \times 3 =$ ____

14. $8 \times 3 =$ ____

15. $7 \times 4 =$ ____

16. $4 \times 4 =$ ____

17. $2 \times 2 =$ ____

18. $9 \times 3 =$ ____

19. $8 \times 4 =$ ____

Find the quotient. Use a related multiplication fact.

20. $21 \div 7 =$ ____

21. $6 \div 6 =$ ____

22. $30 \div 6 =$ ____

23. $49 \div 7 =$ ____

24. $18 \div 6 =$ ____

25. $28 \div 7 =$ ____

26. $7 \div 7 =$ ____

27. $24 \div 6 =$ ____

28. $24 \div 4 =$ ____

Name _____

Multiplication and Division: Mental Math Strategies

Think of a related multiplication or division fact to solve.
Write only the unknown number.

1. ____ $\div 6 = 7$

2. ____ $\times 7 = 35$

3. ____ $\div 7 = 7$

4. ____ $\times 6 = 36$

5. ____ $\times 4 = 24$

6. ____ $\div 3 = 7$

7. ____ $\times 2 = 4$

8. ____ $\div 5 = 3$

9. ____ $\times 7 = 42$

Find the quotient. Think of multiplication.

10. $2\overline{)14}$

11. $6\overline{)36}$

12. $4\overline{)16}$

13. $6\overline{)42}$

14. $5\overline{)20}$

15. $5\overline{)15}$

16. $6\overline{)12}$

17. $5\overline{)35}$

18. $7\overline{)0}$

19. $3\overline{)27}$

20. $4\overline{)32}$

21. $3\overline{)21}$

22. $4\overline{)28}$

23. $7\overline{)42}$

24. $3\overline{)24}$

Use mental math. Write only the answer.

25. $4 \times 16 =$ ____

26. $3 \times 23 =$ ____

27. $6 \times 14 =$ ____

28. $2 \times 38 =$ ____

29. $3 \times 28 =$ ____

30. $7 \times 13 =$ ____

Read each question and choose the best answer.

1. Jill found 8 times as many seashells as sand dollars while walking the beach. Altogether she found 72 seashells and sand dollars. How many seashells did Jill find?

   A 8   **B** 9

   C 56   **D** 64

2. Which comparison sentence best represents the number sentence?

   $$3 \times 4 = 12$$

   A 4 more than 3 is 12.

   B 4 is 3 times as many as 12.

   C 12 is 3 times as many as 4.

   D 4 is 3 times as many as 12.

3. Andrea has 32 coins in her change purse. Eight of the coins are quarters and the rest are pennies. Which equation can be used to determine the number of coins that are pennies?

   A $8 \times p = 32$

   B $32 \div p = 8$

   C $8 + p = 32$

   D $p - 8 = 32$

4. Pete made a table. Which is the rule Pete used to make the table?

Input	j	7	5	3	1
Output	k	42	30	18	6

   A The output is $j + 5$.

   B The output is $j + 15$.

   C The output is $j \times 6$.

   D The output is $j \div 6$.

5. The table shows known depths for several of the deepest caves in the world. If the Cehi and Sarma caves were combined, how many feet deeper would they be than the Krubera Cave?

Cave	Known Depth in Feet
Krubera	7,208
Cehi	4,982
Sarma	5,062
Gouffre Mirolda	5,685
Sima de la Cornisa	4,944

   A 80 feet

   B 2,146 feet

   C 2,746 feet

   D 2,836 feet

GO ON

6. Mrs. Bolton bought more than 96 markers. If each pack of markers holds 12 markers, which inequality could be used to determine the number of packs of markers Mrs. Bolton bought?

 A $96 > 12 + m$

 B $96 < 12 + m$

 C $12 \times m > 96$

 D $12 \times m < 96$

7. Use the pan balance to solve the equation.

$$h + 7 = 9 + 4$$

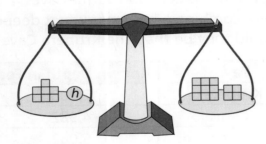

 A 13

 B 8

 C 6

 D 4

8. During the month of March, Toby sold $8,392 worth of products. In April, he sold $2,745 more than in March. How much did Toby sell in March and April?

 A $11,137

 B $14,039

 C $18,329

 D $19,529

9. Use the pan balance to solve the equation.

$$8 + 9 = k + 1$$

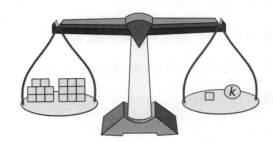

 A 8

 B 16

 C 17

 D 18

GO ON

10. Scott read 32 books this month. This is 4 times as many books as Steve read. How many books did Steve read?

   A 6

   B 7

   C 8

   D 9

11. Which is the solution to the inequality?

   $$8 + n < 24$$

   A $n < 3$

   B $n < 16$

   C $n > 16$

   D $n > 32$

12. Luna makes the table shown. Which shows a rule Luna might have used to make the table?

Input	x	18	15	12	9
Output	y	12	9	6	3

   A The output is $x + 6$.

   B The output is $x - 6$.

   C The output is $x \div 2$.

   D The output is $x \div 3$.

13. Find the unknown value.

   $$y + 4 = 28$$

   A 7

   B 8

   C 24

   D 32

14. On Monday, Megan saw 5 times as many yellow finches as starlings at the bird feeder. Megan saw a total of 42 birds. How many yellow finches did Megan see?

   A 35

   B 30

   C 6

   D 5

15. During a two-day festival, 12,483 people attended on the first day. On the second day, the attendance was 4,922 more than the first day. How many people attended the festival in all?

   A 17,405

   B 20,044

   C 28,788

   D 29,888

GO ON

16. Caleb ate 9 blueberries. He now has 18 blueberries left. Which equation can be used to determine how many blueberries he started with?

   A $18 - n = 9$

   B $18 \div n = 9$

   C $9 + 18 = n$

   D $9 \times n = 18$

17. Kira is wearing 2 bracelets. Alison is wearing 4 times as many bracelets as Kira. How many bracelets is Alison wearing?

   A 2

   B 4

   C 6

   D 8

18. Aliya and her aunt went to the state fair. The cost of her aunt's ticket was 4 times as much as Aliya's ticket. If they spent $20 on the tickets, what was the cost of Aliya's aunt's ticket?

   A $16

   B $15

   C $5

   D $4

19. Which number is a solution for the inequality?

$$3 + 9 > 6 + n$$

   A 4

   B 6

   C 9

   D 10

20. Betty bought 8 packs of yogurt. Each pack has 4 yogurts. Which equation can be used to determine the total number of yogurts Betty bought?

   A $y - 4 = 8$

   B $y \div 8 = 4$

   C $y + 4 = 8$

   D $4 \times y = 8$

STOP

Chapter 5

Geometry and Patterns

Math in the Real World

Explain how a rhombus and a square are alike and how they are different.

What skills do I know that will help me solve this problem?

_____

_____

_____

What do I need to know that can help me solve this problem?

_____

_____

_____

_____

My solution to the problem:

Building Your Math Abilities

Before you begin to explore geometry and patterns, fill in the chart with what you know about geometry and patterns, and then, what you would like to learn. As you go through the chapter, add to the chart the things you have learned.

What I know . . .	What I want to know . . .	What I have learned . . .

Go Deeper

What additional questions do you have about geometry and patterns? Write your questions in the space below.

_____

_____

_____

_____

Lesson **5.1**

Lesson Objective: Identify and draw points, lines, line segments, endpoints, rays, and angles.

Lines, Rays, and Angles

Name	What it looks like	Think
point *D*	*D*•	A **point** names a location in space.
line *AB*; $\overleftrightarrow{AB}$ line *BA*; $\overleftrightarrow{BA}$	*A* *B*	A **line** extends without end in opposite directions.
line segment *AB*; $\overline{AB}$ line segment *BA*; $\overline{BA}$	*A* *B*	"Segment" means part. A **line segment** is part of a line. It is named by its two **endpoints.**
ray *MN*; $\overrightarrow{MN}$ ray *NM*; $\overrightarrow{NM}$	*M* *N* *M* *N*	A **ray** has one endpoint and extends without end in one direction. A ray is named using two points. The endpoint is always named first.
angle *XYZ*; ∠*XYZ* angle *ZYX*; ∠*ZYX* angle *Y*; ∠*Y*	*X* *Y* *Z*	Two rays or line segments that share an endpoint form an angle. The shared point is the vertex of the angle.

A **right angle** forms a square corner.	An **acute angle** opens less than a right angle.	An **obtuse angle** opens more than a right angle and less than a straight angle.	A **straight angle** forms a line.

Draw and label an example of the figure.

1. $\overline{PQ}$

2. $\overrightarrow{KJ}$

3. obtuse ∠*FGH*

Draw and label an example of the figure.

4. obtuse ∠ABC

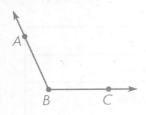

Think: An obtuse angle is greater than a right angle. The middle letter, B, names the vertex of the angle.

5. $\overrightarrow{GH}$

6. acute ∠JKL

7. $\overline{BC}$

Use the figure for 8–11.

8. Name a line segment.

_____

9. Name a right angle.

_____

10. Name an obtuse angle.

_____

11. Name a ray.

_____

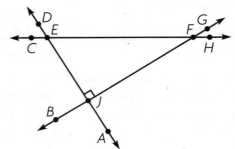

Problem Solving

Use the figure at the right for 12–14.

12. Classify ∠AFD. _____

13. Classify ∠CFE. _____

14. Name two acute angles.

_____

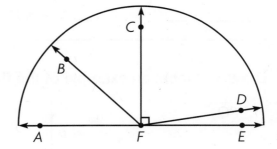

Lesson **5.2**

Lesson Objective: Identify and draw points, lines, line segments, endpoints, rays, and angles.

Parallel Lines and Perpendicular Lines

Parallel lines are lines in a plane that are always the same distance apart. Parallel lines or line segments never meet.

In the figure, lines AB and CD, even if extended, will never meet. The lines are parallel. Write $\overleftrightarrow{AB} \| \overleftrightarrow{CD}$.

Lines __AD__ and __BC__ are also parallel. So, $\overleftrightarrow{AD} \| \overleftrightarrow{BC}$.

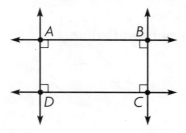

Intersecting lines cross at exactly one point. Intersecting lines that form right angles are **perpendicular.**

In the figure, lines __AD__ and __AB__ are perpendicular because they form right angles at vertex A. Write $\overleftrightarrow{AD} \perp \overleftrightarrow{AB}$.

Lines __BC__ and __CD__ are also perpendicular. So, $\overleftrightarrow{BC} \perp \overleftrightarrow{CD}$.

Use the figure for 1–3.

1. Name two sides that appear to be parallel.

   _____

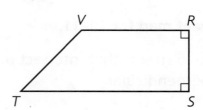

2. Name two sides that appear to be perpendicular.

   _____

3. Name two sides that appear to be intersecting, but not perpendicular.

   _____

Use the figure for 4–6.

4. Name a pair of lines that appear to be perpendicular.

      Think: Perpendicular lines form right angles.

        $\overleftrightarrow{AB}$ and $\overleftrightarrow{EF}$ appear to form right angles.

       $\overleftrightarrow{AB}$ and $\overleftrightarrow{EF}$
_____

5. Name a pair of lines that appear to be parallel.

_____

6. Name another pair of lines that appear to be perpendicular.

_____

Draw and label the figure described.

7. $\overleftrightarrow{MN}$ and $\overleftrightarrow{PQ}$ intersecting at point R

8. $\overleftrightarrow{WX} \parallel \overleftrightarrow{YZ}$

9. $\overleftrightarrow{FH} \perp \overleftrightarrow{JK}$

Problem Solving REAL WORLD

Use the street map for 10–11.

10. Name two streets that intersect but do not appear to be perpendicular.

_____

_____

11. Name two streets that appear to be parallel to each other.

_____

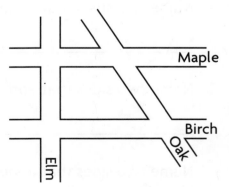

Describe Angles and Sides in Polygons

**Look at this polygon.
Describe the angles.**

There are **2** right angles.

There are **2** obtuse angles.

There is **1** acute angle.

Look at the same polygon.

There is 1 pair of parallel lines.

There are 2 pairs of intersecting lines that are perpendicular.

There are 3 pairs of intersecting lines that are not perpendicular.

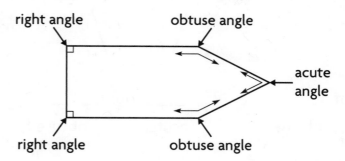

right angle   obtuse angle

acute angle

right angle   obtuse angle

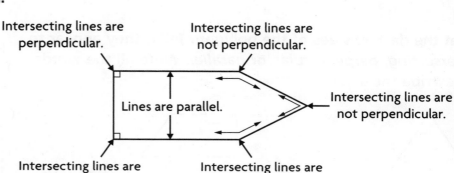

Intersecting lines are perpendicular.

Intersecting lines are not perpendicular.

Lines are parallel.

Intersecting lines are not perpendicular.

Intersecting lines are perpendicular.

Intersecting lines are not perpendicular.

Write how many of each type of angle the shape has.

1.

_____ right, _____ acute, _____ obtuse

2.

_____ right, _____ acute, _____ obtuse

3.

_____ right, _____ acute, _____ obtuse

Look at the dashed sides of the polygon. Tell if they appear to be *intersecting*, *perpendicular*, or *parallel*. Write all the words that describe the sides.

4.

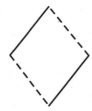

_____

5.

_____

6.

_____

Write how many of each type of angle the shape has.

7.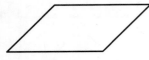

_____0_____ right, _____2_____
acute, _____2_____ obtuse

8.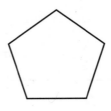

_____ right, _____
acute, _____ obtuse

9.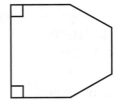

_____ right, _____
acute, _____ obtuse

Look at the dashed sides of the polygon. Tell if they appear to be _intersecting, perpendicular,_ or _parallel._ Write all the words that describe the sides.

10.

_____

11.

_____

12.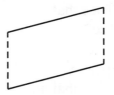

_____

Problem Solving

Draw the shapes described for 13–14.

13. Angles: 2 right, 1 acute, 1 obtuse
    Sides: 1 pair parallel, 2 pairs intersecting
    and perpendicular, 2 pairs intersecting
    but not perpendicular

14. Angles: 8 obtuse
    Sides: 4 pairs of parallel sides.

What shape did you draw?

_____

What shape did you draw?

_____

104

Name _____

Lesson 5.4

Lesson Objective: Use a protractor to measure an angle and to draw an angle with a given measure.

Measure Angles

A **protractor** is a tool for measuring the size of an angle.

A **degree** is a unit used to measure the size of an angle.

Follow the steps below to measure ∠ABC.

Step 1 Place the center point of the protractor on vertex *B* of the angle.

Step 2 Align the 0° mark on the protractor with ray *BC*. Note that the 0° mark is on the outer scale or top scale.

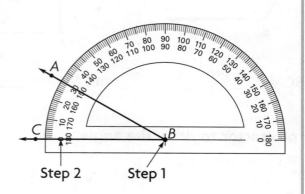

Step 3 Find where ray *BA* intersects the same scale.

Step 4 Read the angle measure on the scale.

m∠ABC = __30°__.

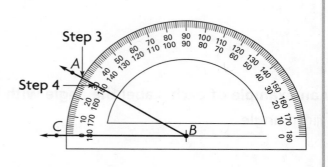

Use a protractor to find the angle measure.

1.

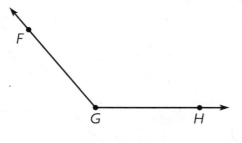

m∠FGH _____

2.

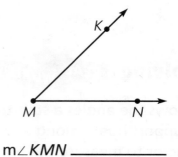

m∠KMN _____

Use a protractor to draw the angle.

3. 110°

4. 55°

Use a protractor to find the angle measure.

5.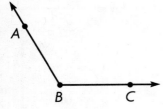

6.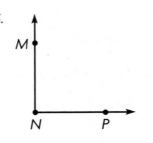

7.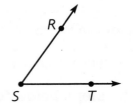

m∠ABC = ___120°___

m∠MNP = _____

m∠RST = _____

Use a protractor to draw the angle.

8. **40°**

9. **170°**

Draw an example of each. Label the angle with its measure.

10. a right angle

11. an acute angle

Problem Solving REAL WORLD

The drawing shows the angles a stair tread makes with a support board along a wall. Use your protractor to measure the angles.

12. What is the measure of ∠A? _____

13. What is the measure of ∠B? _____

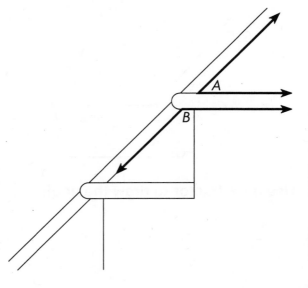

1. Molly needs to write a definition of parallel lines. Which description would best get her started?

   A They only form right angles.

   B They never cross each other.

   C They always form acute angles.

   D They cross at one point.

2. Which of the following terms best describes this figure?

   A ray   **B** line

   C angle   **D** line segment

3. Which describes the angles of the polygon?

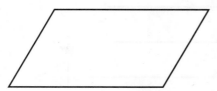

   A 4 acute

   B 2 acute and 2 right

   C 2 right and 2 obtuse

   D 2 acute and 2 obtuse

4. Use a protractor. What is the measure of the greatest angle in the triangle?

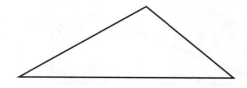

   A 70°   **B** 100°

   C 105°   **D** 115°

5. Which polygon does not have a pair of parallel sides?

   A   **B**

   C   **D**

6. Which two lines are perpendicular?

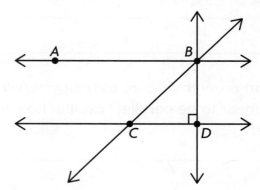

   A $\overleftrightarrow{AB}$ and $\overleftrightarrow{BD}$ **B** $\overleftrightarrow{AB}$ and $\overleftrightarrow{BC}$

   C $\overleftrightarrow{AB}$ and $\overleftrightarrow{CD}$ **D** $\overleftrightarrow{CB}$ and $\overleftrightarrow{BD}$

   GO ON →

Name _____

7. Which is a correct way to name the right angle?

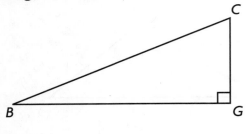

A ∠BC

B ∠CBG

C ∠BGC

D ∠GBC

8. Yvonne is sewing a quilt made of triangles. What is the measure of the angle A?

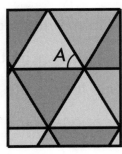

A 30°

B 60°

C 110°

D 120°

9. Luci drew the polygon to the right. How many right, acute, and obtuse angles does it have? Explain.

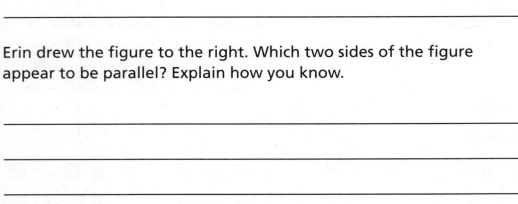

_____

_____

_____

_____

_____

10. Erin drew the figure to the right. Which two sides of the figure appear to be parallel? Explain how you know.

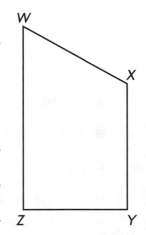

_____

_____

_____

_____

Apply Your Understanding

Classify Quadrilaterals

A **quadrilateral** is a polygon with __4__ sides and __4__ angles.
Some quadrilaterals have special names:

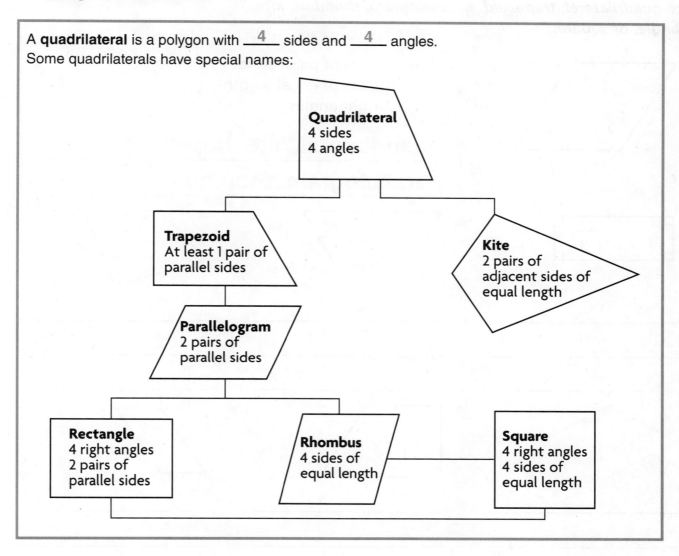

Quadrilateral
4 sides
4 angles

Trapezoid
At least 1 pair of
parallel sides

Kite
2 pairs of
adjacent sides of
equal length

Parallelogram
2 pairs of
parallel sides

Rectangle
4 right angles
2 pairs of
parallel sides

Rhombus
4 sides of
equal length

Square
4 right angles
4 sides of
equal length

Classify each figure as many ways as possible. Write
quadrilateral, trapezoid, parallelogram, rhombus, kite, rectangle, or *square.*

1.

2.

3.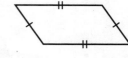

_____   _____   _____

_____   _____   _____

_____   _____   _____

Classify each figure as many ways as possible.
Write *quadrilateral, trapezoid, parallelogram, rhombus, kite,*
rectangle, or *square.*

4.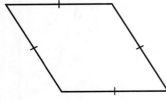

Think: 2 pairs of parallel sides
4 sides of equal length
0 right angles

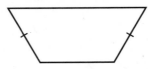

quadrilateral, kite, trapezoid,

parallelogram, rhombus

5.

_____

_____

6.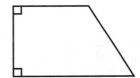

_____

_____

7.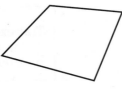

_____

_____

8.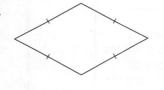

_____

_____

_____

9.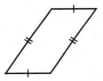

_____

_____

_____

10.

_____

_____

_____

Problem Solving

11. Alan drew a polygon with four sides and four angles. All four sides are equal. None of the angles are right angles. What figure did Alan draw?

_____

12. Teresa drew a quadrilateral with 2 pairs of parallel sides and 4 right angles. What quadrilateral could she have drawn?

_____

110

© Houghton Mifflin Harcourt Publishing Company

Draw Quadrilaterals

Use grid paper to draw a quadrilateral.

Step 1 Use a ruler to draw line segments.
Connect *A* to *B*.

Step 2 Connect *B* to *C*.

Step 3 Connect *C* to *D*.

Step 4 Connect *D* to *A*.

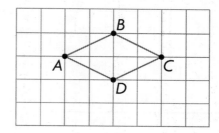

Write the most specific name of your quadrilateral.

rhombus

1. Choose four endpoints that connect to make a square.

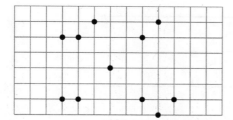

2. Choose four endpoints that connect to make a trapezoid that is not a parallelogram.

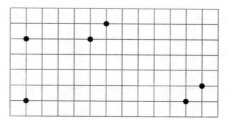

Use grid paper to draw a quadrilateral that is described.
Name the quadrilateral you drew.

3. 4 right angles

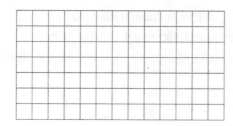

4. 2 pairs of opposite sides that are parallel

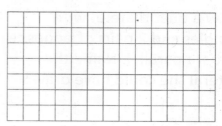

_____

_____

Draw a quadrilateral that is described.
Name the quadrilateral you drew.

5. 4 sides of equal length

square

6. 1 pair of opposite sides that
   are parallel

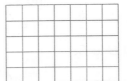

Draw a quadrilateral that does not belong.
Then explain why.

7.

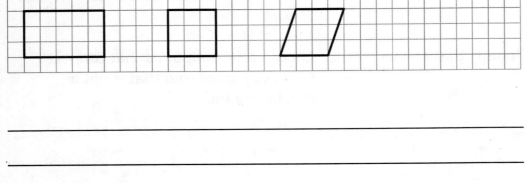

Problem Solving REAL WORLD

8. Layla drew a quadrilateral with
   4 right angles and 2 pairs of opposite
   sides that are parallel. Name the
   quadrilateral she could have drawn.

9. Victor drew a quadrilateral with 2 pairs
   of adjacent sides of equal length. What
   quadrilateral could Victor have drawn?

Algebra • Shape Patterns

Describe a pattern. What is the next figure in your pattern?

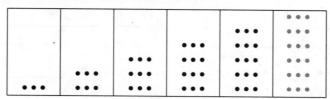

Step 1 Make a table to show the number of dots in each figure.

Figure	1	2	3	4	5	6
Number of Dots	3	6	9	12	15	18

Step 2 Find the rule.

$3 + \underline{\quad 3 \quad} = 6$

Think: The number of dots increase. Try addition.

$6 + \underline{\quad 3 \quad} = 9$

$9 + \underline{\quad 3 \quad} = 12$

$12 + \underline{\quad 3 \quad} = 15$

The rule is to __add 3__.

Step 3 Draw the next figure in your pattern.

Describe a rule. Then draw the next figure in your pattern.

1.

Rule: _____.   _____

2.

Rule: _____.   _____

Describe a rule. Then draw the next figure in your pattern.

3.

Rule: _____.   _____

4.

Rule: _____.   _____

5.

Rule: _____.   _____

Use the rule to draw the next four figures in the pattern.

6. Rule: Add 5.

_____

7. Rule: Multiply by 2.

_____

Problem Solving REAL WORLD

8. Paige made a pattern by drawing shapes. Paige says the rule for her pattern is $s - 1$, where s is the number of sides of the previous shape. Paige's first shape is a hexagon. Draw the next 3 shapes in Paige's pattern.

Name _____

Multiplying and Dividing by 4

Find the unknown factor. Complete.

1. $9 \times$ _____ $= 36$

2. $4 \times$ _____ $= 32$

3. $4 \times$ _____ $= 12$

4. $7 \times 4 = 4 \times$ _____

5. $4 \times 5 = 5 \times$ _____

6. _____ $\times 7 = 28$

7. $4 \times$ _____ $= 16$

8. $2 \times$ _____ $= 4 \times 2$

9. $4 \times$ _____ $= 24$

List the first ten multiples.

10. of 4 _____ _____ _____ _____ _____ _____ _____ _____ _____ _____

Write a related multiplication fact. Then divide.

11. $10 \div 2 =$ _____

_____

12. $8 \div 4 =$ _____

_____

13. $16 \div 4 =$ _____

_____

14. $14 \div 2 =$ _____

_____

15. $24 \div 4 =$ _____

_____

16. $20 \div 4 =$ _____

_____

17. $32 \div 4 =$ _____

_____

18. $18 \div 2 =$ _____

_____

19. $28 \div 4 =$ _____

_____

Name _____

Multiplying and Dividing by 4

Divide. Check by multiplying.

1. $4\overline{)8}$ _____

2. $4\overline{)32}$ _____

3. $4\overline{)24}$ _____

4. $4\overline{)16}$ _____

5. $4\overline{)36}$ _____

6. $4\overline{)12}$ _____

7. $28 \div 4 =$ _____

8. $20 \div 4 =$ _____

9. $12 \div 4 =$ _____

Multiply.

10. $\begin{array}{r} 6 \\ \times\ 4 \\ \hline \end{array}$

11. $\begin{array}{r} 5 \\ \times\ 4 \\ \hline \end{array}$

12. $\begin{array}{r} 7 \\ \times\ 4 \\ \hline \end{array}$

13. $\begin{array}{r} 4 \\ \times\ 8 \\ \hline \end{array}$

14. $\begin{array}{r} 4 \\ \times\ 9 \\ \hline \end{array}$

15. $\begin{array}{r} 3 \\ \times\ 4 \\ \hline \end{array}$

16. $\begin{array}{r} 4 \\ \times\ 4 \\ \hline \end{array}$

17. $\begin{array}{r} 9 \\ \times\ 4 \\ \hline \end{array}$

18. $\begin{array}{r} 8 \\ \times\ 4 \\ \hline \end{array}$

19. $\begin{array}{r} 4 \\ \times\ 5 \\ \hline \end{array}$

20. $4 \times 3 =$ _____

21. $2 \times 7 =$ _____

22. $6 \times 4 =$ _____

Read each question and choose the best answer.

1. Naomi says she is thinking of a quadrilateral with 2 pairs of parallel sides and 4 sides of equal length. Which quadrilateral is she thinking of?

   A rhombus

   B trapezoid

   C rectangle

   D parallelogram

2. Which describes the angles of the polygon?

   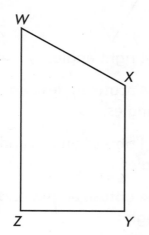

   A 1 acute, 2 right, and 1 obtuse

   B 1 acute, 1 right, and 2 obtuse

   C 2 acute and 2 right

   D 2 acute and 2 obtuse

3. Which of the following terms best describes this figure?

   A ray

   B line

   C angle

   D line segment

4. Neva drew a quadrilateral with 2 pairs of parallel sides and 4 right angles. Which could be the quadrilateral Neva drew?

   A   **B**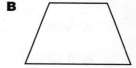

   C    **D**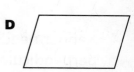

GO ON ➡

5. Li Jing made this pattern using square tiles.

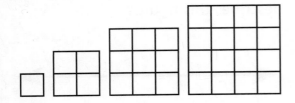

How many square tiles should Li Jing use to make the next figure in the pattern?

A 17

B 19

C 23

D 25

6. Use a protractor. What is the measure of the greatest angle in the triangle?

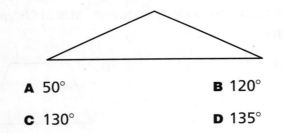

A 50°

B 120°

C 130°

D 135°

7. Xander needs to write a definition of perpendicular lines. Which description would best get him started?

A They cross and form right angles

B They never cross each other

C They always form acute angles

D They cross at more than one point

8. Bindy drew a quadrilateral with 2 pairs of parallel sides that are not all equal. Which is the best name for the quadrilateral she drew?

A parallelogram

B square

C rectangle

D rhombus

9. Which statement is true about the polygon?

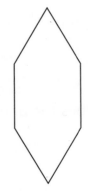

A There are 4 right angles.

B There are 4 acute angles and 2 obtuse angles.

C There are 4 obtuse angles and 2 right angles.

D There are 4 obtuse angles and 2 acute angles.

10. Use a protractor. What is the measure of ∠C?

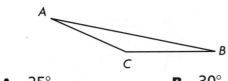

A 25°

B 30°

C 150°

D 155°

GO ON

11. Ariv made a pattern using counters.

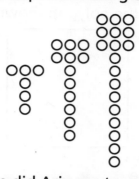

What rule did Ariv use to create the pattern?

A Add 3.

B Add 6.

C Multiply by 2.

D Multiply by 6.

12. Which polygon does not have a pair of perpendicular sides?

A
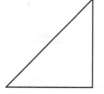

B

C

D
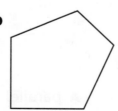

13. Which two lines appear to be parallel?

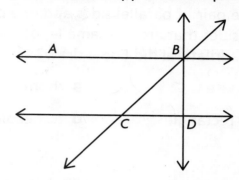

A $\overleftrightarrow{AB}$ and $\overleftrightarrow{BC}$

B $\overleftrightarrow{CD}$ and $\overleftrightarrow{DB}$

C $\overleftrightarrow{AB}$ and $\overleftrightarrow{CD}$

D $\overleftrightarrow{CB}$ and $\overleftrightarrow{BD}$

14. Ethan is building a ramp to use with his dirt bike. Using your protractor, what is the measure of angle *R* on the ramp?

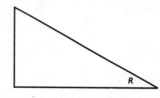

A 30°

B 35°

C 145°

D 150°

15. Which is a correct way to name this angle?

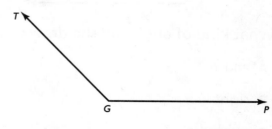

A ∠PT

B ∠PGT

C ∠GPT

D ∠TPG

GO ON

119

16. Eddie drew a quadrilateral with exactly one pair of parallel sides and one pair of sides that are the same length. Which quadrilateral did Eddie draw?

A kite

B rhombus

C rectangle

D trapezoid

17. Jenna drew a quadrilateral has two pairs of sides of equal length that are next to each other and the quadrilateral does not have any parallel sides. What shape did she draw?

A kite

B square

C trapezoid

D rectangle

18. Mrs. Mesiti drew an angle on the chalkboard.

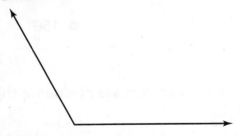

What kind of angle did she draw?

A acute

B right

C obtuse

D straight

19. Which name could not be used to describe the polygon shown?

A square

B rhombus

C rectangle

D triangle

20. Adam started to draw a map of the area. Which words best describe the lines representing Maple Street and East Ave?

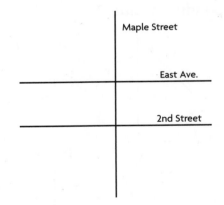

A parallel

B intersecting

C parallel and intersecting

D perpendicular and intersecting

Chapter 6

Decimals and Money

Math in the Real World

Kim spent $\frac{40}{100}$ of a dollar on a snack. Write as a money amount the amount she has left.

What skills do I know that will help me solve this problem??

_____

_____

_____

What do I need to know that can help me solve this problem?

_____

_____

_____

_____

My solution to the problem:

Building Your Math Abilities

Before you begin to explore decimals and money, fill in the chart with what you know about decimals and money, and then, what you would like to learn. As you go through the chapter, add to the chart the things you have learned.

What I know . . .	What I want to know . . .	What I have learned . . .

Go Deeper

What additional questions do you have about decimals and money? Write your questions in the space below.

_____

_____

_____

_____

Make Change

Change is the money you get back if you paid for an item with coins or bills that have a value greater than the cost of the item.

Riana buys a comic book for $3. She pays with a $20 bill. What change should Riana get?

Step 1 Start with the cost of the comic book. Count on to the amount paid.

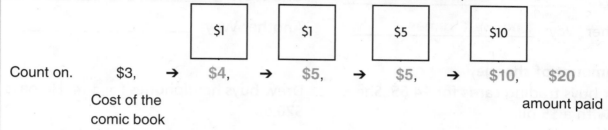

Count on. $3,   → $4,   → $5,   → $5,   → $10, $20

Cost of the comic book

amount paid

Step 2 Count on to find the value of the bills you used.

$10	$5	$1	$1
$10,	$15,	$16,	$17

So, Riana should get $17 in change.
You can show the same amount in a different way.
Show Riana's change in a different way.

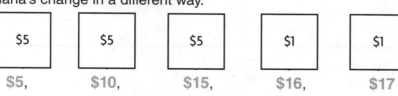

$5, $10, $15, $16, $17

Think: 3 five dollar bills, 2 one dollar bills is also $17 in change.

1. Nevyn buys an apple for 48¢. He pays $1. Find the amount of change. Draw and label each coin.

48¢, _____   _____   _____   _____

Find the amount of change. Write two different ways to make the same amount.

3. Emma buys a notepad for $2.69. She pays $3.00.

   Count on: $2.70, $2.75, $3.00

   _____$0.31_____

   One Way: _1 penny, 1 nickel, 1 quarter_

   Another Way: _1 penny, 3 dimes_____

4. Juan buys an action figure for $3. He pays with a $10 bill.

   _____

   One Way: _____

   Another Way: _____

Find the amount of change.

5. Taylor buys trading cards for $4.65. She pays with a $5 bill.

   _____

6. Drew buys headphones for $14. He pays $20.00.

   _____

7. Inez buys a game for $4. She pays with four $1 bills.

   _____

8. Renzo buys a shirt for $8. He pays with $20.

   _____

Problem Solving REAL WORLD

Use the menu for 9–10.

Menu	
Fruit Salad	$4.35
Sandwich	$4.00
Wrap	$6.00

9. Lou buys a wrap and pays with two $5 bills. How much change should he receive?

   _____

10. Eva buys a fruit salad. Her change is 2 quarters, a dime, and a nickel. How much money did Eva give the cashier?

   _____

Lesson **6.2**

Lesson Objective: Represent money amounts using different combinations of coins.

Make Equivalent Amounts

Samuel has $2 worth of coins. He has 11 coins.
What coins could Samuel have?

Step 1 Use the coin with the greatest value to make $2. It takes __8__ quarters to make $2. There are not enough quarters.	
Step 2 Trade a quarter for __2__ dimes and __1__ nickel. There are __10__ coins. There are not enough coins.	
Step 3 Trade 1 dime for__2__ nickels. Now there are __11__ coins. So, Samuel could have **7 quarters, 1 dime, and 3 nickels.**	

1. List another way Samuel could have $2 with 11 coins.

2. If Samuel had $2 with 14 coins, list the coins he could have.

_____   _____

3. Shaundra has $0.90. Name two different groups of coins she could have.

_____

List one way to make each amount.

4. Use 8 coins to make $2.

_____

_____

5. Use 5 coins to make $0.75.

_____

_____

List three different groups of coins to make each amount.

6. $1

_____

_____

_____

_____

7. $3

_____

_____

_____

_____

8. $0.64

_____

_____

_____

_____

9. $0.83

_____

_____

_____

_____

Problem Solving REAL WORLD

10. Nathaniel has $0.53 in his pocket. He has more than 5 coins, but less than 8 coins. What coins could Nathaniel have?

_____

_____

11. What is the difference between the greatest and least number of coins that make $0.99?

_____

_____

Lesson 6.3

Lesson Objective: Make change using different combinations of bills and coins.

Different Ways to Make Change

Ana has $20. She wants to play the museum entrance fee of $7.
How many different ways can Ana receive change?

Read the Problem	Solve the Problem
What do I need to find? I need to find the number of different ways to make Ana's change. **What information do I need to use?** She has $20 and pays $7 for the entrance fee. $20 − $7 = $13 change **How will I use the information** I will make a table to find all of the different ways to make $13 change.	Show all of the combinations of $10 bills, $5 bills, and $1 bills that equal $13. <table><tr><th>$10 bills</th><th>$5 bills</th><th>$1 bills</th><th>Total Value</th></tr><tr><td>1</td><td>0</td><td>3</td><td>$13</td></tr><tr><td>0</td><td>2</td><td>3</td><td>$13</td></tr><tr><td>0</td><td>1</td><td>8</td><td>$13</td></tr><tr><td>0</td><td>0</td><td>13</td><td>$13</td></tr></table> So, Ana could receive $13 change in ___4___ different ways.

Complete the tables to find how many different ways to make the amount of change.

1. Mei has $3. She pays $2.70 for lunch. How many ways can Mei receive change, using fewer than 10 coins?

Q	D	N	P	Total Value

2. Josh has five $1 bills. He wants to buy a puzzle for $4.75. How many different ways can be receive change using only quarters, dimes, and nickels?

Q	D	N	Total Value

Find the amount of change. Then, if possible, show three ways that amount can be given.

3. Reggie buys an item for $2. He pays with a $10 bill.

$10 bills	$5 bills	$1 bills	Total Value
0	1	3	$8
0	0	8	$8

4. Luz buys an eraser for $0.34. She pays with a $1 bill.

Q	D	N	P	Total Value

5. Lu Chen buys a calendar for $3. She pays with a $20 bill.

$10 bills	$5 bills	$1 bills	Total Value

6. Mario buys a pencil for $0.51. He pays with 3 quarters.

Q	D	N	P	Total Value

Problem Solving REAL WORLD

8. Keenan buys a sandwich for $6 and a drink for $3. He pays with $20. How much change should he get?

_____

9. Rebecca buys an action figure for $8 and a comic book for $4. She pays with $15. How much change should she get?

_____

Name _____

Lesson 6.4

Lesson Objective: Translate among representations of fractions, decimals, and money.

Relate Fractions, Decimals, and Money

Write the total money amount. Then write the amount as a fraction and as a decimal in terms of a dollar.

Step 1 Count the value of coins from greatest to least. Write the total money amount.

$0.25 → $0.35 → $0.40 → $0.45 → $0.50

Step 2 Write the total money amount as a fraction of a dollar.

The total money amount is $0.50, which is the same as 50 cents.

Think: There are 100 cents in a dollar.

So, the total amount written as a fraction of a dollar is:

$$\frac{50 \text{ cents}}{100 \text{ cents}} = \frac{50}{100}$$

Step 3 Write the total money amount as a decimal.

Think: I can write $0.50 as 0.50.

The total money amount is $\frac{50}{100}$ written as a fraction of a dollar, and 0.50 written as a decimal.

Write the total money amount. Then write the amount as a fraction and as a decimal in terms of a dollar.

1.

2.

_____   _____

Write the total money amount. Then write the amount as a fraction and as a decimal in terms of dollars.

3.

$0.18; $\frac{18}{100}$; 0.18
_____

4.

_____

Write as a money amount and as a decimal in terms of dollars.

5. $\frac{25}{100}$ 6. $\frac{79}{100}$ 7. $\frac{31}{100}$ 8. $\frac{8}{100}$ 9. $\frac{42}{100}$

_____ _____ _____ _____ _____

Write the money amount as a fraction in terms of dollars.

10. $0.87   11. $0.03   12. $0.66   13. $0.95   14. $1.00

_____ _____ _____ _____ _____

Write the total money amount. Then write the amount as a fraction and as a decimal in terms of dollars.

15. 2 quarters, 2 dimes   16. 3 dimes, 4 pennies   17. 8 nickels, 12 pennies

_____ _____ _____

Problem Solving REAL WORLD

18. Kate has 1 dime, 4 nickels, and 8 pennies. Write Kate's total amount as a fraction in terms of a dollar.

19. Nolan says he has $\frac{75}{100}$ of a dollar. If he only has 3 coins, what are the coins?

_____ _____

Problem Solving • Money

Use the strategy *act it out* to solve the problem.

Jessica, Carlos, Brian, and Grace earned $9. They want to share the money equally. How much will each person get?

Read the Problem	Solve the Problem
What do I need to find? I need to find the <u>amount of money each person should get</u>.	• Show the total amount, __$9__, using ____9____ one-dollar bills.
What information do I need to use? I need to use the total amount, __$9__, and divide it by ___4___, the number of people sharing the money equally.	• Share the one-dollar bills equally. There is ___1___ one-dollar bill left.
How will I use the information? I will use <u>dollar bills and coins</u> to model the total amount and <u>act out the problem</u>.	• Change the dollar bill that is left for ___4___ quarters. • Share the quarters equally. So, each person gets ___2___ one-dollar bills and ___1___ quarter, or __$1.25__.

Use the strategy *act it out* and coins and bills to solve the problems.

1. Jacob, Dan, and Nathan were given $18 to share equally. How much money will each boy get?

   _____

2. Becky, Marlis, and Hallie each earned $12 raking leaves. How much did they earn together?

   _____

Use the strategy *act it out* and coins and bills to solve the problems.

3. Carl wants to buy a bicycle bell that costs
   $0.95. Carl has saved $0.53 so far. How much
   more money does he need to buy the bell?

   Use 3 quarters and 2 dimes to model
   $0.95. Remove coins that have a value
   of $0.53.

   First, remove 2 quarters. Then exchange
   1 dime for 1 nickel and 5 pennies. Remove
   $0.03.

   Count the amount that is left.
   So, Carl needs to save $0.42 more.

   _____ $0.42 _____

4. Together, Xavier, Yolanda, and Zachary have
   $0.84. If each person has the same amount,
   how much money does each person have?

   _____

5. Marcus, Nan, and Olive each have $7 in
   their pockets. They decide to combine the
   money. How much money do they have
   altogether?

   _____

6. Jessie saves $6 each week. In how many
   weeks will she have saved at least $20?

   _____

7. Becca has $12 more than Cece. Dave has
   $3 less than Cece. Cece has $6. How much
   money do they have altogether?

   _____

Addition and Subtraction Facts

Add.

1. 2 + 4	2. 3 + 5	3. 8 + 1	4. 3 + 4	5. 7 + 2

6. 1 + 0	7. 2 + 6	8. 2 + 8	9. 7 + 1	10. 0 + 6

Add or subtract. Find a pattern. Write the next number sentence.

11. 1 + 6 = _____

    2 + 6 = _____

    3 + 6 = _____

    _____ + _____ = _____

12. 3 + 3 = _____

    4 + 3 = _____

    5 + 3 = _____

    _____ + _____ = _____

13. 7 − 2 = _____

    8 − 2 = _____

    9 − 2 = _____

    _____ − _____ = _____

14. 9 − 5 = _____

    9 − 6 = _____

    9 − 7 = _____

    _____ − _____ = _____

Name _____

Addition and Subtraction Facts

Find the greater number. Count on to add.

1. 6 + 1 = _____   *2.* 3 + 4 = _____   *3.* 5 + 2 = _____

4. 3 + 7 = _____   *5.* 6 + 2 = _____   *6.* 1 + 8 = _____

7. 2 + 9 = _____   *8.* 3 + 5 = _____   *9.* 4 + 2 = _____

Find the difference.

10.	11.	12.	13.	14.
5 − 3	7 − 4	8 − 6	10 − 7	4 − 0

15.	16.	17.	18.	19.
6 − 5	4 − 2	9 − 6	6 − 4	7 − 6

20.	21.	22.	23.	24.
5 − 2	6 − 3	8 − 5	7 − 3	6 − 0

25.	26.	27.	28.	29.
9 − 3	8 − 2	9 − 5	4 − 3	7 − 5

Name _____

Read each question and choose the best answer.

1. Lucas has $15. Erin has $8 more than Lucas. Oliver has $6 more than Erin. How much money do they have altogether?

   A $28   **B** $44

   C $63   **D** $67

2. Sofia buys a new movie for $13. She pays with two $10 bills. How much change should she receive?

   A $3   **B** $7

   C $20   **D** $23

3. Jaxon has the coins shown.

   Which shows his the total amount of money?

   A $0.46   **B** $0.61

   C $0.66   **D** $0.75

4. Natalia pays for a movie ticket. She receives 2 quarters and 6 pennies in change. Which shows another way to make this amount?

   A 26 pennies

   B 5 nickels and 1 penny

   C 11 nickels and 1 penny

   D 6 dimes, 2 nickels, and 11 pennies

5. Elliott spent $0.75 on a pack of gum. Which set of coins could he have used?

   A 3 dimes

   B 2 quarters

   C 7 dimes and 1 nickel

   D 10 nickels and 2 quarters

6. Jorge bought 3 books that each cost $3.99. How much did he spend in all?

   A $1.33

   B $6.99

   C $11.97

   D $14.97

GO ON

7. At the school store, a pencil costs $0.50. Which coins total this amount?

   A 1 quarter

   B 9 nickels and 5 pennies

   C 1 dime, 1 nickel, and 40 pennies

   D 2 quarters, 4 dimes, and 10 pennies

8. A store clerk gave her customer 1 quarter, 1 dime, and 1 nickel in change. What other coins could she have given the customer?

   A 3 dimes and 2 nickels

   B 4 nickels and 5 pennies

   C 2 quarters and 5 nickels

   D 2 nickels and 10 pennies

9. Aiden buys a new shirt for $8.35. He pays with a $10 bill. How much change should he receive?

   A $1.65

   B $2.65

   C $9.35

   D $18.35

10. Paige spent the coins shown to buy a sticker.

   Which shows the total amount of money as a fraction of a dollar?

   A $\frac{62}{100}$ B $\frac{67}{100}$

   C $\frac{72}{100}$ D $\frac{90}{100}$

11. Trevor puts money in a snack machine. The machine gives him 2 dimes and 3 nickels as change. What is another way to make the same amount of change?

   A 13 nickels

   B 65 pennies

   C 1 quarter and 1 dime

   D 3 quarters and 1 nickel

12. Bella has $4. She buys a box of colored pencils for $2.37. How much change should she receive?

   A $0.63

   B $1.63

   C $1.73

   D $2.73

13. Abby and three friends order a pizza that costs $18.60. They share the cost equally. How much does each friend pay?

   A $4.15

   B $4.65

   C $14.60

   D $15.60

14. Max finds 2 dimes, 4 nickels, and 8 pennies. Which set of coins is an equivalent amount?

   A 9 nickels and 3 pennies

   B 10 dimes and 8 pennies

   C 1 quarter, 5 dimes, and 8 pennies

   D 2 quarters, 1 nickel, and 3 pennies

15. Jamal has $\frac{80}{100}$ of a dollar in his pocket. Which shows the fraction as a money amount?

   A $0.08

   B $0.80

   C $8.00

   D $8.80

16. Jacob has $12. He buys a comic book for $5.60. How much change should he receive?

   A $6.40

   B $7.40

   C $15.60

   D $17.60

17. Brian buys a stamp at the post office. He receives 2 quarters and 1 dime as change. What is another way he could receive the same amount of change?

   A 9 nickels

   B 5 dimes and 2 nickels

   C 7 nickels and 10 pennies

   D 1 quarter, 3 nickels, and 5 pennies

18. Kwan spent $0.07 in sales tax. Which fraction shows this amount of money?

   A $\frac{7}{1}$

   B $\frac{7}{10}$

   C $\frac{70}{10}$

   D $\frac{7}{100}$

GO ON

19. Marcus earns $2.75 each day for walking his neighbor's dog. How much will he earn in 7 days?

   A $9.75

   B $14.00

   C $19.25

   D $21.00

20. There are 2 quarters, 3 dimes, and a nickel on the kitchen counter. Which set of coins has an equivalent value?

   A 3 quarters

   B 1 dime and 7 nickels

   C 8 nickels and 5 pennies

   D 1 quarter, 5 dimes, and 2 nickels

STOP

Chapter 7

Add and Subtract Like Fractions

Math in the Real World

Sense or Nonsense? Brian says that when you add or subtract fractions with the same denominator, you can add or subtract the numerators and keep the same denominator. Does Brian's statement make sense? Explain.

What skills do I know that will help me solve this problem?

_____

_____

_____

What do I need to know that can help me solve this problem?

_____

_____

_____

My solution to the problem:

Building Your Math Abilities

Before you begin to explore adding and subtracting like fractions, fill in the chart with what you know about adding and subtracting like fractions, and then, what you would like to learn. As you go through the chapter, add to the chart the things you have learned.

What I know . . .	What I want to know . . .	What I have learned . . .

Go Deeper

What additional questions do you have about adding and subtracting like fractions? Write your questions in the space below.

_____

_____

_____

_____

Name _____

Lesson 7.1

Lesson Objective: Understand that to add or subtract fractions, they must refer to parts of the same whole.

Investigate • Add and Subtract Parts of a Whole

Justin has $\frac{3}{8}$ pound of cheddar cheese and $\frac{2}{8}$ pound of brick cheese. How much cheese does he have in all?

Step 1 Use fraction strips to model the problem. Use three $\frac{1}{8}$-strips to represent $\frac{3}{8}$ pound of cheddar cheese.

Step 2 Join two more $\frac{1}{8}$-strips to represent the amount of brick cheese.

Step 3 Count the number of $\frac{1}{8}$-strips. There are
____ **five** ____ $\frac{1}{8}$-strips. Write the amount as a fraction.

Justin has ___ $\frac{5}{8}$ ___ pound of cheese.

Step 4 Use the model to write an equation.

$$\frac{3}{8} + \frac{2}{8} = \frac{5}{8}$$

Suppose Justin eats $\frac{1}{8}$ pound of cheese. How much cheese is left?

Step 1 Use five $\frac{1}{8}$-strips to represent the $\frac{5}{8}$ pound of cheese.

Step 2 Remove one $\frac{1}{8}$-strip to show the amount eaten.

Step 3 Count the number of $\frac{1}{8}$-strips left. There are
___ **four** ___ $\frac{1}{8}$ fraction strips. There is ___ $\frac{4}{8}$ ___ pound left.

Step 4 Write an equation for the model.

$$\frac{5}{8} - \frac{1}{8} = \frac{4}{8}$$

Use the model to write an equation.

1.

    _____

2.

    _____

Use the model to write an equation.

3.

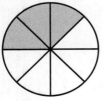 + 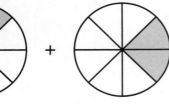 =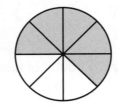

Think: $\frac{3}{8}$ + $\frac{2}{8}$ = $\frac{5}{8}$

$$\frac{3}{8} + \frac{2}{8} = \frac{5}{8}$$

4.

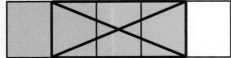

_____

5.

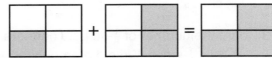

_____

Use the model to solve the equation.

6.

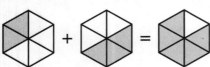

$$\frac{2}{6} + \frac{3}{6} = \underline{\hspace{2cm}}$$

7.

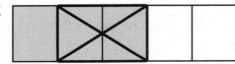

$$\frac{3}{5} - \frac{2}{5} = \underline{\hspace{2cm}}$$

Problem Solving REAL WORLD

8. Jake ate $\frac{4}{8}$ of a pizza. Millie ate $\frac{3}{8}$ of the same pizza. How much of the pizza was eaten by Jake and Millie?

_____

9. Kate ate $\frac{1}{4}$ of her orange. Ben ate $\frac{2}{4}$ of his banana. Did Kate and Ben eat $\frac{1}{4} + \frac{2}{4} = \frac{3}{4}$ of their fruit? Explain.

_____

_____

_____

142

Name _____

Lesson 7.2

Lesson Objective: Decompose a fraction by writing it as a sum of fractions with the same denominators.

Write Fractions as Sums

A **unit fraction** tells the part of the whole that 1 piece represents.
A unit fraction always has a numerator of 1.

Bryan has $\frac{4}{10}$ pound of clay for making clay figures. He wants
to use $\frac{1}{10}$ pound of clay for each figure. How many clay figures can he make?

Use fraction strips to write $\frac{4}{10}$ as a sum of unit fractions.

Step 1 Represent $\frac{4}{10}$ with fraction strips.

Step 2 Each $\frac{1}{10}$ is a unit fraction. Write a $\frac{1}{10}$ addend for
each $\frac{1}{10}$-strip you used to show $\frac{4}{10}$.

Step 3 Count the number of addends. The number of
addends represents the number of clay figures
Bryan can make.

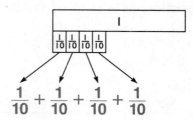

$$\frac{1}{10} + \frac{1}{10} + \frac{1}{10} + \frac{1}{10}$$

So, Bryan can make ___4___ clay figures.

Write the fraction as the sum of unit fractions.

1.

$$\frac{3}{6} = \underline{\quad} + \underline{\quad} + \underline{\quad}$$

2.

$$\frac{2}{4} = \underline{\quad} + \underline{\quad}$$

3.

$$\frac{4}{8} = \underline{\quad} + \underline{\quad} + \underline{\quad} + \underline{\quad}$$

4.

$$\frac{5}{5} = \underline{\quad} + \underline{\quad} + \underline{\quad} + \underline{\quad} + \underline{\quad}$$

Write the fraction as a sum of unit fractions.

5. $\frac{4}{5} = $ _____ $\frac{1}{5} + \frac{1}{5} + \frac{1}{5} + \frac{1}{5}$ _____

Think: Add $\frac{1}{5}$ four times.

6. $\frac{3}{8} = $ _____

7. $\frac{6}{12} = $ _____

_____

8. $\frac{4}{4} = $ _____

Write the fraction as a sum of fractions three different ways.

9. $\frac{7}{10}$

_____

_____

_____

10. $\frac{6}{6}$

_____

_____

_____

Problem Solving REAL WORLD

11. Miguel's teacher asks him to color $\frac{4}{8}$ of his grid. He must use 3 colors: red, blue, and green. There must be more green sections than red sections. How can Miguel color the sections of his grid to follow all the rules?

_____

_____

_____

12. Petra is asked to color $\frac{6}{6}$ of her grid. She must use 3 colors: blue, red, and pink. There must be more blue sections than red sections or pink sections. What are the different ways Petra can color the sections of her grid and follow all the rules?

_____

_____

_____

144

Lesson **7.3**

Lesson Objective: Use models to represent and find sums involving fractions.

Add Fractions Using Models

Fractions with like denominators have the same denominator. You can add fractions with like denominators using a number line.

Model $\frac{4}{6} + \frac{1}{6}$.

Step 1 Draw a number line labeled with sixths. Model the fraction $\frac{4}{6}$ by starting at 0 and shading **4** sixths.

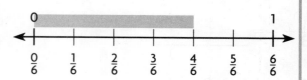

Step 2 Add the fraction $\frac{1}{6}$ by shading **1** more sixth.

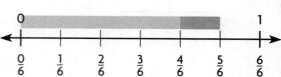

Step 3 How many sixths are there in all? **5** sixths

Write the number of sixths as a fraction.

$5 \text{ sixths} = \frac{5}{6}$ $\qquad$ $\frac{4}{6} + \frac{1}{6} = \frac{5}{6}$

Find the sum. Use a model to help.

1. $\frac{1}{5} + \frac{4}{5}$

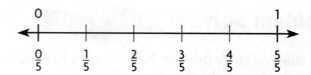

_____

2. $\frac{2}{10} + \frac{4}{10}$

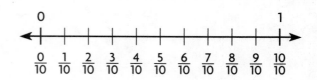

_____

3. $\frac{1}{4} + \frac{1}{4}$

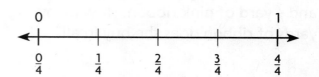

_____

Name _____

Find the sum. Use fraction strips to help.

4. $\frac{2}{6} + \frac{1}{6} =$ _____ $\frac{3}{6}$

$\frac{2}{6}$ $\frac{1}{6}$

5. $\frac{4}{10} + \frac{5}{10} =$ _____

6. $\frac{1}{3} + \frac{2}{3} =$ _____

7. $\frac{2}{4} + \frac{1}{4} =$ _____

8. $\frac{2}{12} + \frac{4}{12} =$ _____

9. $\frac{1}{6} + \frac{2}{6} =$ _____

10. $\frac{3}{12} + \frac{9}{12} =$ _____

11. $\frac{3}{8} + \frac{4}{8} =$ _____

12. $\frac{3}{4} + \frac{1}{4} =$ _____

13. $\frac{1}{5} + \frac{2}{5} =$ _____

Problem Solving REAL WORLD

14. Lola walks $\frac{4}{10}$ mile to her friend's house. Then she walks $\frac{5}{10}$ mile to the store. How far does she walk in all?

_____

15. Evan eats $\frac{1}{8}$ of a pan of lasagna, and his brother eats $\frac{2}{8}$ of it. What fraction of the pan of lasagna do they eat in all?

_____

16. Jacqueline buys $\frac{2}{4}$ yard of green ribbon and $\frac{1}{4}$ yard of pink ribbon. How many yards of ribbon does she buy in all?

_____

17. Shu mixes $\frac{2}{3}$ pound of peanuts with $\frac{1}{3}$ pound of almonds. How many pounds of nuts does Shu mix in all?

_____

1. Cole played the piano for $\frac{1}{3}$ of an hour. Then he played the flute for $\frac{1}{3}$ of an hour and the drums for another $\frac{1}{3}$ of an hour. What fraction shows the total number of hours he play instruments?

   A $\frac{2}{3}$ of an hour

   B $\frac{3}{3}$ of an hour

   C $\frac{1}{9}$ of an hour

   D $\frac{3}{9}$ of an hour

2. Aiden read $\frac{5}{8}$ of his library book over the weekend. What is $\frac{5}{8}$ written as the sum of unit fractions?

   A $\frac{2}{8} + \frac{3}{8}$

   B $\frac{1}{5} + \frac{1}{5}$

   C $\frac{1}{2} + \frac{1}{2} + \frac{1}{2} + \frac{2}{2}$

   D $\frac{1}{8} + \frac{1}{8} + \frac{1}{8} + \frac{1}{8} + \frac{1}{8}$

3. Valeria ran $\frac{3}{10}$ of a mile. Then she walked $\frac{4}{10}$ of a mile. What fraction of a mile did she travel?

   A $\frac{10}{7}$ of a mile

   B $\frac{1}{10}$ of a mile

   C $\frac{7}{10}$ of a mile

   D $\frac{7}{20}$ of a mile

4. The fraction of a yard of ribbon Mia used to make bookmarks for her friends is equal to the sum of the fractions below.

   $$\frac{2}{12} + \frac{3}{12} + \frac{4}{12}$$

Which shows total amount of ribbon Mia used?

   A $\frac{5}{12}$ of a yard

   B $\frac{6}{12}$ of a yard

   C $\frac{7}{12}$ of a yard

   D $\frac{9}{12}$ of a yard

5. Mr. Franklin painted $\frac{3}{5}$ of a table top in the morning. He painted $\frac{1}{5}$ of a table top in the afternoon. Use the model to find the total amount of the table top Mr. Franklin painted.

   $$\frac{3}{5} + \frac{1}{5} = \underline{\quad}$$

   A $\frac{5}{4}$ **B** $\frac{1}{5}$

   C $\frac{4}{5}$ **D** $\frac{4}{10}$

6. Kaitlyn raked leaves. She filled $\frac{3}{12}$ of a bag with leaves in the front yard and $\frac{7}{12}$ of a bag in the back yard. Then she put all of the leaves in a bag together. How much of the bag did she fill?

   A $\frac{12}{10}$ **B** $\frac{4}{12}$

   C $\frac{10}{12}$ **D** $\frac{10}{24}$

GO ON

Name _____

7. Carlos buys a pack of flower seeds. He plants $\frac{2}{5}$ the pack in his garden and $\frac{3}{5}$ of the pack in flower pots. What fraction of seeds does Carlos plant?

A $\frac{1}{5}$

B $\frac{5}{5}$

C $\frac{1}{10}$

D $\frac{5}{10}$

8. Which shows $\frac{4}{4}$ as the sum?

A $\frac{4}{4} + \frac{4}{4}$

B $\frac{1}{4} + \frac{2}{4} + \frac{1}{4}$

C $\frac{3}{4} + \frac{1}{4} + \frac{1}{4}$

D $\frac{1}{1} + \frac{1}{1} + \frac{1}{1} + \frac{1}{1}$

9. Eric had a fraction of a gallon of juice. He poured juice for his family, and had a fraction of a gallon left. Use the model to write an equation to represent Eric's juice. Explain how the equation relates to the model.

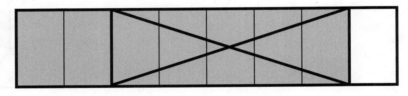

_____

_____

_____

_____

10. The distance from Eva's house to her grandmother's house is $\frac{4}{10}$ of a mile. Write the fraction as a sum of unit fractions.

_____

_____

Apply Your Understanding

Lesson 7.4

Lesson Objective: Use models to represent and find differences involving fractions.

Subtract Fractions Using Models

You can subtract fractions with like denominators using fraction strips.

Model $\frac{5}{8} - \frac{2}{8}$.

Step 1 Shade the eighths you start with.
Shade 5 eighths.

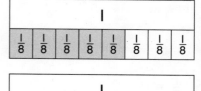

Step 2 Subtract $\frac{2}{8}$.

Think: How many eighths are taken away?
Cross out **2** of the shaded eighths.

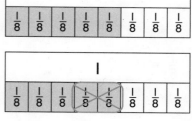

Step 3 Count the shaded eighths that remain.
There are **3** eighths remaining.

Step 4 Write the number of eighths that remain as
a fraction.

3 eighths $= \frac{3}{8}$ $\qquad$ $\frac{5}{8} - \frac{2}{8} = \frac{3}{8}$

1. **Model** $\frac{3}{3} - \frac{2}{3}$.

$\frac{3}{3} - \frac{2}{3} =$ _____

Subtract. Use fraction strips to help.

2. $\frac{5}{6} - \frac{1}{6}$

$\frac{5}{6} - \frac{1}{6} =$ _____

3. $\frac{6}{10} - \frac{3}{10}$

$\frac{6}{10} - \frac{3}{10} =$ _____

Subtract. Use fraction strips to help.

4. $\dfrac{4}{5} - \dfrac{1}{5} = $ _____ $\dfrac{3}{5}$

5. $\dfrac{3}{4} - \dfrac{1}{4} = $ _____

6. $\dfrac{5}{6} - \dfrac{1}{6} = $ _____

7. $\dfrac{7}{8} - \dfrac{1}{8} = $ _____

8. $\dfrac{4}{4} - \dfrac{1}{4} = $ _____

9. $\dfrac{8}{10} - \dfrac{2}{10} = $ _____

10. $\dfrac{3}{4} - \dfrac{1}{4} = $ _____

11. $\dfrac{7}{6} - \dfrac{5}{6} = $ _____

Problem Solving REAL WORLD

Use the table for 12 and 13.

12. Ena is making trail mix. She buys the items shown in the table. How many more pounds of pretzels than raisins does she buy?

_____

13. How many more pounds of granola than banana chips does she buy?

_____

Item	Weight (in pounds)
Pretzels	$\dfrac{7}{8}$
Peanuts	$\dfrac{4}{8}$
Raisins	$\dfrac{2}{8}$
Banana Chips	$\dfrac{3}{8}$
Granola	$\dfrac{5}{8}$

Name _____

Lesson 7.5

Lesson Objective: Solve word problems involving addition and subtraction with fractions.

Add and Subtract Fractions

You can find and record the sums and the differences of fractions.

Add. $\dfrac{2}{6} + \dfrac{4}{6}$

Step 1 Model it.	**Step 2** Think: How many sixths are there in all?	**Step 3** Record it.
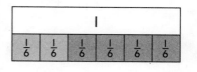	There are **6** sixths. 6 sixths $= \dfrac{6}{6}$	Write the sum as an addition equation. $\dfrac{2}{6} + \dfrac{4}{6} = \dfrac{6}{6}$

Subtract. $\dfrac{6}{10} - \dfrac{2}{10}$

Step 1 Model it.	**Step 2** Think: There are 6 tenths. I take away 2 tenths. How many tenths are left?	**Step 3** Record it.
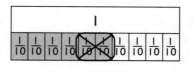	There are **4** tenths left. 4 tenths $= \dfrac{4}{10}$	Write the difference as a subtraction equation. $\dfrac{6}{10} - \dfrac{2}{10} = \dfrac{4}{10}$

Find the sum or difference.

1. 7 eighth-size parts − 4 eighth-size parts = _____

   $\dfrac{7}{8} - \dfrac{4}{8} = $ _____

2. $\dfrac{11}{12} - \dfrac{4}{12} = $ _____

3. $\dfrac{2}{10} + \dfrac{2}{10} = $ _____

4. $\dfrac{6}{8} - \dfrac{4}{8} = $ _____

5. $\dfrac{2}{4} + \dfrac{2}{4} = $ _____

6. $\dfrac{4}{5} - \dfrac{3}{5} = $ _____

7. $\dfrac{1}{3} + \dfrac{2}{3} = $ _____

Find the sum or difference.

8. $\dfrac{4}{12} + \dfrac{8}{12} =$ _____ $\dfrac{12}{12}$

9. $\dfrac{3}{6} - \dfrac{1}{6} =$ _____

10. $\dfrac{4}{5} - \dfrac{3}{5} =$ _____

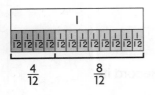

11. $\dfrac{6}{10} + \dfrac{3}{10} =$ _____

12. $1 - \dfrac{3}{8} =$ _____

13. $\dfrac{1}{4} + \dfrac{2}{4} =$ _____

14. $\dfrac{9}{12} - \dfrac{5}{12} =$ _____

15. $\dfrac{5}{6} - \dfrac{2}{6} =$ _____

16. $\dfrac{2}{3} + \dfrac{1}{3} =$ _____

Problem Solving REAL WORLD

Use the table for 17 and 18.

17. Guy finds how far his house is from several locations and makes the table shown. How much farther away from Guy's house is the library than the cafe?

_____

18. If Guy walks from his house to school and back, how far does he walk?

_____

Distance from Guy's House	
Location	**Distance (in miles)**
Library	$\dfrac{9}{10}$
School	$\dfrac{5}{10}$
Store	$\dfrac{7}{10}$
Cafe	$\dfrac{4}{10}$
Yogurt Shop	$\dfrac{6}{10}$

Lesson Objective: Solve multistep problems involving fractions including the use of models.

Problem Solving • Multistep Fraction Problems

Jeff runs $\frac{3}{5}$ mile each day. He wants to know how many days he has to run before he has run a whole number of miles.

Read the Problem	Solve the Problem
What do I need to find? I need to find <u>how many days Jeff</u> <u>needs to run $\frac{3}{5}$ mile</u> until he has run a whole number of miles.	**Describe how to act it out. Use a number line.** $0 \quad \frac{1}{5} \quad \frac{2}{5} \quad \frac{3}{5} \quad \frac{4}{5} \quad 1 \quad \frac{6}{5} \quad \frac{7}{5} \quad \frac{8}{5} \quad \frac{9}{5} \quad 2 \quad \frac{11}{5} \quad \frac{12}{5} \quad \frac{13}{5} \quad \frac{14}{5} \quad 3 \quad \frac{16}{5}$
What information do I need to use? Jeff runs $\frac{3}{5}$ mile a day. He wants the distance run to be a <u>whole number</u>.	Day 1: $\frac{3}{5}$ mile Day 2: $\frac{6}{5}$ mile $\underline{\frac{3}{5}} + \underline{\frac{3}{5}} = \underline{\frac{6}{5}}$ 1 whole mile and $\frac{1}{5}$ mile more Day 3: $\frac{9}{5}$ mile $\underline{\frac{3}{5}} + \underline{\frac{3}{5}} + \underline{\frac{3}{5}} = \underline{\frac{9}{5}}$ 1 whole mile and $\frac{4}{5}$ mile more
How will I use the information? I can use a number line and <u>patterns</u> to <u>act out</u> the problem.	Day 4: $\frac{12}{5}$ mile $\underline{\frac{3}{5}} + \underline{\frac{3}{5}} + \underline{\frac{3}{5}} + \underline{\frac{3}{5}} = \underline{\frac{12}{5}}$ 2 whole miles and $\frac{2}{5}$ mile more Day 5: $\frac{15}{5}$ mile $\underline{\frac{3}{5}} + \underline{\frac{3}{5}} + \underline{\frac{3}{5}} + \underline{\frac{3}{5}} + \underline{\frac{3}{5}} = \underline{\frac{15}{5}}$ 3 whole miles So, Jeff will run a total of <u>3</u> miles in <u>5</u> days.

1. Mack is repackaging $\frac{6}{8}$-pound bags of birdseed into 1-pound bags of birdseed. What is the least number of $\frac{6}{8}$-pound bags of birdseed he needs in order to fill 1-pound bags without leftovers?

2. Lena runs $\frac{2}{3}$ mile each day. She wants to know how many days she has to run before she has run a whole number of miles.

_____   _____

Read each problem and solve.

3. Each child in the Smith family was given an orange cut into 8 equal sections. Each child ate $\frac{5}{8}$ of the orange. After combining the leftover sections, Mrs. Smith noted that there were exactly 3 full oranges left. How many children are in the Smith family?

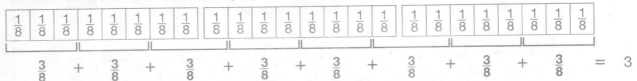

$$\frac{3}{8} + \frac{3}{8} + \frac{3}{8} + \frac{3}{8} + \frac{3}{8} + \frac{3}{8} + \frac{3}{8} + \frac{3}{8} = 3$$

There are 8 addends, so there are 8 children in the Smith family.

_____ 8 children _____

4. Val walks $\frac{13}{5}$ miles each day. Bill runs 10 miles once every 4 days. In 4 days, who covers the greater distance?

_____

5. Chad buys peanuts in 2-pound bags. He repackages them into bags that hold $\frac{5}{6}$ pound of peanuts. How many 2-pound bags of peanuts should Chad buy so that he can fill the $\frac{5}{6}$-pound bags without having any peanuts left over?

_____

6. A carpenter has several boards of equal length. He cuts $\frac{3}{5}$ of each board. After cutting the boards, the carpenter notices that he has enough pieces left over to make up the same length as 4 of the original boards. How many boards did the carpenter start with?

_____

Name _____

Adding and Subtracting Fractions with Like Denominators

Is the fraction less than, equal to, or greater than one half? Write $>$, $<$, or $=$.

1. $\frac{3}{6}$ _____

2. $\frac{5}{8}$ _____

3. $\frac{3}{10}$ _____

4. $\frac{9}{16}$ _____

5. $\frac{5}{12}$ _____

6. $\frac{7}{14}$ _____

7. $\frac{12}{20}$ _____

8. $\frac{6}{18}$ _____

9. $\frac{4}{8}$ _____

Round to the nearest whole number.

10. $3\frac{1}{2}$ _____

11. $4\frac{1}{4}$ _____

12. $8\frac{5}{8}$ _____

13. $13\frac{1}{3}$ _____

14. $7\frac{1}{6}$ _____

15. $9\frac{2}{3}$ _____

16. $11\frac{3}{4}$ _____

17. $10\frac{5}{6}$ _____

18. $5\frac{7}{8}$ _____

Write the closest pair of whole numbers that the sum or difference falls between.

19. $\frac{1}{9} + \frac{4}{9}$

20. $2\frac{1}{5} + \frac{1}{5}$

21. $3\frac{3}{8} - 2\frac{1}{8}$

22. $5\frac{4}{5} - 3\frac{2}{5}$

_____

_____

_____

_____

Name _____

Adding and Subtracting Fractions with Like Denominators

Add or subtract. Write the answer in simplest form.

1.   2 sevenths
    + 3 sevenths
	2. 5 ninths
	    − 2 ninths
		3. 6 tenths
		    − 1 tenth

4.   7 twelfths
    − 3 twelfths
	5. 2 fifths
	    + 1 fifth
		6. 10 fifteenths
		    + 2 fifteenths

7. $\dfrac{5}{8}$ 8. $3\dfrac{3}{5}$ 9. $5\dfrac{2}{7}$ 10. $\dfrac{2}{3}$

   $-\dfrac{2}{8}$ $+2\dfrac{1}{5}$ $-2\dfrac{4}{7}$ $+\dfrac{1}{3}$

11. $6\dfrac{2}{6}$ 12. $9\dfrac{1}{8}$ 13. $\dfrac{2}{6}$ 14. $2\dfrac{7}{8}$

   $+3\dfrac{2}{6}$ $-4\dfrac{3}{8}$ $+\dfrac{3}{6}$ $+4\dfrac{2}{8}$

15. $7\dfrac{3}{9}$ 16. $\dfrac{1}{2}$ 17. $6\dfrac{3}{4}$ 18. $5\dfrac{1}{6}$

   $-2\dfrac{5}{9}$ $+\dfrac{1}{2}$ $-2\dfrac{1}{4}$ $-3\dfrac{5}{6}$

Read each question and choose the best answer.

1. Caden buys a bag of marbles. The bag has $\frac{6}{10}$ red marbles and $\frac{3}{10}$ yellow marbles. The rest of the marbles are blue. What fraction of the marbles are blue?

   A $\frac{1}{10}$

   B $\frac{3}{10}$

   C $\frac{9}{10}$

   D $\frac{10}{10}$

2. Naomi is on a swim team $\frac{4}{12}$ of the year. Which shows $\frac{4}{12}$ as the sum of unit fractions?

   A $\frac{2}{12} + \frac{2}{12}$

   B $\frac{1}{4} + \frac{1}{4} + \frac{1}{4}$

   C $\frac{1}{3} + \frac{1}{3} + \frac{1}{3} + \frac{1}{3}$

   D $\frac{1}{12} + \frac{1}{12} + \frac{1}{12} + \frac{1}{12}$

3. Mrs. Johnson used white sugar and brown sugar to make muffins. The shaded parts of the models show the fraction of a cup for each ingredient that she used.

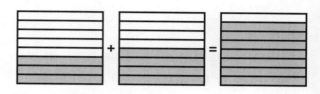

   Which equation do the models show?

   A $\frac{3}{8} + \frac{4}{8} = \frac{7}{8}$

   B $\frac{5}{8} + \frac{4}{8} = \frac{1}{8}$

   C $\frac{3}{5} + \frac{4}{4} = \frac{1}{7}$

   D $\frac{5}{3} + \frac{4}{4} = \frac{7}{1}$

4. Chen pours $\frac{1}{3}$ of a cup of milk on his cereal. He pours $\frac{2}{3}$ of a cup of milk in a glass. How many cups of milk does Chen use in all?

   A $\frac{1}{3}$ cup

   B $\frac{3}{6}$ cup

   C $\frac{3}{3}$ cup

   D $\frac{3}{1}$ cup

GO ON

5. Logan drank $\frac{2}{5}$ of a liter of water before soccer practice. He drank $\frac{1}{5}$ of a liter after practice. How many liters of water did Logan drink?

   A $\frac{1}{10}$ liter   **B** $\frac{1}{5}$ liter

   C $\frac{3}{10}$ liter   **D** $\frac{3}{5}$ liter

6. Chloe has $\frac{5}{8}$ cup of bubble bath in a bottle. She poured $\frac{2}{8}$ cup in the tub. How many cups of bubble bath does she have left? Use the fraction strip to help you.

1							
$\frac{1}{8}$	$\frac{1}{8}$	$\frac{1}{8}$	$\frac{1}{8}$	$\frac{1}{8}$	$\frac{1}{8}$	$\frac{1}{8}$	$\frac{1}{8}$

   A $\frac{1}{8}$ cup   **B** $\frac{3}{8}$ cup

   C $\frac{7}{8}$ cup   **D** $\frac{8}{8}$ cup

7. Each day, Maddie reads for $\frac{1}{4}$ hour before school and $\frac{2}{4}$ hour after school. In how many days will she have read for 3 hours?

   A 4 days

   B 6 days

   C 8 days

   D 12 days

8. Ms. Keller has $\frac{4}{5}$ of a loaf of bread. She uses $\frac{1}{5}$ of the loaf to make sandwiches. What fraction of a loaf of bread is left? Use the fraction model to help you.

1				
$\frac{1}{5}$	$\frac{1}{5}$	$\frac{1}{5}$	$\frac{1}{5}$	$\frac{1}{5}$

   A $\frac{5}{10}$

   B $\frac{3}{5}$

   C $\frac{4}{5}$

   D $\frac{5}{3}$

9. Lamar had a fraction of a gallon of water. He poured some of the water on his mother's plants. A fraction of a gallon of water is left. The model shows Lamar's water.

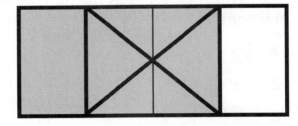

   Which equation is represented by the model?

   A $\frac{2}{4} + \frac{2}{4} = \frac{4}{4}$

   B $\frac{1}{4} + \frac{3}{4} = \frac{4}{4}$

   C $\frac{3}{4} - \frac{2}{4} = \frac{1}{4}$

   D $\frac{4}{4} - \frac{2}{4} = \frac{2}{4}$

GO ON

10. At the beach, Ethan filled $\frac{2}{8}$ of a pail with sand and $\frac{5}{8}$ of a pail with water. What fraction of the pail is full?

A $\frac{3}{8}$

B $\frac{7}{16}$

C $\frac{7}{8}$

D $\frac{8}{1}$

11. Mrs. Hale buys boxes of granola. Her family eats $\frac{6}{8}$ of a box for breakfast each day. What is the least number of boxes Mrs. Hale can buy so her family can eat breakfast without having any granola left over?

A 4

B 6

C 12

D 24

12. At the beach, Samuel collected $\frac{4}{5}$ of a bucket of sea shells. Which shows $\frac{4}{5}$ as a sum of fractions?

A $\frac{1}{2} + \frac{3}{3}$

B $\frac{4}{5} + \frac{4}{5}$

C $\frac{1}{5} + \frac{2}{5} + \frac{1}{5}$

D $\frac{1}{4} + \frac{1}{4} + \frac{1}{4} + \frac{1}{4} + \frac{1}{4}$

13. Sergio bought 1 book at the school book fair. He has read $\frac{1}{3}$ of the book. How much of the book does he have left to read?

A $\frac{1}{3}$

B $\frac{2}{3}$

C $\frac{3}{3}$

D $1\frac{1}{3}$

14. Mr. Sanders has $\frac{7}{10}$ of a bag of potting soil. He uses $\frac{2}{10}$ of a bag in his garden. How much of the bag of soil is left?

A $\frac{5}{20}$

B $\frac{9}{20}$

C $\frac{5}{10}$

D $\frac{9}{10}$

15. Molly's pet frog hopped two times. The first hop was $\frac{7}{12}$ of a yard. The second hop was $\frac{4}{12}$ of a yard. What fraction of a yard did the frog hop?

A $\frac{3}{12}$ yard

B $\frac{11}{24}$ yard

C $\frac{11}{12}$ yard

D $\frac{12}{11}$ yards

GO ON

16. Emma walks east $\frac{3}{10}$ mile, then north $\frac{5}{10}$ mile to get to school. How far does she walk in all?

   A $\frac{2}{10}$ mile

   B $\frac{8}{20}$ mile

   C $\frac{8}{10}$ mile

   D $\frac{10}{8}$ mile

17. Jaden makes $\frac{6}{8}$ of a gallon of punch using three different items. Which shows the fractions of a gallon of each item he could have used?

   A $\frac{1}{8}$ gallon of soda, $\frac{3}{8}$ gallon of pineapple juice, and $\frac{2}{8}$ gallon of orange juice

   B $\frac{1}{2}$ gallon of soda, $\frac{3}{4}$ gallon of pineapple juice, and $\frac{2}{2}$ gallon of orange juice

   C $\frac{3}{8}$ gallon of soda, $\frac{2}{8}$ gallon of pineapple juice, and $\frac{3}{8}$ gallon of orange juice

   D $\frac{2}{4}$ gallon of soda, $\frac{1}{2}$ gallon of pineapple juice, and $\frac{3}{2}$ gallon of orange juice

18. Noah picks $\frac{1}{4}$ pound of blackberries and $\frac{2}{4}$ pound of blueberries. How many pounds of berries does he pick in all?

   A $\frac{3}{8}$ pound   B $\frac{3}{4}$ pound

   C $\frac{4}{4}$ pound   D $\frac{4}{3}$ pound

19. Olivia and her dad jog $\frac{8}{10}$ a mile each day. How many days will it take them to jog a total of 4 miles?

   A 5 days

   B 6 days

   C 8 days

   D 10 days

20. A roll of tape is 1 yard in length. Sasha uses $\frac{3}{12}$ of a yard of tape. How much tape is left on the roll?

   A $\frac{2}{12}$ yard

   B $\frac{4}{12}$ yard

   C $\frac{9}{12}$ yard

   D $1\frac{3}{12}$ yards

STOP

160

Chapter 8

Measurement and Data

Math in the Real World

The students in the third-grade classes recorded the lengths of their shoes to the nearest centimeter. The data are in the tally table.

What if the length of 5 more boys' shoes measured 21 centimeters? Explain how the table would change.

What skills do I know that will help me solve this problem?

_____

_____

_____

What do I need to know that can help me solve this problem?

_____

_____

_____

_____

_____

_____

My solution to the problem:

Shoe Lengths		
Length in Centimeters	**Tally**	
	Boys	**Girls**
18	卌 I	IIII
19	卌	IIII
20	卌 III	卌 IIII
21	卌 II	卌
22	卌 IIII	卌 II

Shoe Lengths		
Length in Centimeters	**Number**	
	Boys	**Girls**
18		
19		
20		
21		
22		

Building Your Math Abilities

Before you begin to explore measurement and data, fill in the chart with what you know about measurement and data, and then, what you would like to learn. As you go through the chapter, add to the chart the things you have learned.

What I know . . .	What I want to know . . .	What I have learned . . .

Go Deeper

What additional questions do you have about measurement and data? Write your questions in the space below.

_____

_____

_____

_____

Lesson **8.1**

Lesson Objective: Choose and use appropriate customary and metric units and tools to measure length.

Choose an Appropriate Measurement Instrument and Unit

There are different units and tools for measuring length.

Customary Tools: inch ruler, yard stick, measuring tape Customary Units: inches, feet

Metric Tools: centimeter ruler, meter stick Metric Units: centimeters, meters

---

Tate wants to find out what size baseball cap he should buy. The cap sizes are customary measures. So, he needs to measure the distance around his head. What tool should Tate use?

Step 1 Tate wants to measure the distance around his head.

The distance around Tate's head is curved and the measurement needs to be precise to get the correct fit.

So, Tate should use a ____measuring tape____ .

Step 2 Think about the units you can choose from.

The cap sizes are customary measures, so Tate should measure using ____inches____ .

Think: The smaller the unit you use, the more precise the measurement.

So, Tate should use a ____measuring tape____ and ____inches____ to measure the distance around his head.

Choose an appropriate tool and unit. Choose metric units.

1. Christopher needs to know the height of a book to see if it will fit on a shelf.

   _____

2. Daniel wants to know if his water skis are too long to fit in the trunk of his car.

   _____

3. Monica wants to find the length of two paper clips.

   _____

4. Annie needs to know the width of her truck to see if it will fit through the paddock gate.

   _____

5. List 3 items that could be measured in centimeters using a centimeter ruler.

   length of a pencil, width of a book, height of a small action figure
   _____

   _____

6. List 3 items that could be measured in inches using an inch ruler.

   _____

   _____

7. List 3 items that could be measured in meters using a meter stick.

   _____

   _____

8. List 3 items that could be measured in feet using a yard stick.

   _____

   _____

9. List 3 items that could be measured in inches or feet using a measuring tape.

   _____

   _____

Problem Solving REAL WORLD

10. Camryn measures the length of her bedroom. She says that it is 16 inches long. Is this correct? Explain.

   _____

   _____

   _____

   _____

Lesson **8.2**

Lesson Objective: Use a ruler to measure objects to the nearest inch, half-inch, and quarter-inch.

Measure to the Nearest Quarter-Inch

Measure the length of the leaf to the nearest inch, half-inch, and quarter-inch.

Step 1 The right end of the leaf is between 3 and 4 inches. It is closer to the 3-inch mark. To the nearest inch, the leaf is **3 inches** long.

Step 2 The right end is between 3 and $3\frac{1}{2}$ inches. It is closer to the $3\frac{1}{2}$-inch mark.

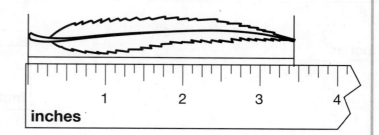

inches

To the nearest half-inch, the leaf is $3\frac{1}{2}$ **inches** long.

Step 3 The right end is between $3\frac{1}{4}$ and $3\frac{1}{2}$ inches.

It is closer to the $3\frac{1}{2}$-inch mark. To the nearest quarter-inch, the leaf is $3\frac{1}{2}$ **inches** long.

Use the inch ruler to estimate the length of each object to the nearest inch, half-inch, and quarter-inch.

1.

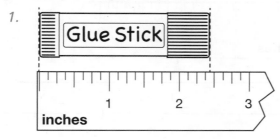

_____

_____

2.

_____

_____

Use the inch ruler to estimate the length of each object to the nearest inch, half-inch, and quarter-inch.

3.

inches

_____

_____

4.

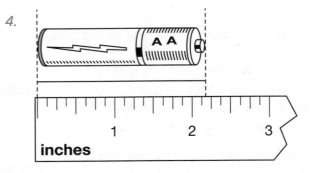

inches

_____

_____

5.

inches

_____

_____

6.

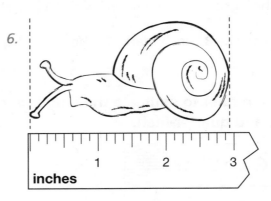

inches

_____

_____

Problem Solving REAL WORLD

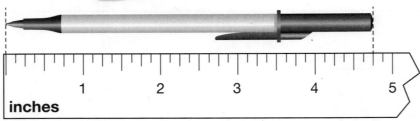

inches

7. Mia is making a case to carry her pens. Measure the pen to the nearest half-inch. How long should Mia make her case? Explain.

_____

_____

Measure to the Nearest Centimeter

Measure the length of the pencil to the nearest centimeter.

Step 1 Line the pencil up with the ruler so that the left end is at the 0 centimeter mark.

Step 2 The right end of the pencil is between 6 and 7 centimeters. It is closer to the __7__ –centimeter mark.

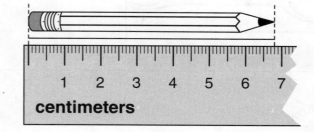

So, to the nearest centimeter, the pencil is ___7 centimeters___ long.

Estimate the length in centimeters. Then use a centimeter ruler to measure to the nearest centimeter.

1.

_____

2.

_____

3.

_____

© Houghton Mifflin Harcourt Publishing Company

Estimate the length in centimeters. Then use a centimeter ruler to measure to the nearest centimeter.

4.

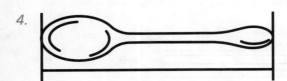

about 5 centimeters; 6 centimeters

5.

6.

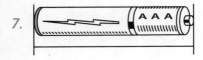

7.

Problem Solving REAL WORLD

8. Eloise made a paper-clip chain using paper clips. Each paper clip was the length of the paper clip shown. About how many centimeters long was the chain if Eloise used 12 paper clips?

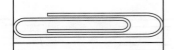

168

© Houghton Mifflin Harcourt Publishing Company

1. Abigail used a glue stick to make a poster for her science project.

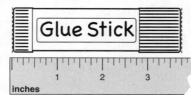

   What is the length of the glue stick to the nearest quarter-inch?

   A 3 inches   **B** $3\frac{1}{2}$ inches

   C $3\frac{3}{4}$ inches   **D** 4 inches

2. Nyden uses his house key to unlock the front door.

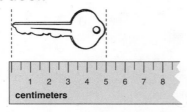

   What is the length of the key to the nearest centimeter?

   A 4 centimeters

   B 5 centimeters

   C 6 centimeters

   D 7 centimeters

3. Which of these items would best be measured in centimeters using a centimeter ruler?

   A the length of a pencil

   B the width of a doorway

   C the length of a soccer field

   D the depth of a swimming pool

4. Mason has a pet goldfish.

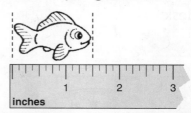

   What is the length of the goldfish to the nearest quarter-inch?

   A 1 inch

   B $1\frac{1}{4}$ inches

   C $1\frac{1}{2}$ inches

   D $1\frac{3}{4}$ inches

5. Ling found a caterpillar in the garden.

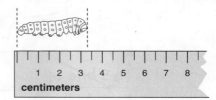

   What is the length of the caterpillar to the nearest centimeter?

   A 2 centimeters

   B 3 centimeters

   C 4 centimeters

   D 5 centimeters

6. Which item would best be measured using a meter stick?

   A the height of a desk

   B the length of a ladybug

   C the width of your notebook

   D the length of a piece of chalk

GO ON

Name _____

7. Addison has the eraser shown in her desk.

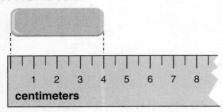

centimeters

What is the length of the eraser to the nearest centimeter?

A 2 centimeters   B 3 centimeters

C 4 centimeters   D 5 centimeters

8. Luis wants to measure the distance around his basketball. Which tool would be best for him to use?

A yard stick

B inch ruler

C measuring tape

D centimeter ruler

9. While on a hike, Emily found a feather.

inches

What is the length of the feather to the nearest quarter-inch? Explain.

_____

_____

_____

10. Lily chewed a piece of gum after lunch. What is the length of the gum to the nearest centimeter? Explain.

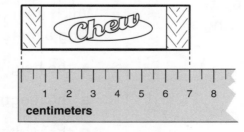

centimeters

_____

_____

Apply Your Understanding

STOP

Name _____

Lesson 8.4

Lesson Objective: Collect, organize, and analyze data in tally tables and frequency tables.

Collect and Organize Data in Tables

Data is a set of numbers or pieces of information.
Conducting a survey is a way to collect data.

A tally table shows the results of the data you collect.
Another way to show data is in a frequency table.
A frequency table uses numbers to record data.

Conduct a survey of students in your class and record the results in a tally table and a frequency table.

Step 1 Think of a survey question that has at least three possible answers. Write your question.

Survey question: _____

Step 2 Complete the labels of the tally table. Include a title and headings. List at least three possible answers to your question.

Make a prediction about which choice will get the most tally marks.

Prediction: _____

Step 3 Survey the students in your class. Record the results in your tally table. Then use your tally table to complete your frequency table.

Step 4 Analyze your data.

Which choice got the most tally marks?

_____

How many students did you survey?

_____

Favorite Color	
Color	Tally
Blue	|||| |||| ||
Green	|||| ||
Orange	|||
Other	|||| |||

Favorite Color	
Color	Number
Blue	12
Green	6
Orange	3
Other	8

Use the table for 1–4.

The students in two fourth-grade classes recorded their favorite school subject. The data are in the tally table.

How many fewer students chose science than chose social studies as their favorite subject?

Favorite School Subject	
Subject	**Tally**
Math	ⵊ⵰⵰⵰ ⵊ⵰⵰⵰ Ⅰ
Science	ⵊ⵰⵰⵰
Language Arts	ⵊ⵰⵰⵰ ⅠⅠ
Reading	ⵊ⵰⵰⵰ ⅠⅠⅠⅠ
Social Studies	ⵊ⵰⵰⵰ ⵊ⵰⵰⵰ ⅠⅠ

1. How many fewer students chose science than chose social studies as their favorite subject?

   Think: Use the data in the tally table to record the data in the frequency table. Then solve the problem.

   social studies: _____12_____ students

   science: _____5_____ students

   _____12_____ – _____5_____ = _____7_____

   So, _____7_____ fewer students chose science.

2. What subject did the least number of students choose?

   _____

3. How many more students chose math than language arts as their favorite subject? _____ more students

4. Suppose 3 students changed their vote from math to science. Describe how the frequency table would change.

   _____

   _____

Favorite School Subject	
Subject	**Number**
Math	
Science	5
Language Arts	
Reading	
Social Studies	12

Problem Solving REAL WORLD

5. Make a tally table about three sports. Ask your classmates which activity they like best. For each answer, make a tally mark beside the sport.

6. Use the data from your tally table to make a frequency table.

7. What is the difference between the sport with the greatest favorite choice and the least favorite choice?

_____

Favorite Sport	
Sport	**Tally**

Favorite Sport	
Sport	**Number**

Lesson **8.5**

Lesson Objective: Create, read, and analyze data in a Venn diagram.

Venn Diagrams

You can use a **Venn diagram** to sort and describe data. The section where the circles overlap shows data the circles have in common.

Use the Venn diagram to list the numbers less than 20 that belong in the diagram.

Step 1 Label Section B. Section A contains multiples of 2. Section C contains contains multiples of 3. So, the label for Section B should be *Multiples of 2 and 3*.

Step 2 List the multiples of 2 and the multiples of 3 up to 20.

Circle the multiples of both 2 and 3.

Multiples of 2: 2, 4, ⑥, 8, 10, ⑫, 14, 16, ⑱, 20

Multiples of 3: 3, ⑥, 9, ⑫, 15, ⑱

Step 3 Write the numbers in the diagram.

Write the circled multiples in Section B.

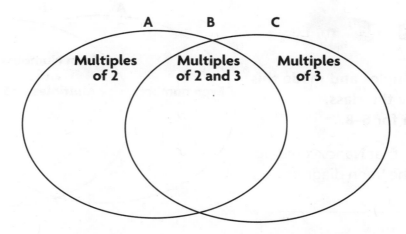

Use the Venn diagram to answer the questions.

1. Why are the numbers 6, 12, and 18 sorted in Section B of the diagram?

   _____

2. Where in the diagram would you find the number 17? Explain how you know.

   _____

   _____

Use the Venn diagram for 3–5.

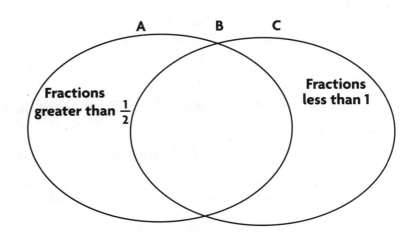

3. What label could be used for Section B?

   Fractions _____

   _____

   _____

4. Name a fraction that belongs in Section B.

   _____

5. Can the fraction $\frac{1}{2}$ be written in Section A? Explain.

   _____

   _____

Problem Solving REAL WORLD

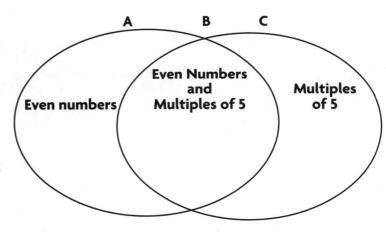

Nancy is studying multiples and made this Venn diagram to show the class. Use the Venn diagram for 6–8.

6. Write two numbers that Nancy could put in each section of the Venn diagram.

   _____

   _____

7. In what section should Nancy write the number 45? Explain.

   _____

   _____

   _____

   _____

8. The multiples of what number belong in Section B? Explain.

   _____

   _____

   _____

   _____

Lesson 8.6

Lesson Objective: Draw and analyze data shown in scaled bar graphs.

Bar Graphs

Use data in a table to make a bar graph.

Step 1 Write the title for the bar graph.

Step 2 Label the side and the bottom.

Step 3 Write the names of the sports.

Step 4 Choose a scale for your graph.

• The scale must be able to show the least number, **3**, and the greatest number, **17**.

• The numbers must be equally spaced. Start with 0 and count by twos until you reach **18**.

Step 5 Draw the bar for ice skating. The bar will end halfway between **16** and **18** at **17**.

Step 6 Then use the results in the table to draw the rest of the bars.

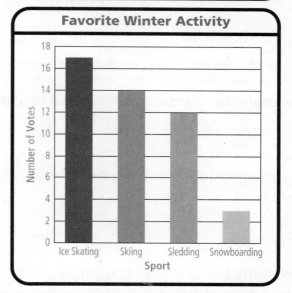

Favorite Winter Activity	
Sport	Number of Votes
Ice Skating	17
Skiing	14
Sledding	12
Snowboarding	3

Use your bar graph to answer the questions.

1. How many students in all answered the survey?

_____ students

2. How many more students chose ice skating or sledding than chose skiing?

_____ more students

3. How many students did not choose snowboarding?

_____ students

4. Some more students were surveyed and they all said snowshoeing. They were 6 fewer students than who said sledding. How many students said snowshoeing?

_____ students

Use the After-Dinner Reading bar graph for 5–10.

The fourth-grade students at Case Elementary School were asked how much time they spent reading last week after dinner. The results are shown in the bar graph at the right.

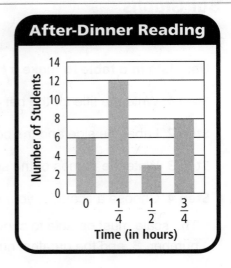

After-Dinner Reading

5. How many students spent $\frac{1}{2}$ hour reading after dinner?

_____3 students_____

6. How many students in all answered the survey?

_____

7. How many students in all spent 0 hours or $\frac{3}{4}$ hour reading

_____

8. How many fewer students spent 0 hours reading than spent $\frac{1}{4}$ hour reading

_____

9. How many more students spent 0 hours reading than spent $\frac{1}{2}$ hour reading

_____

Problem Solving REAL WORLD

10. Suppose 3 students changed their answers to 0 hours instead of $\frac{1}{4}$ hour. Where would the bar for 0 hours end?

_____

Name _____

Lesson **8.7**
Lesson Objective: Make and interpret line plots with whole-number and fractional data.

Line Plots

Howard gave a piece of paper with several survey questions to his friends. Then he made a list to show how long it took for his friends to answer the survey. Howard wants to know how many surveys took longer than $\frac{2}{12}$ hour.

Time for Survey Answers (in hours)
$\frac{1}{12}$ $\frac{3}{12}$ $\frac{1}{12}$ $\frac{2}{12}$ $\frac{6}{12}$ $\frac{3}{12}$ $\frac{5}{12}$

Make a line plot to show the data.

Step 1 Order the data from least to greatest.

$$\frac{1}{12}, \frac{1}{12}, \frac{2}{12}, \frac{3}{12}, \frac{3}{12}, \frac{5}{12}, \frac{6}{12}$$

Step 2 Make a tally table of the data.

Step 3 Label the fractions of an hour on the number line from least to greatest. Notice that $\frac{4}{12}$ is included even though it is not in the data.

Step 4 Plot an X above the number line for each piece of data. Write a title for the line plot.

Step 5 Count the number of Xs that represent data points greater than $\frac{2}{12}$ hour.

There are ____4____ data points greater than $\frac{2}{12}$ hour.

So, ____4____ surveys took more than $\frac{2}{12}$ hour.

Survey	
Time (in hours)	Tally
$\frac{1}{12}$	||
$\frac{2}{12}$	|
$\frac{3}{12}$	||
$\frac{5}{12}$	|
$\frac{6}{12}$	|

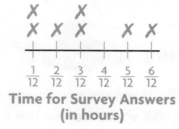

Time for Survey Answers (in hours)

Use the line plot above for 1 and 2.

1. How many of the surveys that Howard gave to his friends were answered? _____

2. What is the difference in hours between the longest time and the shortest time that it took Howard's friends to answer the survey?

_____

3. Some students compared the number of books they read last week. Complete the tally table and line plot to show the data.

Number of Books Read	
Number	Tally
1			
2	
3	
4	

Number of Books Read
1, 3, 4, 2, 3, 1, 3, 3

✗
✗
┼──┼──┼──┼
1   2   3   4
Number of Books Read

Use your line plot for 4 and 5.

4. How many students compared the number of books they read?

_____

5. How many more students read 3 or more books than read fewer than 3 books?

_____

Problem Solving  REAL WORLD

**For 6–7, make a tally table on a separate sheet of paper.
Make a line plot in the space below the problem.**

6.
Milk Drunk at Lunch (in quarts)
$\frac{1}{8}, \frac{2}{8}, \frac{2}{8}, \frac{4}{8}, \frac{1}{8}, \frac{3}{8}, \frac{4}{8}, \frac{2}{8}, \frac{3}{8}, \frac{2}{8}$

7.
Number of Miles Walked
3, 4, 5, 1, 5, 4, 4, 3

┼──┼──┼──┼
$\frac{1}{8}$ $\frac{2}{8}$ $\frac{3}{8}$ $\frac{4}{8}$
**Milk Drunk at Lunch
(in quarts)**

┼──┼──┼──┼──┼
1   2   3   4   5
Number of Miles Walked

Solve Problems Using Data

Some students compared the time they spend riding the school bus. The line plot shows the data. How many more students spend $\frac{3}{4}$ hour or more on the bus than spend less than $\frac{3}{4}$ hour on the bus?

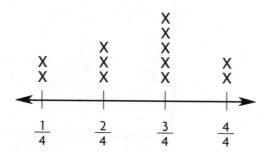

Time Spent on School Bus (in hours)

Step 1 Count the number of students that spend $\frac{3}{4}$ hour or more on the school bus.
Think: $\frac{3}{4}$ hour or more includes the students that spend $\frac{3}{4}$ hour on the bus.

There are **7** students that spend $\frac{3}{4}$ hour or more on the school bus.

Step 2 Count the number of students that spend less than $\frac{3}{4}$ hour on the school bus.

There are **5** students that spend less than $\frac{3}{4}$ hour on the school bus.

Step 3 Think: There are **7** students who spend $\frac{3}{4}$ hour or more on the bus. There are **5** students that spend less than $\frac{3}{4}$ hour on the bus.

$$7 - 5 = 2$$

So, **2** more students spend $\frac{3}{4}$ hour or more on the school bus than students that spend less than $\frac{3}{4}$ hour on the school bus.

Use the bus time line plot to answer the questions.

1. How many students compared times?

2. How many students spend between at least $\frac{2}{4}$ hour and at most $\frac{4}{4}$ hour on the school bus?

_____ students   _____ students

A fourth-grade class measures the height of plants several weeks after planting. The heights of the plants are shown in the frequency table. Use the table for 3–5.

3. How many plants did the students measure?

   _____ plants

4. How many more plants had the most common height than the least common height?

   _____ plants

Heights of Plants	
Height (in cm)	Frequency
5.8	5
5.9	2
6.0	7
6.1	9
6.2	3
6.3	5

5. If the number of plants with a height of 6.3 cm is tripled, how many more plants would have a height of 6.3 cm than a height of 6.2 cm?

   _____ plants

Problem Solving REAL WORLD

Two fourth-grade classes collected data about the length of students' first names. Use the data for 6–7.

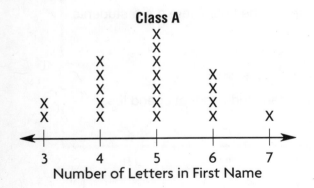

Class A

Number of Letters in First Name

Number of Letters in First Name	
Number of Letters	Frequency
3	4
4	8
5	3
6	1
7	4

Class B

6. Which class has more students? How many more?

7. How many more students in Class A have a name length of 5 letters or more than in Class B?

_____

_____

Multiplying and Dividing by 7

Write a related multiplication fact. Then divide.

1. 7 ÷ 7 = ____

   ____ × ____ = ____

2. 21 ÷ 7 = ____

   ____ × ____ = ____

3. 35 ÷ 7 = ____

   ____ × ____ = ____

4. 56 ÷ 7 = ____

   ____ × ____ = ____

5. 42 ÷ 7 = ____

   ____ × ____ = ____

6. 63 ÷ 7 = ____

   ____ × ____ = ____

7. 14 ÷ 7 = ____

   ____ × ____ = ____

8. 28 ÷ 7 = ____

   ____ × ____ = ____

9. 49 ÷ 7 = ____

   ____ × ____ = ____

Write four number sentences for each set of related facts.

10. 7, 9, 63

   _____ × _____ = _____

   _____ × _____ = _____

   _____ ÷ _____ = _____

   _____ ÷ _____ = _____

11. 7, 8, 56

   _____ × _____ = _____

   _____ × _____ = _____

   _____ ÷ _____ = _____

   _____ ÷ _____ = _____

Name _____

Multiplying and Dividing by 7

Multiply.

1. $7 \times 2 =$ _____

2. $7 \times 5 =$ _____

3. $7 \times 7 =$ _____

4. $7 \times 4 =$ _____

5. $7 \times 3 =$ _____

6. $7 \times 8 =$ _____

7. $7 \times 9 =$ _____

8. $7 \times 6 =$ _____

9. $7 \times 1 =$ _____

10.
$$\begin{array}{r} 7 \\ \times\ 0 \\ \hline \end{array}$$

11.
$$\begin{array}{r} 2 \\ \times\ 7 \\ \hline \end{array}$$

12.
$$\begin{array}{r} 6 \\ \times\ 7 \\ \hline \end{array}$$

13.
$$\begin{array}{r} 8 \\ \times\ 7 \\ \hline \end{array}$$

14.
$$\begin{array}{r} 4 \\ \times\ 7 \\ \hline \end{array}$$

15.
$$\begin{array}{r} 1 \\ \times\ 7 \\ \hline \end{array}$$

16.
$$\begin{array}{r} 9 \\ \times\ 7 \\ \hline \end{array}$$

17.
$$\begin{array}{r} 5 \\ \times\ 7 \\ \hline \end{array}$$

18.
$$\begin{array}{r} 7 \\ \times\ 7 \\ \hline \end{array}$$

19.
$$\begin{array}{r} 3 \\ \times\ 7 \\ \hline \end{array}$$

20.
$$\begin{array}{r} 0 \\ \times\ 7 \\ \hline \end{array}$$

21.
$$\begin{array}{r} 7 \\ \times\ 1 \\ \hline \end{array}$$

Divide.

22. $63 \div 7 =$ _____

23. $21 \div 7 =$ _____

24. $7 \div 7 =$ _____

25. $14 \div 7 =$ _____

26. $56 \div 7 =$ _____

27. $42 \div 7 =$ _____

28. $28 \div 7 =$ _____

29. $49 \div 7 =$ _____

30. $35 \div 7 =$ _____

Read each question and choose the best answer.

1. Brayden asked some of the fourth-grade students what activities they do after school. He made a bar graph to display the data.

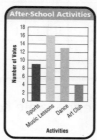

How many students answered the survey?

   A 18   B 38

   c 40   D 42

2. Liam used the crayon below during art class.

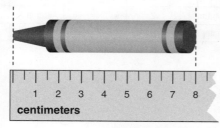

What is the length of the crayon to the nearest centimeter?

   A 6 centimeters

   B 7 centimeters

   c 8 centimeters

   D 9 centimeters

3. The Venn diagram displays data about odd numbers and multiples of 3.

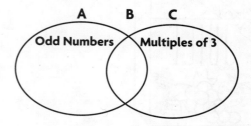

Which statement is correct?

   A 15 belongs in section B.

   B 21 belongs in section A.

   c 30 belongs in section B.

   D 32 belongs in section C.

4. The line plot shows how long the students in Ms. Chester's class read last night, to the nearest quarter-hour.

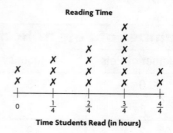

How many students read for $\frac{3}{4}$ hour?

   A 4

   B 6

   c 8

   D 9

GO ON

5. Andrew had a juice box with his lunch. He wanted to find the width of the juice box.

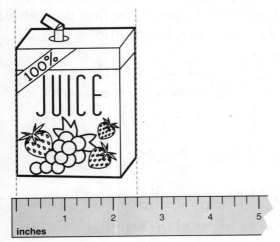

What is the width of the juice box to the nearest quarter-inch?

A 2 inches

B $2\frac{1}{4}$ inches

C $2\frac{1}{2}$ inches

D $2\frac{3}{4}$ inches

6. Mr. Lopez asks his students how many pets they each have at home. The numbers of pets are shown in the frequency table.

Number of Pets at Home	
Number of Pets	**Frequency**
0	3
1	7
2	9
3	4
4	1
5	2

What is the total number of students that have 3 or more pets?

A 0

B 3

C 4

D 7

7. Mr. Irvin's students collected data on their favorite season of the year. They displayed the data in the tally table shown.

Favorite Season	
Season	Tally
Spring	ⵊ⵱
Summer	ⵊ⵱ ⵊ⵱ I
Autumn	II
Winter	ⵊ⵱ III

Which frequency table correctly displays the data?

A

Favorite Season	
Season	**Number**
Spring	5
Summer	11
Autumn	2
Winter	8

B

Favorite Season	
Season	**Number**
Spring	4
Summer	9
Autumn	2
Winter	7

C

Favorite Season	
Season	**Number**
Spring	5
Summer	10
Autumn	2
Winter	5

D

Favorite Season	
Season	**Number**
Spring	5
Summer	10
Autumn	2
Winter	8

GO ON

8. Jack got a new toy race car. He wants to find the length of the car.

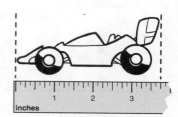

What is the length of the car to the nearest quarter-inch?

A $3\frac{1}{4}$ inches

B $3\frac{1}{2}$ inches

C $3\frac{3}{4}$ inches

D $4\frac{1}{4}$ inches

9. Ms. Moffitt asked her students how far they live from school rounded to the nearest $\frac{1}{4}$ of a mile. She displayed the data in a bar graph.

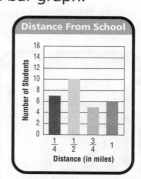

How many students live less than $\frac{3}{4}$ mile from school?

A 5

B 7

C 16

D 17

10. The fourth-grade students ran laps at P.E. The line plot shows the number of laps each student ran.

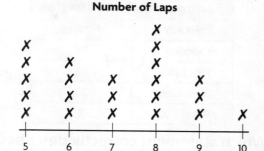

Awards were given to the four students who ran the most laps. What is the total number of laps these students ran?

A 10

B 19

C 37

D 40

11. The line plot shows how much apple juice each student drank at a class party.

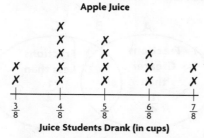

How many students drank apple juice at the party?

A 2   B 5

C 14   D 16

GO ON

12. Students at Adventure Summer Camp chose their favorite activities. The frequency table shows the data.

Summer Camp Activities	
Activity	Number
Canoeing	16
Kick Ball	13
Swimming	25
Wood Shop	7

Which statement correctly describes the data?

A 9 campers chose wood shop or canoeing.

B 41 campers chose canoeing or swimming.

C 38 more students chose swimming than kick ball.

D 13 fewer students chose kick ball than wood shop.

13. The Venn diagram displays data about fractions.

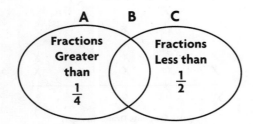

Which statement is true?

A $\frac{4}{5}$ belongs in circle A.

B $\frac{1}{8}$ belongs in circle B.

C $\frac{3}{10}$ belongs in circle A.

D $\frac{7}{12}$ belongs in circle C.

14. Rico makes a line plot to show how many books he reads each month.

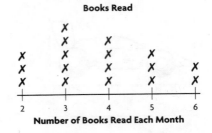

What is the greatest number of books Rico read in one month?

A 2

B 4

C 5

D 6

15. Zoe measured the lengths of her colored pencils to the nearest 0.25 foot. She used a bar graph to display the data.

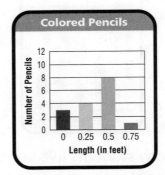

How many colored pencils are 0.5 or 0.75 foot long?

A 1   **B** 2

C 9   **D** 10

186

Chapter 9

Multiply by 1-Digit Numbers

Math in the Real World

Tanya says that the difference in the cost of 4 flowering cherry trees and 4 Muskogee crape myrtles is $80. Is she correct? Explain.

SaccoNursery Plant Sale Prices per Tree		
Tree	Regular Price	Discounted Price (4 or more)
Flowering Cherry	$59	$51
Italian Cypress	$79	$67
Muskogee Crape Myrtle	$39	$34
Royal Empress	$29	$25

What skills do I know that will help me solve this problem?

_____

_____

_____

What do I need to know that can help me solve this problem?

_____

_____

_____

My solution to the problem:

Building Your Math Abilities

Before you begin to explore multiplying by 1-digit numbers, fill in the chart with what you know about multiplying by 1-digit numbers, and then, what you would like to learn. As you go through the chapter, add to the chart the things you have learned.

What I know . . .	What I want to know . . .	What I have learned . . .

Go Deeper

What additional questions do you have about multiplying by 1-digit numbers? Write your questions in the space below.

_____

_____

_____

_____

Lesson 9.1

Lesson Objective: Multiply tens, hundreds, and thousands by whole numbers through 10.

Multiply Tens, Hundreds, and Thousands

One Way Use patterns.

Count the number of zeros in the factors.

$4 \times 6 = 24$ ← basic fact

$4 \times 60 = 240$ ← When you multiply by tens, the last digit in the product is 0.

$4 \times 600 = 2,400$ ← When you multiply by hundreds, the last ___two___ digits in the product are 0.

$4 \times 6,000 = 24,000$ ← When you multiply by thousands, the last ___three___ digits in the product are 0.

When the basic fact has a zero in the product, there will be an extra zero in the final product:

$5 \times 4 = 20$, so $5 \times 4,000 = 20,000$

Another Way Use place value.

$4 \times 6,000 = 4 \times 6$ thousands

            $= 24$ thousands

            $= 24,000$

Complete the pattern.

1. $9 \times 2 = 18$

     $9 \times 20 = $ _____

     $9 \times 200 = $ _____

     $9 \times 2,000 = $ _____

2. $8 \times 4 = 32$

     $8 \times 40 = $ _____

     $8 \times 400 = $ _____

     $8 \times 4,000 = $ _____

Find the product.

3. $7 \times 300 = 7 \times$ _____ hundreds

            $= $ _____ hundreds

            $= $ _____

4. $5 \times 8,000 = 5 \times$ _____ thousands

            $= $ _____ thousands

            $= $ _____

Draw a quick picture to find the product.

5. $2 \times 500 =$ _1,000_

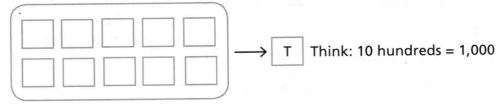

$\longrightarrow$ | T | Think: 10 hundreds = 1,000

6. $8 \times 200 =$ _____

7. $5 \times 6,000 =$ _____

8. $7 \times 800 =$ _____

9. $8 \times 90 =$ _____

10. $6 \times 3,000 =$ _____

11. $3 \times 8,000 =$ _____

12. $5 \times 500 =$ _____

13. $9 \times 4,000 =$ _____

Problem Solving REAL WORLD

14. A bank teller has 7 rolls of coins. Each roll has 40 coins. How many coins does the bank teller have? Explain the strategy you used to solve the problem.

_____

_____

_____

15. Theo buys 5 packages of paper. There are 500 sheets of paper in each package. How many sheets of paper does Theo buy? Explain the strategy you used to solve the problem.

_____

_____

_____

Lesson 9.2

Lesson Objective: Estimate products by rounding and determine if exact answers to multiplication problems are reasonable.

Estimate Products

You can use rounding to estimate products.

Round the greater factor. Then use mental math to estimate the product.

6×295

Step 1 Round 295 to the nearest thousand.   295 rounds to 300.

Step 2 Use patterns and mental math.

$6 \times 3 = 18$

$6 \times 30 = 180$

$6 \times 300 = 1,800$

Find two numbers the exact answer is between.

7×759

Step 1 Estimate by rounding to the lesser hundred.

7×759

$7 \times 700 = 4,900$

Think: $7 \times 7 = 49$
$7 \times 70 = 490$
$7 \times 700 = 4,900$

Step 2 Estimate by rounding to the greater hundred.

7×759

$7 \times 800 = 5,600$

Think: $7 \times 8 = 56$
$7 \times 80 = 560$
$7 \times 800 = 5,600$

So, the product is between __4,900__ and __5,600__.

Estimate the product by rounding.

1. 6×316

2. 5×29

3. 4×703

_____   _____   _____

Estimate the product by finding two numbers the exact answer is between.

4. 3×558

5. 7×252

6. 8×361

_____   _____   _____

_____   _____   _____

Estimate the product by rounding.

7. 4×472

4×472

$\downarrow$

4×500

2,000

8. 2×365

9. 9×54

10. 5×503

11. 3×832

12. 6×98

13. 8×250

14. 7×777

Find two numbers the exact answer is between.

15. 3×567

16. 6×381

17. 4×94

18. 8×684

Problem Solving REAL WORLD

19. Isaac drinks 8 glasses of water each day. He says he will drink 2,920 glasses of water in a year that has 365 days. Is the exact answer reasonable? Explain.

20. Jess delivers 138 newspapers each day. Is it reasonable to estimate that Jess delivers about 1,500 newspapers in 7 days? Explain.

© Houghton Mifflin Harcourt Publishing Company

Lesson 9.3

Lesson Objective: Use expanded form to multiply a multidigit number by a 1-digit number.

Multiply Using Expanded Form

You can use expanded form or a model to find products.

Multiply. 3×124

Think and Write	**Use a Model**
Step 1 Write 124 in expanded form.	**Step 1** Separate 124 by place value.

Step 1 Write 124 in expanded form.

$124 = 100 + 20 + 4$

$3 \times 124 = 3 \times (100 + 20 + 4)$

Step 2 Use the Distributive Property.

$3 \times 124 = (3 \times 100) + (3 \times 20) + (3 \times 4)$

Step 3 Multiply the hundreds. Multiply the tens. Multiply the ones.

$3 \times 124 = (3 \times 100) + (3 \times 20) + (3 \times 4) =$
$\underline{\ 300\ } + \underline{\ 60\ } + \underline{\ 12\ }$

Step 4 Add the partial products.

So, $3 \times 124 = \underline{\ 372\ }$.

$$\begin{array}{r} 300 \\ 60 \\ +12 \\ \hline 372 \end{array}$$

Use a Model

Step 1 Separate 124 by place value.

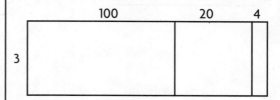

Step 2 Multiply the hundreds, the tens, and the ones.

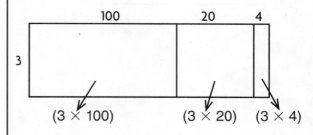

(3×100) (3×20) (3×4)

Step 3 Add to find the total product.

$\underline{\ 300\ } + \underline{\ 60\ } + \underline{\ 12\ } = \underline{\ 372\ }$

Record the product. Use expanded form to help.

1. $6 \times 14 = $ _____

    _____

    _____

2. $4 \times 52 = $ _____

    _____

    _____

3. $5 \times 162 = $ _____

    _____

    _____

4. $3 \times 279 = $ _____

    _____

    _____

Record the product. Use expanded form to help.

5. $7 \times 14 = $ _____98_____

$7 \times 14 = 7 \times (10 + 4)$

$\qquad = (7 \times 10) + (7 \times 4)$

$\qquad = 70 + 28$

$\qquad = 98$

6. $8 \times 543 = $ _____

7. $6 \times 532 = $ _____

8. $5 \times 923 = $ _____

9. $4 \times 371 = $ _____

10. $7 \times 829 = $ _____

Problem Solving  REAL WORLD

11. The fourth-grade students at Riverside School are going on a field trip. There are 68 students on each of the 4 buses. How many students are going on the field trip?

12. There are 168 hours in a week. Hannah will be spending 6 weeks at camp this summer. How many hours will Hannah spend at camp?

_____

_____

1. Quinn earns $22 for mowing lawns. Which is the best estimate of how much he will earn mowing 8 lawns?

   A $160

   B $220

   C $240

   D $300

2. Mr. Simons volunteers at his son's school 40 hours each month. How many hours will he volunteer in 6 months?

   A 24 hours

   B 240 hours

   C 2,400 hours

   D 24,000 hours

3. A garden hose drips 8 ounces of water every hour. Which expression can be used to find how many ounces of water will drip in 24 hours?

   A $8 \times (20 + 4)$

   B $8 \times (20 \times 4)$

   C $(8 \times 20) + 4$

   D $(8 + 20) \times 4$

4. Carmen wrote the multiplication pattern below.

   $$3 \times 7 = 21$$
   $$3 \times 70 = 210$$
   $$3 \times 700 = 2,100$$
   $$3 \times 7,000 = $$

   What is the unknown number in the pattern?

   A 21

   B 210

   C 21,000

   D 210,000

5. Kari uses place value and the expanded form $(3 \times 200) + (3 \times 90) + (3 \times 5)$ to solve a multiplication problem. Which is Kari's multiplication problem?

   A $3 \times 259 = 777$

   B $3 \times 295 = 885$

   C $3 \times 2,095 = 6,285$

   D $3 \times 2,950 = 8,850$

6. Mr. Jackson travels 127 miles per day for work. Which is the best estimate of how far he travels in 5 days?

   A less than 500 miles

   B between 500 and 700 miles

   C between 700 and 1,000 miles

   D more than 1,000 miles

GO ON

7. Liz scored 900 points playing a game. She played 5 times and had the same score each time. What is the total number of points Liz scored?

   A 45 ones

   B 45 tens

   C 45 hundreds

   D 45 thousands

8. Olivia reads 172 pages each week for 4 weeks. Which expression shows how to multiply 4 × 172 by using place value and expanded form?

   A (4 × 100) + (4 × 70) + (4 × 2)

   B (4 × 100) + (4 × 72) + (4 × 1)

   C (4 × 170) + (4 × 72) + (4 × 2)

   D (4 × 200) + (4 × 70) + (4 × 1)

9. A baker makes 385 muffins each day. Write and solve an expression that estimates how many muffins the baker makes in 7 days. Is your estimate greater than or less than the actual product? Explain.

_____

_____

_____

10. A company packs 2,000 pens in each box. How many pens are in 8 boxes? Explain your answer.

_____

_____

_____

Apply Your Understanding

Lesson 9.4

Lesson Objective: Use place value and partial products to multiply a multidigit number by a 1-digit number.

Multiply Using Partial Products

Use partial products to multiply.

Multiply. 6 × 182

Step 1 Estimate the product.

182 is between 100 and 200.

6 × 100 = 600 and 6 × 200 = 1,200

	100	80	2
6			

Step 2 Make an area model.

Step 3 Multiply the hundreds.

6 × 1 hundred __6 hundreds__

$$\begin{array}{r} 182 \\ \times \quad 6 \\ \hline 600 \end{array}$$

Step 4 Multiply the tens

6 × 8 tens __48 tens__

$$\begin{array}{r} 182 \\ \times \quad 6 \\ \hline 600 \\ 480 \end{array}$$

Step 5 Multiply the ones.

6 × 2 ones __12 ones__

$$\begin{array}{r} 182 \\ \times \quad 6 \\ \hline 600 \\ 480 \\ 12 \end{array}$$

Step 6 Add the partial products.

$$\begin{array}{r} 182 \\ \times \quad 6 \\ \hline 600 \\ 480 \end{array}$$

So, 6 × 182 = 1,092. Since 1,092 is between the estimates of 600 and 1,200, it is reasonable.

$$\begin{array}{r} 182 \\ \times \quad 6 \\ \hline 600 \\ 480 \\ 12 \\ \hline 1,092 \end{array}$$

Estimate. Then record the product.

1. Estimate: _____

$$\begin{array}{r} 181 \\ \times \quad 2 \\ \hline \end{array}$$

2. Estimate: _____

$$\begin{array}{r} 156 \\ \times \quad 4 \\ \hline \end{array}$$

3. Estimate: _____

$$\begin{array}{r} \$210 \\ \times \quad 5 \\ \hline \end{array}$$

Estimate. Then record the product.

4. Estimate: <u>1,200 to 1,800</u>

$$\begin{array}{r} 243 \\ \times \quad 6 \\ \hline 1,200 \\ 240 \\ +\quad 18 \\ \hline 1,458 \end{array}$$

5. Estimate: _____

$$\begin{array}{r} 640 \\ \times \quad 3 \\ \hline \end{array}$$

6. Estimate: _____

$$\begin{array}{r} \$149 \\ \times \quad 5 \\ \hline \end{array}$$

7. Estimate: _____

$$\begin{array}{r} 721 \\ \times \quad 8 \\ \hline \end{array}$$

8. Estimate: _____

$$\begin{array}{r} 293 \\ \times \quad 4 \\ \hline \end{array}$$

9. Estimate: _____

$$\begin{array}{r} \$416 \\ \times \quad 6 \\ \hline \end{array}$$

10. Estimate: _____

$$\begin{array}{r} 961 \\ \times \quad 2 \\ \hline \end{array}$$

11. Estimate: _____

$$\begin{array}{r} 837 \\ \times \quad 9 \\ \hline \end{array}$$

12. Estimate: _____

$$\begin{array}{r} 652 \\ \times \quad 4 \\ \hline \end{array}$$

13. Estimate: _____

$$\begin{array}{r} 307 \\ \times \quad 3 \\ \hline \end{array}$$

14. Estimate: _____

$$\begin{array}{r} 543 \\ \times \quad 7 \\ \hline \end{array}$$

15. Estimate: _____

$$\begin{array}{r} \$822 \\ \times \quad 5 \\ \hline \end{array}$$

Problem Solving  REAL WORLD

16. A maze at a county fair is made from 275 bales of hay. The maze at the state fair is made from 4 times as many bales of hay. How many bales of hay are used for the maze at the state fair?

17. Pedro gets 8 hours of sleep each night. How many hours does Pedro sleep in a year with 365 days?

_____

_____

Lesson Objective: Use mental math and properties to multiply a multidigit number by a 1-digit number.

Multiply Using Mental Math

Use addition to break apart the larger factor.	Use subtraction to break apart the larger factor.
Find 8 × 214.	**Find 6 × 298.**
Think: 214 = 200 + 14	**Think:** 298 = 300 − 2
8 × 214 = (8 × 200) + (8 × 14)	6 × 298 = (6 × 300) − (6 × 2)
$\quad\quad$ = __1,600__ + __112__	$\quad\quad$ = __1,800__ − __12__
$\quad\quad$ = __1,712__	$\quad\quad$ = __1,788__
Use halving and doubling.	When multiplying more than two numbers, use the Commutative Property to change the order of the factors.
Find 14 × 50.	**Find 2 × 9 × 50.**
Think: 14 can be evenly divided by 2.	**Think:** 2 × 50 = __100__
14 ÷ 2 = __7__	$\quad$ 2 × 9 × 50 = 2 × __50__ × 9
7 × 50 = __350__	$\quad\quad\quad\quad$ = __100__ × 9
2 × 350 = __700__	$\quad\quad\quad\quad$ = __900__

Find the product. Tell which strategy you used.

1. 5 × 7 × 20

2. 6 × 321

_____

_____

3. 86 × 50

4. 9 × 399

_____

_____

Find the product. Tell which strategy you used.

5. 6×297 **Think:** $297 = 300 - 3$
$$6 \times 297 = 6 \times (300 - 3)$$
$$= (6 \times 300) - (6 \times 3)$$
$$= 1,800 - 18$$
$$= 1,782$$

____1,782; use subtraction____

6. 389×7

7. 8×604

8. 50×28

_____

_____

9. 9×199

10. $20 \times 72 \times 5$

11. 695×4

_____

_____

Problem Solving REAL WORLD

12. Section J in an arena has 9 rows. Each row has 15 seats. All tickets cost $18 each. If all the seats are sold, how much money will the arena collect for Section J?

13. In a high-school gym, the bleachers are divided into 6 equal sections. Each section can seat 395 people. How many people can be seated in the gym?

_____

_____

Name _____

Lesson **9.6**

Lesson Objective: Use the *draw a diagram*
strategy to solve multistep problems.

Problem Solving • Multistep
Multiplication Problems

Use the strategy *draw a diagram* to solve a multistep multiplication problem.

Amy planted 8 rows with 18 tulips in each row. In each of the 4 middle rows, there are 4 red tulips. All of the other tulips are yellow. How many of the tulips are yellow?

Read the Problem	Solve the Problem
What do I need to find? I need to find the total number of __yellow__ tulips.	I drew a diagram for each color of tulip. 18 tulips 4 rows — R R R R / R R R R / R R R R / R R R R — 8 rows 4 tulips
What information do I need to use? There are __8__ rows of tulips with __18__ tulips in each row. There are __4__ rows of tulips with __4__ red tulips in each row.	Next, I found the number in each section. **All Tulips** **Red Tulips** $8 \times 18 = 144$ $4 \times 4 = 16$
How will I use the information? I can ___multiply___ to find the total number of tulips and the number of red tulips. Then I can ___subtract___ to find the number of yellow tulips.	Last, I subtracted the number of red tulips from the total number of tulips. __144__ − __16__ = __128__ So, there are __128__ yellow tulips.

1. A car dealer has 4 rows of cars with 205 cars in each row. In each of the first 3 rows, 6 are used cars. The rest of the cars are new cars. How many new cars does the dealer have?

2. An orchard has 4 rows of apple trees with 125 trees in each row. There are also 6 rows of pear trees with 134 trees in each row. How many apple and pear trees are in the orchard?

_____   _____

Solve each problem.

3. A community park has **6** tables with a chessboard painted on top. Each board has **8** rows of **8** squares. When a game is set up, **4** rows of **8** squares on each board are covered with chess pieces. If a game is set up on each table, how many total squares are NOT covered by chess pieces?

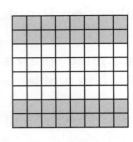

192 squares

$4 \times 8 = 32$

$32 \times 6 = $ ▨

How do you know your answer is correct?

There are 384 total squares. When I add the number of squares that are covered with chess pieces, 192, to the number of chess squares that are not covered by chess pieces, 192, the sum is 384. So, my answer is correct.

4. Jonah and his friends go apple picking. Jonah fills **5** baskets. Each basket holds **15** apples. If **4** of Jonah's friends pick the same amount as Jonah, how many apples do Jonah and his friends pick in all? Draw a diagram to solve the problem.

How do you know your answer is correct?

Lesson **9.7**

Lesson Objective: Use regrouping to multiply a multidigit number by a 1-digit number.

Multiply 3-Digit Numbers with Regrouping

When you multiply 3-digit numbers, you may need to regroup.

Estimate. Then find the product.

$$\begin{array}{r} \$324 \\ \times \qquad 7 \end{array}$$

Step 1 Estimate the product.

324 is between 300 and 400;

$7 \times 300 =$ ___$2,100___ and $7 \times 400 =$ ___$2,800___

Step 2 Multiply the 4 ones by 7.
Regroup the 28 ones as 2 tens 8 ones.

$$\begin{array}{r} {\scriptstyle 2} \\ \$32\!4 \\ \times \qquad 7 \\ \hline 8 \end{array}$$

Step 3 Multiply the 2 tens by 7.
Add the regrouped tens.
Regroup the 16 tens as 1 hundred 6 tens.

$$\begin{array}{r} {\scriptstyle 1\ 2} \\ \$32\!4 \\ \times \qquad 7 \\ \hline 68 \end{array}$$

Step 4 Multiply the 3 hundreds by 7.
Add the regrouped hundred.

$$\begin{array}{r} {\scriptstyle 1\ 2} \\ \$32\!4 \\ \times \qquad 7 \\ \hline \$2,268 \end{array}$$

So, $7 \times \$324 = \$2,268$.

Since $2,268 is between the estimates of $2,100 and $2,800, the answer is reasonable.

Estimate. Then find the product.

1. Estimate: _____

$$\begin{array}{r} 184 \\ \times \quad 2 \\ \hline \end{array}$$

2. Estimate: _____

$$\begin{array}{r} \$828 \\ \times \quad 4 \\ \hline \end{array}$$

3. Estimate: _____

$$\begin{array}{r} 637 \\ \times \quad 5 \\ \hline \end{array}$$

4. Estimate: _____

$$\begin{array}{r} \$690 \\ \times \qquad 7 \\ \hline \end{array}$$

Estimate. Then find the product.
1,600 to 2,000

5. Estimate: _____

$$\begin{array}{r} 467 \\ \times\quad 4 \\ \hline 1,868 \end{array}$$

6. Estimate: _____

$$\begin{array}{r} 339 \\ \times\quad 6 \\ \hline \end{array}$$

7. Estimate: _____

$$\begin{array}{r} \$879 \\ \times\quad 8 \\ \hline \end{array}$$

8. Estimate: _____

$$\begin{array}{r} 616 \\ \times\quad 3 \\ \hline \end{array}$$

9. Estimate: _____

$$\begin{array}{r} \$854 \\ \times\quad 9 \\ \hline \end{array}$$

10. Estimate: _____

$$\begin{array}{r} 750 \\ \times\quad 2 \\ \hline \end{array}$$

11. Estimate: _____

$$\begin{array}{r} 752 \\ \times\quad 6 \\ \hline \end{array}$$

12. Estimate: _____

$$\begin{array}{r} 550 \\ \times\quad 9 \\ \hline \end{array}$$

13. Estimate: _____

$$\begin{array}{r} 839 \\ \times\quad 4 \\ \hline \end{array}$$

Problem Solving  REAL WORLD

14. Laura reads a report that has 722 words. The next report she reads has 8 times as many words as the first report. How many words are in the second report?

_____

15. A seafood company sold 925 pounds of fish last week. If 6 seafood companies sold the same amount of fish, how much fish did the 6 companies sell last week in all?

_____

Name _____

Adding 2- and 3-Digit Whole Numbers

Estimate the sum.

1. $\begin{array}{r} 74 \\ + 87 \\ \hline \end{array}$
2. $\begin{array}{r} 38 \\ + 28 \\ \hline \end{array}$
3. $\begin{array}{r} 62 \\ + 31 \\ \hline \end{array}$
4. $\begin{array}{r} 54 \\ + 28 \\ \hline \end{array}$
5. $\begin{array}{r} 12 \\ + 35 \\ \hline \end{array}$

6. $\begin{array}{r} 93 \\ + 24 \\ \hline \end{array}$
7. $\begin{array}{r} 48 \\ + 48 \\ \hline \end{array}$
8. $\begin{array}{r} 76 \\ + 28 \\ \hline \end{array}$
9. $\begin{array}{r} 29 \\ + 46 \\ \hline \end{array}$
10. $\begin{array}{r} 70 \\ + 32 \\ \hline \end{array}$

11. $\begin{array}{r} 35 \\ 23 \\ + 36 \\ \hline \end{array}$
12. $\begin{array}{r} 42 \\ 36 \\ + 14 \\ \hline \end{array}$
13. $\begin{array}{r} 65 \\ 61 \\ + 11 \\ \hline \end{array}$
14. $\begin{array}{r} 24 \\ 73 \\ + 32 \\ \hline \end{array}$
15. $\begin{array}{r} 18 \\ 17 \\ + 21 \\ \hline \end{array}$

16. $\begin{array}{r} 16 \\ 21 \\ + 32 \\ \hline \end{array}$
17. $\begin{array}{r} 25 \\ 26 \\ + 31 \\ \hline \end{array}$
18. $\begin{array}{r} 49 \\ 32 \\ + 15 \\ \hline \end{array}$
19. $\begin{array}{r} 31 \\ 42 \\ + 10 \\ \hline \end{array}$
20. $\begin{array}{r} 38 \\ 17 \\ + 17 \\ \hline \end{array}$

Find the sum.

21. $86 + 7 =$ _____

22. $75 + 8 =$ _____

23. $26 + 6 =$ _____

24. $55 + 9 =$ _____

25. $26 + 38 =$ _____

26. $57 + 23 =$ _____

27. $64 + 28 =$ _____

28. $39 + 12 =$ _____

29. $647 + 228 =$ _____

30. $696 + 135 =$ _____

31. $443 + 278 =$ _____

32. $285 + 127 =$ _____

Name _____

Adding 2- and 3-Digit Whole Numbers

Find the sum.

1.   14
   + 29

2.   16
   + 35

3.   25
   + 35

4.   29
   + 24

5.   36
   + 14

6.   72
   + 19

7.   11
     72
   + 18

8.   21
     63
   + 18

9.   12
     28
   + 26

10. 31
     47
   + 23

11. 42
     66
   + 14

12. 11
     49
   + 27

13. 175
   + 226

14. 284
   + 176

15. 297
   + 244

16. 375
   + 268

17. 329
   + 186

18. 295
   + 124

19. 141
     257
   + 338

20. 114
     726
   + 175

21. 693
     46
   + 241

22. 728
     210
   + 146

23. 654
     31
   + 206

24. 123
     881
   + 27

25. 216
     270
   + 9

26. $307 + 256 =$ _____

27. $198 + 198 =$ _____

28. $326 + 85 =$ _____

29. $458 + 271 =$ _____

30. $329 + 116 =$ _____

31. $458 + 67 =$ _____

Read each question and choose the best answer.

1. Matthew makes 4 payments of $195 each to pay for his new TV. Which expression shows a strategy for finding the product of 4 × 195?

   A 4 × (200 − 5) = 780

   B 4 × (200 + 5) = 820

   C 4 × (195 + 5) = 800

   D 4 × (195 − 5) = 760

2. Ms. Roma bought 7 new tablets for her company. Each tablet cost $400. What is the total cost of the tablets?

   A $28

   B $280

   C $2,800

   D $28,000

3. Peyton buys 3 packages of stickers. Each package has 8 pages with 8 stickers on a page. How many stickers does Peyton buy?

   A 19

   B 48

   C 88

   D 192

4. Riley runs 4 miles each day. She used partial products to find the total number of miles she will run in one year, or 365 days. Which shows the sum of the partial products?

   A 12 + 24 + 20 = 56

   B 120 + 240 + 20 = 380

   C 1,200 + 24 + 20 = 1,244

   D 1,200 + 240 + 20 = 1,460

5. In one hour, 78 meals were served in a restaurant. Which is the best estimate of how many meals will be served in 6 hours?

   A 350

   B 420

   C 480

   D 600

6. There are 345 centimeters of ribbon on a roll. Hannah buys 7 rolls. How many centimeters of ribbon does she buy?

   A 2,115 centimeters

   B 2,185 centimeters

   C 2,355 centimeters

   D 2,415 centimeters

GO ON

7. A baker uses 4 cups of flour for each cake he makes. Which expression can be used to find how many cups of flour he will use to make 36 cakes?

   A $4 \times (30 + 6)$

   B $4 \times (30 \times 6)$

   C $(4 \times 30) + 6$

   D $(4 + 30) \times 6$

8. A company pays about $395 per month for office supplies. Which is the best estimate of the cost of office supplies for 6 months?

   A less than $1,500

   B between $1,500 and $2,000

   C between $2,000 and $2,500

   D more than $2,500

9. A theater has 3,000 seats. All of the seats were filled for 5 performances of a play. How many people attended the play?

   A 15

   B 150

   C 1,500

   D 15,000

10. There are 128 students in each grade at Twin Oaks School. The school has 6 grades, including kindergarten through fifth grade. Which sum of partial products shows the total number of students at the school?

   A $600 + 40 + 8 = 648$

   B $600 + 12 + 48 = 660$

   C $600 + 120 + 8 = 728$

   D $600 + 120 + 48 = 768$

11. In a video game, Mia earns 74 tokens that are worth 50 points each. Which is the best mental math strategy for her to use to find the total number of points she earned?

   A use addition

   B use subtraction

   C halving and doubling

   D Commutative Property

GO ON

12. LeRoy uses place value and the expanded form $(9 \times 600) + (9 \times 20) + (9 \times 4)$ to solve a multiplication problem. Which is LeRoy's multiplication problem?

   A $9 \times 624 = 5,616$

   B $9 \times 642 = 5,778$

   C $9 \times 6,024 = 54,216$

   D $9 \times 6,204 = 55,836$

13. A music store sells 287 CDs the first week it is open. It sells 6 times as many CDs the next week. How many CDs does the music store sell the second week?

   A 1,282

   B 1,682

   C 1,704

   D 1,722

14. Kaylie's scout troop sold 856 boxes of cookies for $7 each. Which sum of partial products shows the total amount of money they collected?

   A $\$560 + \$35 + \$42 = \$637$

   B $\$560 + \$350 + \$42 = \$952$

   C $\$5,600 + \$35 + \$42 = \$5,677$

   D $\$5,600 + \$350 + \$42 = \$5,992$

15. Jared has 9 albums for his sports cards. Each album holds 80 cards. He writes the equation below to find the total number of cards.

   $$9 \times 80 = \boxed{} \text{ tens}$$

   What is the unknown number?

   A 72

   B 720

   C 7,200

   D 72,000

16. For the school bake sale, Nathan and his dad baked 9 apples pies. They used 5 apples in each pie. They also baked 14 peach pies and used 6 peaches in each. How many pieces of fruit did they use in all?

   A 115   B 129

   C 253   D 280

17. The students at Kennedy School rode on 9 buses for a field trip. There were 53 students on each bus. Which expression shows the best estimate for the number of students on the trip?

   A 9×50

   B 9×60

   C 10×50

   D 10×60

GO ON

18. Ms. Rodriguez buys 36 packages of paint brushes for her art students. There are 25 brushes in each pack. Which expression shows a strategy she could use to find the total number of brushes?

   A $3 \times 6 \times 25 = 450$

   B $9 \times 4 \times 25 = 900$

   C $36 \times 2 \times 5 = 360$

   D $32 \times 4 \times 25 = 3{,}200$

19. For the school play, there were 9 rows with 15 yellow chairs in each. There were also 13 rows with 8 blue chairs in each. How many more yellow than blue chairs were there?

   A 31

   B 41

   C 229

   D 239

20. Dylan's family visits his grandmother 4 times each year. Each round-trip to her house is 192 miles. How many miles do they travel each year to visit Dylan's grandmother?

   A 438 miles

   B 468 miles

   C 768 miles

   D 848 miles

STOP

210

Chapter 10

Multiply 2-Digit Numbers and Area

Math in the Real World

On each of Maggie's bird-watching trips, she has seen at least 24 birds. If she has taken 4 trips each year over the past 16 years, at least how many birds has Maggie seen?

What skills do I know that will help me solve this problem?

_____

_____

_____

What do I need to know that can help me solve this problem?

_____

_____

_____

_____

My solution to the problem:

Building Your Math Abilities

Before you begin to explore multiplying 2-digit numbers and area, fill in the chart with what you know about multiplying 2-digit numbers and area, and then, what you would like to learn. As you go through the chapter, add to the chart the things you have learned.

What I know . . .	What I want to know . . .	What I have learned . . .

Go Deeper

What additional questions do you have about multiplying 2-digit numbers and area? Write your questions in the space below.

_____

_____

_____

_____

Lesson **10.1**

Lesson Objective: Use place value and
multiplication properties to multiply by tens.

Multiply by Tens

One section of seating at an arena has 40 rows. Each row has 30 seats.
How many seats in all are in that section?

Multiply. 30 × 40

Step 1 Think of each factor as a multiple
of 10 and as a repeated addition.

$40 = \underline{4} \times \underline{10}$ or $\underline{10} + \underline{10} + \underline{10} + \underline{10}$

$30 = \underline{3} \times \underline{10}$ or $\underline{10} + \underline{10} + \underline{10}$

Step 2 Draw a diagram to show
the multiplication.

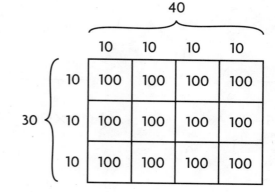

Step 3 Each small square in the diagram
shows 10 × 10, or $\underline{100}$. Count the
squares.
There are $\underline{12}$ squares of $\underline{100}$.

Step 4 Use patterns and mental math to find
12 × 100.

$12 \times 1 = \underline{12}$

$12 \times 10 = \underline{120}$

$12 \times 100 = \underline{1,200}$

There are $\underline{1,200}$ seats in that section.

Choose a method. Then find the product.

1. 20 × 90 = _____

2. 40 × 40 = _____

3. 60 × 70 = _____

4. 50 × 30 = _____

5. 80 × 60 = _____

6. 90 × 40 = _____

Choose a method. Then find the product.

7. 16×60

Use the halving-and-doubling strategy.

Find half of 16: $16 \div 2 = 8$.

Multiply this number by 60: $8 \times 60 = 480$

Double this result: $2 \times 480 = 960$

_____960_____

8. 80×22

9. 30×52

10. 60×20

_____

_____

_____

11. 40×35

12. 10×90

13. 31×50

_____

_____

_____

Problem Solving REAL WORLD

14. Kenny bought 20 packs of baseball cards. There are 12 cards in each pack. How many cards did Kenny buy?

15. The Hart family drove 10 hours to their vacation spot. They drove an average of 48 miles each hour. How many miles did they drive in all?

_____

_____

Name _____

Lesson 10.2

Lesson Objective: Estimate products by rounding or by using compatible numbers.

Estimate Products

You can use rounding and compatible numbers to estimate products.

Use mental math and rounding to estimate the product.

Estimate. $62 \times \$23$

Step 1 Round each factor down to the nearest ten to find the lower estimate. $60 \times \$20$

Step 2 Use mental math.

$6 \times \$2 = \$12$
$6 \times \$20 = \$120$
$60 \times \$20 = \$1,200$

Step 3 Round each factor up to the nearest ten to find the upper estimate. $70 \times \$30$

Step 4 Use mental math.

$7 \times \$3 = \$21$
$7 \times \$30 = \$210$
$70 \times \$30 = \$2,100$

So, $62 \times \$23$ is between __\$1,200__ and __\$2,100__.

Use mental math and compatible numbers to estimate the product.

Estimate. 24×78

Step 1 Use compatible numbers. 25×80

Step 2 Use $25 \times 4 = 100$ to help find 25×8.
$25 \times 8 = $ **200**

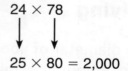

Step 3 Since 80 has 1 zero, write 1 zero to the right of the product.

$25 \times 80 = 2,000$

So, 24×78 is about __2,000__.

Estimate the product by finding two numbers the exact answer is between.

1. 78×21 　　　　*2.* $59 \times \$46$ 　　　　*3.* 81×33 　　　　*4.* 67×21

_____ 　　 _____ 　　 _____ 　　 _____

5. $88 \times \$42$ 　　　*6.* 51×36 　　　　*7.* 73×73 　　　　*8.* $99 \times \$44$

_____ 　　 _____ 　　 _____ 　　 _____

Estimate the product. Choose a method.

9. 38 × 21

   38 × 21

   ↓   ↓

   40 × 20

   _____800_____

10. 63 × 19

   _____

11. 27 × $42

   _____

12. 73 × 67

   _____

13. 37 × $44

   _____

14. 85 × 71

   _____

15. 88 × 56

   _____

16. 97 × 13

   _____

17. 92 × 64

   _____

Problem Solving

18. A dime has a diameter of about 18 millimeters. About how many millimeters long would a row of 34 dimes be?

   _____

19. A half-dollar has a diameter of about 31 millimeters. About how many millimeters long would a row of 56 half-dollars be?

   _____

© Houghton Mifflin Harcourt Publishing Company

216

Name _____

Lesson **10.3**

Lesson Objective: Use area models and partial products to multiply 2-digit numbers.

Investigate • Area Models and Partial Products

You can use area models to multiply 2-digit numbers by 2-digit numbers.

Use the model and partial products to solve.

Draw a rectangle to find 19 × 18.

The rectangle is 19 units long and 18 units wide.

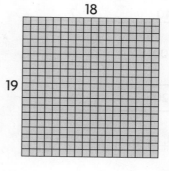

Step 1 Break apart the factors into tens and ones. Divide the area model into four smaller rectangles to show the factors.

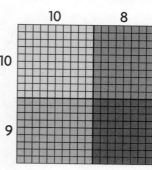

Step 2 Find the products for each of the smaller rectangles.

$10 \times 10 = 100$ $10 \times 8 = 80$ $9 \times 10 = 90$ $9 \times 8 = 72$

Step 3 Find the sum of the products. $100 + 80 + 90 + 72 = 342$

So, $19 \times 18 = 342$.

Draw a model to represent the product. Then record the product.

1. 21 × 25

2. 16 × 14

3. 24 × 15

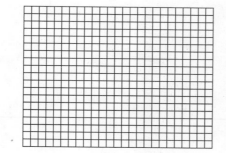

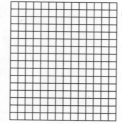

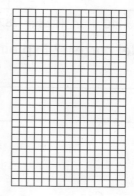

Draw a model to represent the product.
Then record the product.

4. 13 × 42

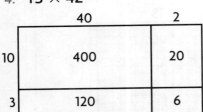

	40	2
10	400	20
3	120	6

400 + 20 + 120 + 6 = <u>546</u>

5. 18 × 34

_____

6. 22 × 26

_____

7. 15 × 33

_____

8. 23 × 29

_____

9. 19 × 36

_____

Problem Solving REAL WORLD

10. Sebastian made the following model to find the product 17 × 24.

	20	4
10	200	40
7	14	28

200 + 40 + 14 + 28 = 282

Is his model correct? Explain.

_____

_____

11. Each student in Ms. Sike's kindergarten class has a box of crayons. Each box has 36 crayons. If there are 18 students in Ms. Sike's class, how many crayons are there in all?

_____

_____

Lesson 10.4

Lesson Objective: Use place value and partial products to multiply 2-digit numbers.

Multiply Using Partial Products

Multiply 25 × 43. Record the product.

tens ones

$$
\begin{array}{r}
4\ 3 \\
\times\ 2\ 5 \\
\hline
8\ 0\ 0 \\
6\ 0 \\
2\ 0\ 0 \\
+\ \ \ 1\ 5 \\
\hline
1,0\ 7\ 5
\end{array}
$$

Think: I can use partial products to find 25 × 43.

Step 1 Multiply the tens by the tens.
20 × 4 tens = 80 tens, or 800. ⟶

Step 2 Multiply the ones by the tens.
20 × 3 ones = 60 ones, or 60. ⟶

Step 3 Multiply the tens by the ones.
5 × 4 tens = 20 tens, or 200. ⟶

Step 4 Multiply the ones by the ones.
5 × 3 ones = 15 ones, or 15. ⟶

Step 5 Add the partial products. ⟶
800 + 60 + 200 + 15 = 1,075.

So, 25 × 43 = ___1,075___.

Record the product.

1.   25
    × 62

2.   59
    × 38

3.   85
    × 72

4.   46
    × 52

5.   76
    × 23

6.   38
    × 95

Record the product.

7.
```
      23
  ×   79
   1,400
     210
     180
  +   27
   1,817
```

8.
```
      56
  ×   32
```

9.
```
      87
  ×   64
```

10.
```
      33
  ×   25
```

11.
```
      94
  ×   12
```

12.
```
      51
  ×   77
```

13.
```
      69
  ×   49
```

14.
```
      86
  ×   84
```

15.
```
      98
  ×   42
```

16.
```
      73
  ×   37
```

17.
```
      85
  ×   51
```

Problem Solving

18. Evelyn drinks 8 glasses of water a day, which is 56 glasses of water a week. How many glasses of water does she drink in a year? (1 year = 52 weeks)

19. Joe wants to use the Hiking Club's funds to purchase new walking sticks for each of its 19 members. The sticks cost $26 each. The club has $480. Is this enough money to buy each member a new walking stick? If not, how much more money is needed?

_____

_____

Multiply with Regrouping

Estimate. Then use regrouping to find 28 × 43.

Step 1 Round to estimate the product.

$30 \times 40 = 1,200$

Step 2 Think: 28 = 2 tens 8 ones.
Multiply 43 by 8 ones.
8 × 3 = 24. Record the 4. Write the
regrouped 2 above the tens place.
8 × 40 = 320. Add the regrouped tens:
320 + 20 = 340.

$$\begin{array}{r} {}^{2} \\ 43 \\ \times\ 28 \\ \hline 344 \end{array}$$ ⟵ 8 × 43

Step 3 Multiply 43 by 2 tens.
20 × 3 = 60 and 20 × 40 = 800.
Record 860 below 344.

$$\begin{array}{r} {}^{\cancel{2}} \\ 43 \\ \times\ 28 \\ \hline 344 \\ 860 \end{array}$$ ⟵ 20 × 43

Step 4 Add the partial products.

1,204 ⟵ 344 + 860

So, 28 × 43 = __1,204__. 1,204 is close to 1,200. The answer is reasonable.

Estimate. Then find the product.

_1._ Estimate: _____

$$\begin{array}{r} 36 \\ \times\ 12 \\ \hline \end{array}$$

_2._ Estimate: _____

$$\begin{array}{r} 43 \\ \times\ 29 \\ \hline \end{array}$$

_3._ Estimate: _____

$$\begin{array}{r} 51 \\ \times\ 47 \\ \hline \end{array}$$

Estimate. Then find the product.

4. Estimate: _____2,700_____

    $$\begin{array}{r} \overset{2}{\overset{1}{}} \\ 87 \\ \times\quad 32 \\ \hline 174 \\ +\ 2{,}610 \\ \hline 2{,}784 \end{array}$$

    Think: 87 is close to 90 and 32 is close to 30.

    $$90 \times 30 = 2{,}700$$

5. Estimate: _____

    $$\begin{array}{r} 73 \\ \times\quad 28 \\ \hline \end{array}$$

6. Estimate: _____

    $$\begin{array}{r} 48 \\ \times\quad 38 \\ \hline \end{array}$$

7. Estimate: _____

    $$\begin{array}{r} 59 \\ \times\quad 52 \\ \hline \end{array}$$

8. Estimate: _____

    $$\begin{array}{r} 84 \\ \times\quad 40 \\ \hline \end{array}$$

9. Estimate: _____

    $$\begin{array}{r} 83 \\ \times\quad 77 \\ \hline \end{array}$$

10. Estimate: _____

    $$\begin{array}{r} 91 \\ \times\quad 19 \\ \hline \end{array}$$

Problem Solving REAL WORLD

11. Baseballs come in cartons of 84 baseballs. A team orders 18 cartons of baseballs. How many baseballs does the team order?

12. There are 16 tables in the school lunch room. Each table can seat 22 students. How many students can be seated at lunch at one time?

_____   _____

1. The pet store has 49 fish tanks. Each fish tank holds 12 gallons of water. Which is the best estimate of the total amount of water needed to fill the fish tanks?

   A 100 gallons

   B 400 gallons

   C 500 gallons

   D 1,000 gallons

2. Isaiah draws this model to help him find 17 × 19.

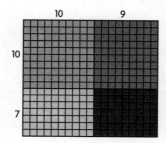

   What is the product?

   A 133

   B 190

   C 323

   D 423

3. Animation for a computer drawn cartoon requires about 20 frames per second. How many frames would need to be drawn for a 60-second cartoon?

   A 120

   B 600

   C 1,200

   D 1,800

4. Each of the 42 football players did 75 crunches. How many crunches did the football players do in all?

   A 504

   B 2,040

   C 3,040

   D 3,150

5. Each of the students in the book club read a 234-page book. There are 8 students in the book club. How many pages did the students read altogether?

   A 1,636

   B 1,840

   C 1,872

   D 7,600

6. Luis jogs 10 miles a week. How far will he have jogged in 52 weeks?

   A 100 miles

   B 500 miles

   C 520 miles

   D 5,200 miles

GO ON

7. There are 487 students at Plainview Elementary. Each student collected 5 cans for the food drive. How many cans did the students collect in all?

A 9,500

B 2,435

C 2,400

D 2,035

8. Nicole draws this model to find 32 × 19.

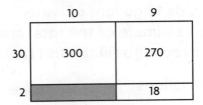

What partial product is missing from the model?

A 12

B 20

C 60

D 100

9. A total of 58 teams attended a soccer tournament. Each team brought 17 players. Explain how you would estimate the total number of soccer players at the tournament.

_____

_____

_____

_____

10. Landon needs 1,300 plates for the teacher appreciation dinner. He buys 18 boxes of plates. There are 75 plates in each box. Will Landon have enough plates? Explain.

_____

_____

_____

_____

STOP

Apply Your Understanding

Lesson **10.6**

Lesson Objective: Choose a method to
multiply 2-digit numbers.

Choose a Multiplication Method

Estimate. Then use regrouping to find 47 × 89.

$$\begin{array}{r} 89 \\ \times\ 47 \end{array}$$

Step 1 Estimate the product. $\qquad$ $50 \times 90 = 4,500$

Step 2 Multiply the 9 ones by the 7 ones.
Regroup the 63 ones as 6 tens
3 ones.

$$\begin{array}{r} {}^{6}89 \\ \times\ 47 \\ \hline 3 \end{array}$$

Step 3 Multiply the 8 tens, or 80, by the
7 ones, or 7. Add the regrouped tens.
Regroup the 62 tens as 6 hundreds
2 tens.

$$\begin{array}{r} {}^{6}89 \\ \times\ 47 \\ \hline 623 \end{array}$$

Step 4 Multiply the 9 ones by the 4 tens,
or 40. Regroup the 36 tens as
3 hundreds 6 tens.

$$\begin{array}{r} {}^{3}\cancel{8}9 \\ \times\ 47 \\ \hline 623 \\ 60 \end{array}$$

Step 5 Multiply the 8 tens, or 80, by the 4 tens,
or 40. Add the regrouped tens. Regroup
the 35 hundreds as 3 thousands
5 hundreds.

$$\begin{array}{r} {}^{3}\cancel{8}9 \\ \times\ 47 \\ \hline 623 \\ 3,560 \end{array}$$

Step 6 Add the partial products.

$$\begin{array}{r} {}^{3}\cancel{8}9 \\ \times\ 47 \\ \hline 623 \\ +\ 3,560 \\ \hline 4,183 \end{array}$$

So, 47 × 89 = __4,183__ . Since 4,183 is close to
the estimate of 4,500, it is reasonable.

Estimate. Then choose a method to find the product.

1. Estimate: _____

$$\begin{array}{r} 76 \\ \times\ 31 \end{array}$$

2. Estimate: _____

$$\begin{array}{r} 24 \\ \times\ 35 \end{array}$$

3. Estimate: _____

$$\begin{array}{r} 14 \\ \times\ 28 \end{array}$$

4. Estimate: _____

$$\begin{array}{r} 64 \\ \times\ 56 \end{array}$$

Estimate. Then choose a method to find the product.

5. Estimate: <u>1,200</u>

$$\begin{array}{r} 31 \\ \times\ 43 \\ \hline 93 \\ +\ 1,240 \\ \hline 1,333 \end{array}$$

6. Estimate: _____

$$\begin{array}{r} 67 \\ \times\ 85 \\ \hline \end{array}$$

7. Estimate: _____

$$\begin{array}{r} 68 \\ \times\ 38 \\ \hline \end{array}$$

8. Estimate: _____

$$\begin{array}{r} 95 \\ \times\ 17 \\ \hline \end{array}$$

9. Estimate: _____

$$\begin{array}{r} 49 \\ \times\ 54 \\ \hline \end{array}$$

10. Estimate: _____

$$\begin{array}{r} 91 \\ \times\ 26 \\ \hline \end{array}$$

11. Estimate: _____

$$\begin{array}{r} 82 \\ \times\ 19 \\ \hline \end{array}$$

12. Estimate: _____

$$\begin{array}{r} 46 \\ \times\ 27 \\ \hline \end{array}$$

13. Estimate: _____

$$\begin{array}{r} 41 \\ \times\ 33 \\ \hline \end{array}$$

14. Estimate: _____

$$\begin{array}{r} 97 \\ \times\ 13 \\ \hline \end{array}$$

15. Estimate: _____

$$\begin{array}{r} 75 \\ \times\ 69 \\ \hline \end{array}$$

16. Estimate: _____

$$\begin{array}{r} 58 \\ \times\ 27 \\ \hline \end{array}$$

Problem Solving  REAL WORLD

17. A movie theatre has 26 rows of seats. There are 18 seats in each row. How many seats are there in all? Estimate, then solve the problem.

_____

18. For Exercise 17, how do you know your answer is reasonable?

_____

_____

_____

_____

_____

Problem Solving • Multiply
2-Digit Numbers

A library ordered 17 cases with 24 books in each case. In 12 of the cases, 18 books were fiction books. The rest of the books were nonfiction. How many nonfiction books did the library order?

Read the Problem	Solve the Problem
What do I need to find? I need to find <u>how many nonfiction</u> <u>books</u> were ordered.	• First, find the total number of books ordered. <u>17</u> × <u>24</u> = <u>408</u> books ordered • Next, find the number of fiction books. <u>12</u> × <u>18</u> = <u>216</u> fiction books
What information do I need to use? <u>17</u> cases of <u>24</u> books each were ordered. In <u>12</u> cases, <u>18</u> books were fiction books.	• Last, draw a bar model. I need to subtract. <table><tr><td>408 books ordered</td></tr></table> <table><tr><td>216 fiction books</td></tr></table> ? 408 − 216 = <u>192</u> So, the library ordered <u>192</u> nonfiction books.
How will I use the information? I can find the <u>total number of books</u> <u>ordered</u> and the <u>number of fiction</u> <u>books ordered</u>. Then I can draw a bar model to compare the <u>total number of books</u> to the <u>number of fiction books</u>.	• Check your answer for reasonableness: Round and multiply. <u>20</u> × <u>20</u> = <u>400</u> books <u>10</u> × <u>20</u> = <u>200</u> fiction books Subtract the estimated numbers. <u>400</u> − <u>200</u> = <u>200</u> nonfiction books 192 is close to 200, so my answer is reasonable.

1. A grocer ordered 32 cases with 28 small cans of fruit in each case. The grocer also ordered 24 cases with 18 large cans of fruit in each case. How many more small cans of fruit did the grocer order?

_____

Solve each problem. Use a bar model to help.

2. Mason counted an average of 18 birds at his bird feeder each day for 20 days. Gloria counted an average of 21 birds at her bird feeder each day for 16 days. How many more birds did Mason count at his feeder than Gloria counted at hers?

360 birds counted by Mason

336 birds counted by Gloria

?

Birds counted by Mason: 18 × 20 = 360

Birds counted by Gloria: 21 × 16 = 336

Draw a bar model to compare.

So, Mason counted ___24___ more birds.

Subtract. 360 − 336 = 24

Is your answer reasonable? Explain.

_____

_____

3. The 24 students in Ms. Lee's class each collected an average of 18 cans for recycling. The 21 students in Mr. Galvez's class each collected an average of 25 cans for recycling. How many more cans were collected by Mr. Galvez's class than Ms. Lee's class?

_____

Is your answer reasonable? Explain.

_____

_____

4. A zoo gift shop orders 18 boxes of 75 monkey key rings each, 15 boxes of 80 elephant key rings each, and 12 boxes of 65 giraffe key rings each. How many key rings in all does the gift shop order?

_____

Is your answer reasonable? Explain.

_____

_____

Name _____

Lesson 10.8

Lesson Objective: Use a formula to find the area of a rectangle.

Area

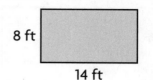

Area is the number of **square units** needed to cover a flat surface.

Find the area of the rectangle at the right.

8 ft
14 ft

You can use the formula **Area = length × width**.

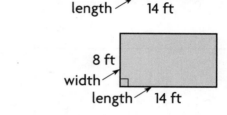

8 ft
length   14 ft

Step 1 Identify the length.

The length is __14__ feet.

Step 2 Identify a perpendicular side as the width.

8 ft
width
length   14 ft

The width is __8__ feet.

Step 3 Use the formula to find the area.

Area = length × width

= **14 × 8**

= **112**

So, the area of the rectangle is 112 square feet.

Find the area of the rectangle or square.

1.

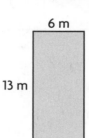

6 m

13 m

_____

2.

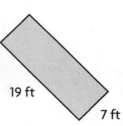

19 ft

7 ft

_____

3.

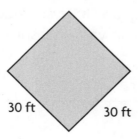

30 ft   30 ft

_____

4.

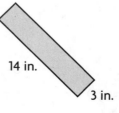

14 in.

3 in.

_____

Find the area of the rectangle or square.

5.

12 ft

9 ft

$A = l \times w$
$= 12 \times 9$
108 square feet

6.

8 yd

8 yd

7.

15 m

3 m

8.

17 in.

6 in.

9.

30 cm

5 cm

10.

14 ft

4 ft

Problem Solving 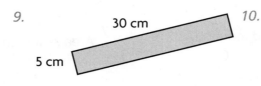 REAL WORLD

11. Meghan is putting wallpaper on a wall that measures 8 feet by 12 feet. How much wallpaper does Meghan need to cover the wall?

12. Bryson is laying down sod in his yard to grow a new lawn. Each piece of sod is a 1-foot by 1-foot square. How many pieces of sod will Bryson need to cover his yard if his yard measures 30 feet by 14 feet?

Area of Combined Rectangles

Find the area of the combined rectangles.

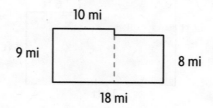

10 mi

9 mi

8 mi

18 mi

Step 1 First, find the area of each section of the shape.

LEFT	RIGHT	
$A = l \times w$	$A = l \times w$	
$= 10 \times 9$	$= 8 \times 8$	**Think:** $18 - 10 = 8$
$= 90$	$= 64$	

Step 2 Add the two areas. $90 + 64 = 154$

So, the total area is __154__ square miles.

Find the area of the combined rectangles.

1.
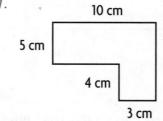
10 cm

5 cm

4 cm

3 cm

_____

2.
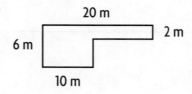
20 m

6 m

2 m

10 m

_____

3.
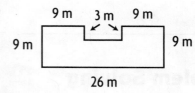
9 m   3 m   9 m

9 m   9 m

26 m

_____

4.
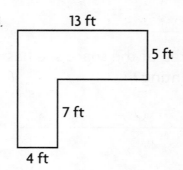
13 ft

5 ft

7 ft

4 ft

_____

5.
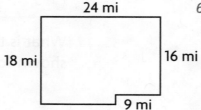
24 mi

18 mi   16 mi

9 mi

_____

6.
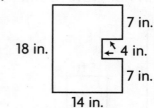
7 in.

18 in.   4 in.

7 in.

14 in.

_____

Find the area of the combined rectangles.

7.

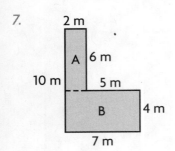

Area A = 2 × 6,
Area B = 7 × 4
12 + 28 = 40
40 square meters

8.

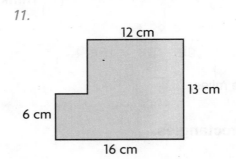

9.

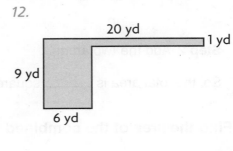

10.

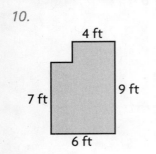

11.

12 cm

6 cm

13 cm

16 cm

12.

20 yd

1 yd

9 yd

6 yd

Problem Solving REAL WORLD

Use the diagram for 13–14.
Nadia makes the diagram below to represent the counter space she wants to build in her craft room.

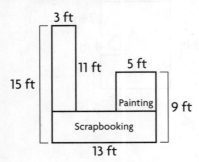

13. What is the area of the space that Nadia has shown for scrapbooking?

_____

14. What is the area of the space she has shown for painting?

_____

© Houghton Mifflin Harcourt Publishing Company

Lesson **10.10**

Lesson Objective: Use the strategy *solve a simpler problem* to solve area problems.

Problem Solving • Find the Area

Use the strategy *solve a simpler problem*.

Marilyn is going to paint a wall in her bedroom. The wall is
15 feet long and 8 feet tall. The window takes up an area
6 feet long and 4 feet high. How many square feet of the wall
will Marilyn have to paint?

Read the Problem	Solve the Problem
What do I need to find? I need to find how many square feet of the wall Marilyn will paint.	First, find the area of the wall. $A = l \times w$ $= 15 \times 8$ $= 120$ square feet Next, find the area of the window.
What information do I need to use? The paint will cover the wall. The paint will not cover the window. The base of the wall is 15 feet, and the height is 8 feet. The base of the window is 6 feet, and the height is 4 feet.	$A = l \times w$ $= 6 \times 4$ $= 24$ square feet Last, subtract the area of the window from the area of the wall.
How will I use the information? I can solve simpler problems. Find the area of the wall. Then, find the area of the window. Last, subtract the area of the window from the area of the wall.	$\begin{array}{r} 120 \\ -\ \ 24 \\ \hline 96 \end{array}$ square feet So, Marilyn will paint 96 square feet of her bedroom wall.

1. Ned wants to wallpaper the wall
   of his bedroom that has the door.
   The wall is 14 feet wide and 9 feet
   high. The door is 3 feet wide and 7
   feet high. How many square feet of
   wallpaper will Ned need for the wall?

   _____

2. Nicole has a rectangular canvas
   that is 12 inches long and 10 inches
   wide. She paints a blue square in the
   center of the canvas. The square is
   3 inches on each side. How much of
   the canvas is NOT painted blue?

   _____

Solve each problem.

3. A room has a wooden floor. There is a rug in the center of the floor. The diagram shows the room and the rug. How many square feet of the wood floor still shows?

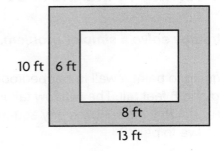

_____**82 square feet**_____

Area of the floor: 13 × 10 = 130 square feet
Area of the rug: 8 × 6 = 48 square feet
Subtract to find the area of the floor still showing: 130 − 48 = 82 square feet

4. A rectangular wall has a square window, as shown in the diagram.

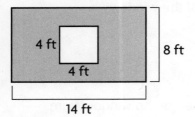

What is the area of the wall NOT including the window?

_____

5. Bob wants to put down new sod in his backyard, except for the part set aside for his flower garden. The diagram shows Bob's backyard and the flower garden.

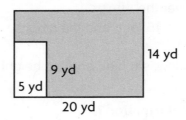

How much sod will Bob need?

_____

6. A rectangular painting, including the frame, is 28 inches wide and 24 inches tall. The opening inside the frame is 24 inches wide and 20 inches tall. What is the area covered by the frame?

_____

7. One wall in Jeanne's bedroom is 13 feet long and 8 feet tall. There is a door 3 feet wide and 6 feet tall. She has a poster on the wall that is 2 feet wide and 3 feet tall. How much of the wall is visible?

_____

Multiplying 2- and 3-Digit Numbers

Find the product. Look for a pattern.

1. $45 \times 10 = $ _____

2. $45 \times 100 = $ _____

3. $45 \times 1,000 = $ _____

4. $234 \times 20 = $ _____

5. $234 \times 200 = $ _____

6. $234 \times 2,000 = $ _____

Estimate the product.

7.
$$\begin{array}{r} 37 \\ \times\ 2 \\ \hline \end{array}$$

8.
$$\begin{array}{r} 81 \\ \times\ 6 \\ \hline \end{array}$$

9.
$$\begin{array}{r} 721 \\ \times\ 9 \\ \hline \end{array}$$

10.
$$\begin{array}{r} 58 \\ \times\ 22 \\ \hline \end{array}$$

11.
$$\begin{array}{r} 289 \\ \times\ 4 \\ \hline \end{array}$$

Is the product reasonable? Write _yes_ or _no_.

12.
$$\begin{array}{r} 43 \\ \times\ 20 \\ \hline 960 \end{array}$$ _____

13.
$$\begin{array}{r} 500 \\ \times\ 70 \\ \hline 350 \end{array}$$ _____

14.
$$\begin{array}{r} 60 \\ \times\ 70 \\ \hline 350 \end{array}$$ _____

15.
$$\begin{array}{r} 200 \\ \times\ 14 \\ \hline 280 \end{array}$$ _____

Find the product.

16. $100 \times 219 = $ _____

17. $775 \times 10 = $ _____

18. $4,100 \times 2 = $ _____

19.
$$\begin{array}{r} 76 \\ \times\ 10 \\ \hline \end{array}$$

20.
$$\begin{array}{r} 300 \\ \times\ 5 \\ \hline \end{array}$$

21.
$$\begin{array}{r} 47 \\ \times\ 200 \\ \hline \end{array}$$

22.
$$\begin{array}{r} 314 \\ \times\ 600 \\ \hline \end{array}$$

23.
$$\begin{array}{r} 190 \\ \times\ 100 \\ \hline \end{array}$$

Name _____

Multiplying 2- and 3-Digit Numbers

Find the product. Use mental math.

1. $10 \times 20 =$ _____

2. $50 \times 100 =$ _____

3. $41 \times 10 =$ _____

4. $100 \times 43 =$ _____

5. $6 \times 10 =$ _____

6. $200 \times 30 =$ _____

7. $39 \times 10 =$ _____

8. $100 \times 77 =$ _____

9. $400 \times 2 =$ _____

Estimate the product.

10. $22 \times 79 =$ _____

11. $15 \times 12 =$ _____

12. $27 \times 31 =$ _____

13.
$$\begin{array}{r} 32 \\ \times\ 12 \\ \hline \end{array}$$

14.
$$\begin{array}{r} 49 \\ \times\ 27 \\ \hline \end{array}$$

15.
$$\begin{array}{r} 662 \\ \times\ 11 \\ \hline \end{array}$$

16.
$$\begin{array}{r} 61 \\ \times\ 57 \\ \hline \end{array}$$

17.
$$\begin{array}{r} 544 \\ \times\ 8 \\ \hline \end{array}$$

Find the product.

18.
$$\begin{array}{r} 10 \\ \times\ 91 \\ \hline \end{array}$$

19.
$$\begin{array}{r} 200 \\ \times\ 4 \\ \hline \end{array}$$

20.
$$\begin{array}{r} 32 \\ \times\ 100 \\ \hline \end{array}$$

21.
$$\begin{array}{r} 701 \\ \times\ 10 \\ \hline \end{array}$$

22.
$$\begin{array}{r} 543 \\ \times\ 100 \\ \hline \end{array}$$

23.
$$\begin{array}{r} 62 \\ \times\ 7 \\ \hline \end{array}$$

24.
$$\begin{array}{r} 104 \\ \times\ 9 \\ \hline \end{array}$$

25.
$$\begin{array}{r} 80 \\ \times\ 33 \\ \hline \end{array}$$

26.
$$\begin{array}{r} 31 \\ \times\ 62 \\ \hline \end{array}$$

27.
$$\begin{array}{r} 17 \\ \times\ 19 \\ \hline \end{array}$$

Name _____

Read each question and choose the best answer.

1. A choir needs new robes for each of its 35 singers. The cost of each robe is $21. What will be the total cost for the new robes?

   A $105

   B $635

   C $735

   D $800

2. Robert reads for 30 minutes per day. How many minutes will Robert read in 14 days?

   A 140 minutes

   B 300 minutes

   C 420 minutes

   D 4,200 minutes

3. Riley is buying a carpet for a room that measures 16 feet by 12 feet. How many square feet of carpet does Riley need to buy?

   A 27 feet

   B 54 feet

   C 172 square feet

   D 192 square feet

4. Audrey walks 3 miles a day. How many miles will Audrey walk in 185 days?

   A 315 miles

   B 540 miles

   C 555 miles

   D 690 miles

5. A landscaper is putting down a rubber mat at a playground. The rubber mat will cover the whole playground except for a square sandbox. The diagram shows the playground and the sandbox.

   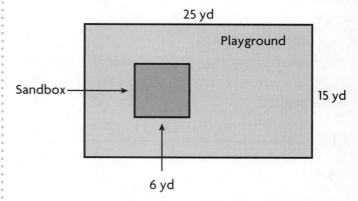

   How many square yards of rubber mat will the landscaper use?

   A 36 square yards

   B 339 square yards

   C 375 square yards

   D 411 square yards

6. Ace Manufacturing ordered 17 boxes with 85 gears in each box. How many gears did Ace Manufacturing order?

   A 680

   B 1,415

   C 1,445

   D 1,800

7. In an auditorium there are 38 rows of chairs. There are 12 chairs in each row. Which is the *best* estimate of the total number of chairs in the auditorium?

   A about 400

   B about 300

   C about 200

   D about 100

8. Ashlyn is laying carpet in her office. The diagram shows where the carpet will be installed.

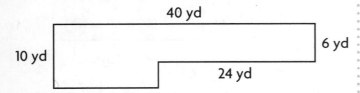

   What is the area of the space where the carpet will be installed?

   A 80 square yards

   B 272 square yards

   C 304 square yards

   D 400 square yards

9. There are 12 inches in a foot. In April, Mrs. Harris used 32 feet of ribbon for an arts club. In May, she used 45 feet of ribbon. How many more inches of ribbon did Mrs. Harris use in May than in April?

   A 540 inches

   B 384 inches

   C 156 inches

   D 39 inches

10. Carter draws this model to help him find 12 × 14.

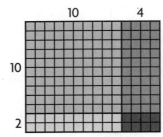

   What is the product?

   A 28

   B 120

   C 148

   D 168

GO ON

11. Each class at Dove Creek Elementary made 22 Valentine's Day cards. There are 23 classes in the school. How many cards did the classes make?

A 110   B 400

C 406   D 506

12. Jackets cost $32 each. Coach Daniels bought 17 jackets. Which is the **best** estimate of the total cost of the jackets?

A $320   B $300

C $600   D $1,200

13. There is a rose garden and an herb garden at the park. The diagram shows the two gardens at the park.

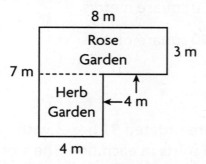

What is the total area of the two gardens?

A 16 square meters

B 24 square meters

C 40 square meters

D 56 square meters

14. Nicole draws this model to find 25 × 23.

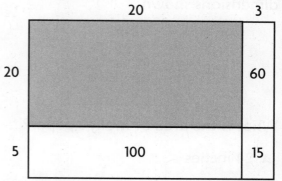

What partial product is missing from the model?

A 40   B 60

C 400   D 600

15. Sophie earns $20 per week mowing lawns. How much money will Sophie earn in 30 weeks?

A $6,000

B $600

C $500

D $60

16. Lillian sold 44 tickets for the school carnival. Each ticket cost $12. How much money did Lillian collect?

A $132

B $400

C $428

D $528

GO ON

17. Molly cut a piece of paper with the dimensions shown.

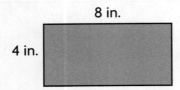

8 in.

4 in.

What is the area of Molly's paper?

A 24 inches

B 32 inches

C 24 square inches

D 32 square inches

18. Ms. Chase buys 7 packages of markers for the students in her art class. Each package has 125 markers. How many markers did Ms. Chase buy?

A 840

B 875

C 910

D 1,190

19. Max is laying a rectangular brick patio for a restaurant. He will cover the whole area in bricks, except for a rectangular fountain. The diagram shows the patio and fountain.

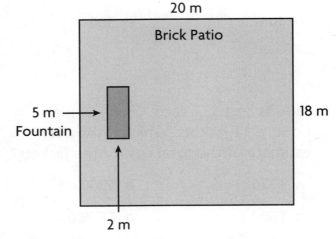

20 m

Brick Patio

5 m → Fountain

18 m

2 m

How many square meters of bricks are needed?

A 10 square meters

B 350 square meters

C 360 square meters

D 370 square meters

20. A store ordered 51 boxes with 17 small shirts in each box. The store also ordered 34 boxes with 13 large shirts in each box. How many more small shirts than large shirts did the store order?

A 272

B 425

C 442

D 867

STOP

Chapter 11

Length, Liquid Volume, Mass, Temperature, and Time

Math in the Real World

Bethany finished her math homework at 4:20 P.M. She did 25 multiplication problems in all. If each problem took her 3 minutes to do, at what time did Bethany start her math homework?

What skills do I know that will help me solve this problem?

_____

_____

_____

What do I need to know that can help me solve this problem?

_____

_____

_____

My solution to the problem:

Building Your Math Abilities

Before you begin to explore length, liquid volume, mass, temperature, and time, fill in the chart with what you know about length, liquid volume, mass, temperature, and time, and then, what you would like to learn. As you go through the chapter, add to the chart the things you have learned.

What I know . . .	What I want to know . . .	What I have learned . . .

Go Deeper

What additional questions do you have about length, liquid volume, mass, temperature, and time? Write your questions in the space below.

_____

_____

_____

_____

Lesson 11.1

Lesson Objective: Add, subtract, multiply, or divide to solve problems involving length.

Solve Problems Related to Length

You can use a model or write an equation to solve problems about length.

> Carla has two lengths of ribbon. The red ribbon is two feet long. The blue ribbon is 30 inches long. Which length of ribbon is longer? How much longer?
>
> **Step 1** Find which ribbon is longer.
>
> **Use a model.**
>
> **Red ribbon**
>
> | 24 inches |
> |---|
>
> **Blue ribbon**
>
> | 30 inches |
> |---|
>
> So, the blue ribbon is longer.
>
> **Step 2** Find how much longer.
>
> **Think:** I can subtract to find the difference.
>
> 30 − 24 = 6 inches
>
> So, the blue ribbon is 6 inches longer.
>
> **Write an equation.**
>
> **Think:** 1 foot = 12 inches. To find how many inches in 2 feet, I can multiply 2 × 12.
>
> 2 × 12 = 12
>
> The red ribbon is 24 inches.
>
> 24 < 30
>
> So, the blue ribbon is longer.

Write an equation and solve the problem.

1. Harry drives 137 miles on Tuesday. He drives 156 miles on Wednesday. How many miles does he drive in all?

   _____

2. Ingrid has a piece of board that is 96 centimeters long. She and her mom cut it into 8 pieces that are each the same length. How long is each piece?

   _____

Use a model to solve the problem.

3. Sierra ties a piece of yarn that is $\frac{3}{10}$ meter in length in her hair. She ties a piece of yarn that is $\frac{5}{10}$ of a meter in length in her sister's hair. What is the total length of yarn Sierra uses?

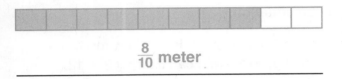

$\frac{8}{10}$ meter

4. Toby rolled his toy car $\frac{11}{12}$ yard. Marcus rolled his toy car $\frac{5}{12}$ yard. How much farther did Toby's car roll?

Solve the problems.

5. The fourth-grade students painted two murals at school. One had a length of 7 feet. The other had a length of 4 yards. What is the total length of both murals?

   Think: There are 3 feet in 1 yard.

6. Abby buys 4 rolls of tape that are each 5 meters in length. How many centimeters of tape does she buy?

   Think: There are 100 centimeters in 1 meter.

Problem Solving

7. Mrs. Chen buys 4 yards of fabric. She uses 27 inches of the fabric to make book covers for her daughter and 18 inches for a craft project. How many inches of fabric does Mrs. Chen have left?

   Think: There are 12 inches in 1 foot. There are 3 feet in 1 yard.

8. Andrew rode his bike $\frac{5}{4}$ miles from his house to the park. Then he rode $\frac{7}{4}$ miles to the library. Becca rode her bike $\frac{13}{4}$ miles to a friend's house. Who rode a greater distance? How much farther did that person ride?

Lesson **11.2**

Lesson Objective: Add, subtract, multiply, or divide to solve problems involving liquid volumes or masses.

Solve Problems Related to Liquid Volume and Mass

You can use a model or write an equation to solve problems about liquid volume and mass.

Tina's watering can holds 4 liters of water. Todd's watering can holds 6 liters of water. What is the total liquid volume of both watering cans?

Tina's Watering Can

4 L

Todd's Watering Can

6 L

Use a bar model.

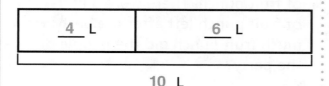

| _4_ L | _6_ L |

10 L

Think: Add to find the total.

4 L + 6 L = 10 L

So, the total liquid volume is _10_ L.

Write an equation.

Think: I can write an addition equation to find the sum of the liquid volumes.

_4_ $\oplus$ _6_ = _10_

So, the total liquid volume is _10_ L.

Write an equation and solve the problem.

1. Kyra has a small bucket that holds 96 ounces of water and a large bucket that holds 384 ounces of water. Altogether, how many ounces of water do the two buckets hold?

____ ◯ ____ = ____ _____

2. Rick's recipe calls for 25 grams of raisins and 40 grams of nuts. How many more grams of nuts than raisins does the recipe call for?

____ ◯ ____ = ____ _____

Write an equation and solve the problem.

3. Luis was served 145 grams of meat and 217 grams of vegetables at a meal. What was the total mass of the meat and the vegetables?

   Think: Add to find how much in all.

   <u>145</u> (+) <u>217</u> = <u>362</u>   <u>362</u>
   _____grams_____

4. The gas tank of a riding mower holds 5 liters of gas. How many 5-liter gas tanks can you fill from a full 20-liter gas can?

   _____ ◯ _____ = _____   _____

5. To make a lemon-lime drink, Mac mixed 36 cups of lemonade with 28 cups of limeade. How much lemon-lime drink did Mac make?

6. A nickel has a mass of 5 grams. There are 40 nickels in a roll of nickels. What is the mass of a roll of nickels?

   _____ ◯ _____ = _____   _____

7. Four families share 48 kilograms of apples equally. How many kilograms of apples does each family get?

   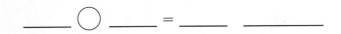

8. For a party, Julia made 12 liters of fruit punch. There were 3 liters of fruit punch left after the party. How much fruit punch did the people drink at the party?

   _____ ◯ _____ = _____   _____

Problem Solving REAL WORLD

9. Zoe has two fish tanks. One holds 27 gallons of water, and the other holds 36 gallons of water. She uses a 3-gallon container to fill the tanks. How many times does she have to fill the 3-gallon container in order to fill both fish tanks?

   _____

10. Adrian's backpack has a mass of 15 kilograms. Theresa's backpack has a mass of 8 kilograms. What is the total mass of both backpacks?

    _____

Lesson **11.3**

Lesson Objective: Add, subtract, multiply, or divide to solve problems involving temperature.

Solve Problems Related to Temperature

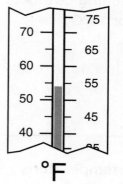

The thermometer shows the temperature when Adam woke up. When he rode his bike after school, the temperature was 80°F. How many degrees warmer was it?

Think: What operation can you use to find how many degrees warmer it was when Adam rode his bike than when he woke up?

You can subtract to find the difference in the two temperatures.

Step 1 Find the temperature when Adam woke up.

Each mark on the thermometer shows one degree. The red line reaches the mark before 55, so the temperature was 54°F.

Step 2 Subtract the temperature when Adam woke up from the temperature when he rode his bike.

80 − 54 = 26

So, it was _____ 26°F _____ warmer when Adam rode his bike than when he woke up.

Choose the better temperature for the activity.

1. Ice skating outdoors
   24°F or 52°F

2. Outdoor soccer game
   22°C or 62°C

3. Reading a book
   outdoors 25°F or 75°F

_____

_____

_____

Choose the better temperature for the activity.

4. Gardening outdoors
   0°C or 15°C

   Think: 0°C is freezing, and 20°C is normal room temperature.

   _____ 15°C _____

5. Snowboarding outdoors
   2°C or 32°C

   _____

6. Flying a kite outdoors
   28°F or 58°F

   _____

Find the temperature.

7. The thermometer shows the low temperature on Monday. The high temperature was 32 degrees warmer. What was the high temperature on Monday?

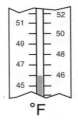

8. It was 85°F when Megan's family was at the beach. The thermometer shows the temperature when they got home. How many degrees cooler was it when Megan's family gor home?

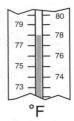

9. The thermometer shows the temperature of the water in a pot. How many degrees must the water increase before it boils? Water boils at 100°C.

10. The thermometer shows the temperature in Lamar's city. It is 15 degrees cooler in the city where his aunt lives. What is the temperature in his aunt's city?

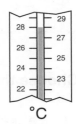

Problem Solving

11. The thermometer shows the evening temperature. The morning temperature was 6°C cooler. What was the temperature in the morning?

12. The thermometer shows the temperature at a mountain peak. The temperature at the base is 36°F warmer than the temperature at the peak. What is the temperature at the base?

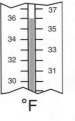

1. Wyatt walks $1\frac{3}{4}$ miles. Kate walks $2\frac{1}{4}$ miles. How much farther did Kate walk than Wyatt?

   A $\frac{1}{4}$ mile

   B $\frac{1}{2}$ mile

   C $\frac{3}{4}$ mile

   D 1 mile

2. Masako is swimming outdoors. Which is most likely the temperature?

   A 12°F

   B 35°F

   C 40°F

   D 95°F

3. Xavier uses 48 fluid ounces of water to make juice and 64 fluid ounces of water to make tea. How many fluid ounces of water did Xavier use in all?

   A 14 fluid ounces

   B 16 fluid ounces

   C 102 fluid ounces

   D 112 fluid ounces

4. The thermometer shows the temperature outside. The temperature in Aaliyah's house is 10° warmer.

   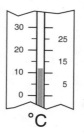

   °C

   What is the temperature in Aaliyah's house?

   A 2°F

   B 2°C

   C 22°F

   D 22°C

5. Seth buys 30 feet of rope. He cuts the rope into 5 equal pieces. How long is each piece of rope?

   A 6 feet

   B 7 feet

   C 25 feet

   D 35 feet

6. Danielle is walking around a store. Which is the most likely temperature inside the store?

   A 0°C

   B 10°C

   C 20°C

   D 40°C

GO ON

7. Mary is tripling her granola recipe. Her recipe calls for 60 grams of dried apples. How many grams of dried apples will Mary use?

   A 20 grams

   B 60 grams

   C 120 grams

   D 180 grams

8. Blake has 3 chains. Each chain is 7 meters long. How many meters of chain does Blake have?

   A 4 meters

   B 10 meters

   C 21 meters

   D 28 meters

9. Ellie looks at the thermometer. It is 4°C warmer than it was one hour before. What was the temperature one hour before? Explain how you found your answer.

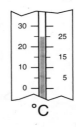

°C

_____

_____

_____

_____

10. William makes 32 cups of lemonade. Then he pours the lemonade into glasses. He pours 2 cups of lemonade into each glass. How many glasses did William fill? Explain how you found your answer.

_____

_____

_____

_____

STOP

Apply Your Understanding

Units of Time

Some analog clocks have an hour hand,
a minute hand, and a **second** hand.

There are 60 seconds in a minute. The
second hand makes 1 full turn every minute.
There are 60 minutes in an hour. The minute
hand makes 1 full turn every hour. The hour
hand makes 1 full turn every 12 hours.

You can think of the clock as unrolling to become a number line.

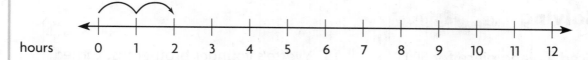

The hour hand moves from one number to the next in 1 hour.

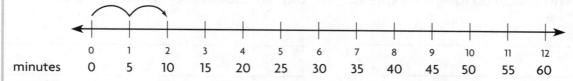

The minute hand moves from one number to the next in 5 minutes.

Use the table at the right to change between units of time.

1 hour = 60 minutes, or 60 × 60 seconds, or
___3,600___ seconds.

So, 1 hour is ___3,600___ times as long as 1 second.

1 day = 24 hours, so 3 days = 3 × 24 hours, or
___72___ hours.

1 year = 12 months, so 5 years = 5 × 12 months, or ___60___ months.

Units of Time
1 minute = 60 seconds
1 hour = 60 minutes
1 day = 24 hours
1 week = 7 days
1 year = 12 months
1 year = 52 weeks

Complete.

1. 3 hours = _____ minutes

2. 2 minutes 15 seconds = _____ seconds

3. 6 hours = _____ seconds

4. 5 weeks = _____ days

5. 8 minutes = _____ seconds

6. 7 years = _____ months

Complete.

7. 6 minutes = _____360_____ seconds

Think: 1 minute = 60 seconds,
so 6 minutes = 6 × 60 seconds,
or 360 seconds.

8. 24 hours = _____ minutes

9. 3 years = _____ weeks

10. 9 hours = _____ minutes

11. 9 minutes 25 seconds = _____ seconds

12. 3 hours 45 minutes = _____ minutes

13. 7 days = _____ hours

Problem Solving  REAL WORLD

14. Jody practiced a piano piece for 500 seconds. Bill practiced a piano piece for 8 minutes. Who practiced longer? **Explain.**

_____

_____

_____

15. Yvette's younger brother just turned 3 years old. Fred's brother is now 30 months old. Whose brother is older? **Explain.**

_____

_____

_____

16. Marcus is going on a field trip to a wildlife preserve. He will spend a total of 1 hour 20 minutes on the bus, and 4 hours 45 minutes at the wildlife preserve. How many minutes will Marcus be on the field trip? **Explain.**

_____

_____

_____

_____

_____

17. Leila and Kai watch a movie that is 3 hours long. Leila says the movie is less than 10,000 seconds. Kai says the movie is more than 10,000 seconds. Which friend is correct? **Explain.**

_____

_____

_____

_____

_____

Convert Mixed Measures of Time

Gabrielle's puppy is 6 weeks 3 days old. How many days old is the puppy?

Step 1 Think of 6 weeks 3 days as 6 weeks + 3 days.

Step 2 Change the weeks to days.

Think: 1 week = ___7___ days.

So, 6 weeks = 6 × 7 days, or ___42___ days.

Step 3 Add like units to find the answer.

So, Gabrielle's puppy is ___45___ days old.

$$\begin{array}{r} 42 \text{ days} \\ + 3 \text{ days} \\ \hline 45 \text{ days} \end{array}$$

Gabrielle played with her puppy for 2 hours 10 minutes yesterday and 1 hour 25 minutes today. How much longer did she play with the puppy yesterday than today?

Step 1 Subtract the mixed measures. Write the subtraction with like units lined up.

Think: 25 minutes is greater than 10 minutes.

$$\begin{array}{r} 2 \text{ hr } 10 \text{ min} \\ - 1 \text{ hr } 25 \text{ min} \\ \hline \end{array}$$

Step 2 Rename 2 hours 10 minutes to subtract.

1 hour = 60 minutes

So, 2 hr 10 min = 1 hr + 60 min + 10 min, or ___1___ hr ___70___ min.

$$\begin{array}{r} 1 \quad 70 \\ \cancel{2} \text{ hr } \cancel{10} \text{ min} \\ - 1 \text{ hr } 25 \text{ min} \\ \hline 0 \text{ hr } 45 \text{ min} \end{array}$$

Step 3 Subtract like units.

1 hr − 1 hr = 0 hr; 70 min − 25 min = ___45 min___

So, she played with the puppy ___45___ minutes longer yesterday than today.

Complete.

1. 2 min 8 s = _____ s   2. 1 hr 20 min = _____ min   3. 3 yr 5 mo = _____ mo

Add or subtract.

4. $\begin{array}{r} 6 \text{ h } 24 \text{ min} \\ + 1 \text{ h } 10 \text{ min} \\ \hline \end{array}$

5. $\begin{array}{r} 9 \text{ wk } 6 \text{ d} \\ - 3 \text{ wk } 4 \text{ d} \\ \hline \end{array}$

6. $\begin{array}{r} 4 \text{ yr } 9 \text{ mo} \\ - 1 \text{ yr } 10 \text{ mo} \\ \hline \end{array}$

Complete.

7. 8 years 6 months = _____102_____ months

> Think: 8 years = 8 × 12 months, or 96 months.
> 96 months + 6 months = 102 months

8. 5 weeks 3 days = _____ days

9. 4 minutes 45 seconds = _____ seconds

10. 4 hours 30 minutes = _____ minutes

11. 3 weeks 6 days = _____ days

12. 3 days 2 hours = _____ hours

13. 6 minutes 15 seconds = _____ seconds

Add or subtract.

14. 2 d 9 hr
   + 4 d 3 hr
   _____

15. 5 min 10 sec
   − 2 min 40 sec
   _____

16. 8 hr 3 min
   + 4 hr 12 min
   _____

Problem Solving REAL WORLD

17. Michael's basketball team practiced for 2 hours 40 minutes yesterday and 3 hours 15 minutes today. How much longer did the team practice today than yesterday?

_____

18. Rihanna worked for 3 hours 35 minutes on Monday. She worked for 2 hours 50 minutes on Wednesday. She wants to work enough hours on Friday so she works a total of 8 hours. How much longer does she need to work?

_____

Name _____

Lesson Objective: Use the strategy *draw a diagram* to solve elapsed time problems.

Problem Solving • Elapsed Time

Opal finished her art project at 2:25 P.M. She spent 50 minutes working on her project. What time did she start working on her project?

Read the Problem		
What do I need to find?	**What information do I need to use?**	**How will I use the information?**
I need to find Opal's start time.	End time: __2:25 P.M.__ Elapsed time: __50__ minutes	I can draw a diagram of a clock. I can then count back 5 minutes at a time until I reach 50 minutes.
Solve the Problem		

I start by showing 2:25 P.M. on the clock.
Then I count back 50 minutes by 5s.

Think: As I count back, I go past the 12.
The hour must be 1 hour less than the ending time.

The hour will be __1 o'clock__.

So, Opal started on her project at __1:35 P.M.__.

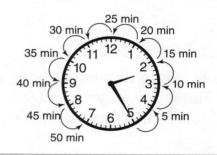

Draw hands on the clock to help you solve the problem.

1. Bill wants to be at school at 8:05 A.M. It takes him 20 minutes to walk to school. At what time should Bill leave his house?

   Bill should leave his house at _____.

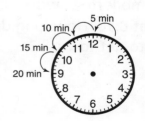

2. Mr. Gleason's math class lasts 40 minutes. Math class starts at 9:55 A.M. At what time does math class end?

   Math class ends at _____.

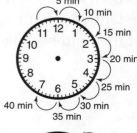

3. Hannah rode her bike for 1 hour and 15 minutes until she got a flat tire at 2:30 P.M. What time did Hannah start riding her bike?

   Hannah started riding her bike at _____.

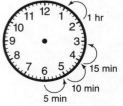

Read each problem and solve.

4. Molly started her piano lesson at 3:45 P.M. The lesson lasted 20 minutes. What time did the piano lesson end?

   Think: What do I need to find? How can I draw a diagram to help?

   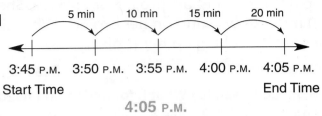

   4:05 P.M.

5. Brendan starting playing a computer game at 2:17 P.M. He stopped playing at 3:55 P.M. and went outside to ride his bike. How long did Brendan play the computer game?

6. Aimee's karate class lasts 1 hour and 15 minutes and is over at 5:00 P.M. What time does Aimee's karate class start?

7. Mr. Giarmo left for work at 7:15 A.M. He arrived at 8:10. How long did it take Mr. Giarmo to get to work?

8. Ms. Brown's flight left at 11:20 A.M. Her plane landed 1 hour and 23 minutes later. What time did her plane land?

Timelines

A **timeline** shows when events took place and in what order. The order of events is called the **sequence**.

Hannah wants to make a timeline of her day. The table shows the events she wants to include.

Use the steps to place the first event on the timeline.

Step 1 Compare the times and find the one that happened first. Remember, A.M. is the label for the hours before noon, and P.M. is the label for the hours after noon.

First event: ___Wake up 6:45 A.M.___

Step 2 Find the location of the first event on the timeline.

Will the event be closer to 6 A.M. or 7 A.M.? ___7 A.M.___

Step 3 Add the point for this event to the timeline. Then, label it.

Hannah's Day	
Event	**Time**
Volleyball practice	3:45 P.M.
Lunch	11:30 A.M.
Breakfast	7:15 A.M.
Wake up	6:45 A.M.
Start school	8:00 A.M.
Dinner	5:45 P.M.

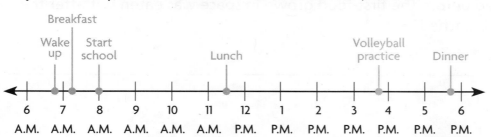

Step 4 Add points to the timeline for the other events in the table. Label each point with the event.

Use your timeline to answer the questions.

1. Name an event that happened before lunch.

   _____

2. Name an event that happened after volleyball practice.

   _____

Use the table for 3–8.

3. Add points to the timeline for each event listed in the table.

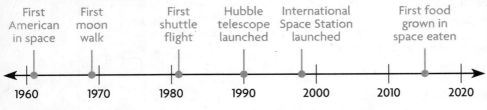

First American in space | First moon walk | First shuttle flight | Hubble telescope launched | International Space Station launched | First food grown in space eaten

1960   1970   1980   1990   2000   2010   2020

Events in Space	
Event	**Year**
International Space Station launched	1998
First shuttle flight	1981
First moon walk	1969
First American in space	1961
First food grown in space eaten	2015
Hubble telescope launched	1990

4. Which event(s) occurred after the International Space Station was launched?

_____

5. Which event(s) occurred between the first American in space and the launching of the Hubble telescope?

_____

6. Which event(s) occurred before the first food grown in space was eaten but after the Hubble telescope was launched?

_____

Problem Solving REAL WORLD

7. In 1983 Sally Ride became the first American woman to go into space. Between which two events should this event be on your timeline?

_____

_____

_____

8. Which event(s) occurred more than 20 years before the Hubble telescope was launched?

_____

_____

_____

Name _____

Review 6, 7, 8, and 9

Multiply.

1. $\begin{array}{r} 4 \\ \times\, 8 \\ \hline \end{array}$ 2. $\begin{array}{r} 9 \\ \times\, 2 \\ \hline \end{array}$ 3. $\begin{array}{r} 5 \\ \times\, 8 \\ \hline \end{array}$ 4. $\begin{array}{r} 9 \\ \times\, 4 \\ \hline \end{array}$ 5. $\begin{array}{r} 8 \\ \times\, 8 \\ \hline \end{array}$

6. $\begin{array}{r} 9 \\ \times\, 3 \\ \hline \end{array}$ 7. $\begin{array}{r} 9 \\ \times\, 7 \\ \hline \end{array}$ 8. $\begin{array}{r} 1 \\ \times\, 8 \\ \hline \end{array}$ 9. $\begin{array}{r} 5 \\ \times\, 9 \\ \hline \end{array}$ 10. $\begin{array}{r} 7 \\ \times\, 9 \\ \hline \end{array}$

11. $\begin{array}{r} 9 \\ \times\, 9 \\ \hline \end{array}$ 12. $\begin{array}{r} 8 \\ \times\, 6 \\ \hline \end{array}$ 13. $\begin{array}{r} 9 \\ \times\, 8 \\ \hline \end{array}$ 14. $\begin{array}{r} 3 \\ \times\, 9 \\ \hline \end{array}$ 15. $\begin{array}{r} 8 \\ \times\, 7 \\ \hline \end{array}$

16. $\begin{array}{r} 6 \\ \times\, 8 \\ \hline \end{array}$ 17. $\begin{array}{r} 9 \\ \times\, 5 \\ \hline \end{array}$ 18. $\begin{array}{r} 2 \\ \times\, 8 \\ \hline \end{array}$ 19. $\begin{array}{r} 7 \\ \times\, 7 \\ \hline \end{array}$ 20. $\begin{array}{r} 8 \\ \times\, 5 \\ \hline \end{array}$

21. $\begin{array}{r} 7 \\ \times\, 8 \\ \hline \end{array}$ 22. $\begin{array}{r} 3 \\ \times\, 8 \\ \hline \end{array}$ 23. $\begin{array}{r} 4 \\ \times\, 9 \\ \hline \end{array}$ 24. $\begin{array}{r} 7 \\ \times\, 4 \\ \hline \end{array}$ 25. $\begin{array}{r} 9 \\ \times\, 6 \\ \hline \end{array}$

26. $\begin{array}{r} 6 \\ \times\, 7 \\ \hline \end{array}$ 27. $\begin{array}{r} 3 \\ \times\, 9 \\ \hline \end{array}$ 28. $\begin{array}{r} 4 \\ \times\, 6 \\ \hline \end{array}$ 29. $\begin{array}{r} 6 \\ \times\, 6 \\ \hline \end{array}$ 30. $\begin{array}{r} 2 \\ \times\, 7 \\ \hline \end{array}$

Name _____

Review 6, 7, 8, and 9

Divide.

1. $9\overline{)36}$ 2. $6\overline{)30}$ 3. $8\overline{)8}$ 4. $8\overline{)64}$ 5. $6\overline{)24}$

6. $6\overline{)54}$ 7. $7\overline{)42}$ 8. $9\overline{)9}$ 9. $8\overline{)56}$ 10. $9\overline{)72}$

11. $7\overline{)21}$ 12. $8\overline{)72}$ 13. $9\overline{)45}$ 14. $8\overline{)0}$ 15. $6\overline{)12}$

16. $9\overline{)0}$ 17. $9\overline{)54}$ 18. $6\overline{)0}$ 19. $7\overline{)49}$ 20. $9\overline{)81}$

21. $6\overline{)36}$ 22. $6\overline{)48}$ 23. $7\overline{)35}$ 24. $7\overline{)7}$ 25. $7\overline{)28}$

26. $8\overline{)16}$ 27. $9\overline{)18}$ 28. $8\overline{)48}$ 29. $8\overline{)32}$ 30. $7\overline{)63}$

31. $6\overline{)18}$ 32. $7\overline{)56}$ 33. $5\overline{)30}$ 34. $3\overline{)21}$ 35. $8\overline{)24}$

Read each question and choose the best answer.

1. Brooklyn used a 1-liter bottle to fill a birdbath with 3 liters of water. How many times did Brooklyn refill the 1-liter bottle?

   A 1 time

   B 2 times

   C 3 times

   D 4 times

2. Kendall spent 1 hour and 25 minutes doing yard work. Then she stopped for lunch at 1:10 P.M. At what time did Kendall start doing yard work?

   A 11:45 P.M.

   B 12:45 A.M.

   C 12:45 P.M.

   D 11:45 A.M.

3. Charlie is leaving on trip in 3 days 7 hours. How many hours until Charlie leaves on his trip?

   A 10 hours

   B 43 hours

   C 79 hours

   D 97 hours

4. Bryce is skiing outdoors. Which is most likely the temperature?

   A 28°F

   B 80°F

   C 95°F

   D 100°F

5. Brady rode his bike for 3 hours. How many minutes did Brady ride his bike?

   A 21 minutes

   B 60 minutes

   C 63 minutes

   D 180 minutes

6. Mr. Green drives 248 miles on Thursday and 187 miles on Friday. How many miles does he drive in all?

   A 61 miles

   B 325 miles

   C 435 miles

   D 570 miles

GO ON

7. Parker is painting his bedroom. He draws a timeline to show his day.

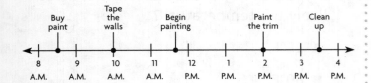

Which event happened after painting the trim?

A buy paint

B tape the walls

C begin painting

D clean up

8. It took Gianna 1 minute 2 seconds to swim a lap. How many seconds did it take Gianna to swim a lap?

A 62 seconds   **B** 58 seconds

C 14 seconds   **D** 9 seconds

9. Alexa works at the zoo. She is measuring the mass of two koala bears. The male koala bear has a mass of 8 kilograms. The female koala bear has a mass of 7 kilograms. How much greater is the mass of the male koala bear than the female?

A 1 kilogram   **B** 2 kilograms

C 15 kilograms   **D** 56 kilograms

10. A traveling exhibit will be at the art museum for 84 days. How many weeks will the exhibit be at the museum?

A 7 weeks

B 12 weeks

C 60 weeks

D 77 weeks

11. Kendall says there are 3 weeks and 4 days until her birthday. How many days are left until Kendall's birthday?

A 17 days

B 22 days

C 25 days

D 76 days

12. Destiny has a piece of ribbon that is 71 inches long. She cuts off a piece of ribbon that is 12 inches long. How long is Destiny's ribbon now?

A 12 inches

B 59 inches

C 61 inches

D 83 inches

GO ON

13. Alicia has lived in her house for 60 months. How many years has Alicia lived in her house?

   A 1 year

   B 5 years

   C 7 years

   D 9 years

14. Fransico participates in several sports. He makes a timeline to show part of his year.

Which sport does Fransico participate in before tennis?

   A soccer

   B basketball

   C baseball

   D swimming

15. The thermometer shows the temperature at the end of a football game. The temperature at the beginning of the game was 4°C cooler.

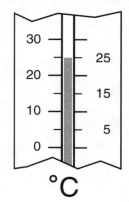

What was the temperature at the beginning of the game?

   A 21°C

   B 29°C

   C 21°F

   D 29°F

16. Jordan went snowboarding with his friends at 10:10 A.M. They snowboarded for 2 hours and 45 minutes. Then they stopped to eat lunch. What time did they stop for lunch?

   A 7:25 A.M.

   B 12:55 A.M.

   C 7:25 P.M.

   D 12:55 P.M.

GO ON ➡

17. Sebastian buys 18 gallons of gas in May. That is 3 times as many gallons of gas as Jada bought. How many gallons of gas did Jada buy?

 A 3 gallons

 B 6 gallons

 C 15 gallons

 D 21 gallons

18. Jackson makes a timeline to show important events in his life.

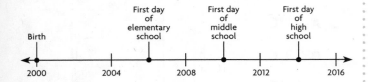

Which event occurred first?

 A birth

 B first day of elementary school

 C first day of middle school

 D first day of high school

19. A movie starts at 11:45 A.M. The movie is 1 hour and 50 minutes long. At what time does the movie end?

 A 9:55 P.M.

 B 1:35 P.M.

 C 9:55 A.M.

 D 1:35 A.M.

20. Julian paints a line that is 44 centimeters long. Reagan paints a line that is 19 centimeters shorter than Julian's line. How long is Reagan's line?

 A 63 centimeters

 B 36 centimeters

 C 35 centimeters

 D 25 centimeters

STOP

Chapter 12

Three-Dimensional Figures and Volume

Math in the Real World

Pia built a rectangular prism with cubes. The base of her prism has 12 centimeter cubes. If the prism was built with 108 centimeter cubes, what is the height of her prism?

What skills do I know that will help me solve this problem?

_____

_____

_____

What do I need to know that can help me solve this problem?

_____

_____

_____

_____

My solution to the problem:

Building Your Math Abilities

Before you begin to explore three-dimensional figures and volume, fill in the chart with what you know about three-dimensional figures and volume, and then, what you would like to learn. As you go through the chapter, add to the chart the things you have learned.

What I know . . .	What I want to know . . .	What I have learned . . .

Go Deeper

What additional questions do you have about three-dimensional figures and volume? Write your questions in the space below.

_____

_____

_____

_____

Three-Dimensional Figures

Solid figures have length, width, and height. They are also called **three-dimensional figures**.
Solid figures can be classified by the number of faces, edges, and vertices.
A **face** is a flat surface of a solid figure.
An **edge** is a line segment formed where two faces meet.
A **vertex** is a point where three or more edges meet. The plural of *vertex* is *vertices*.

sphere	There is no base.	

cylinder	The two bases are circles.	

A **pyramid** is a solid figure with one polygon base. The faces of a pyramid are triangles that meet at a common vertex.

A **prism** is a solid figure with two congruent polygons as bases. The faces of a prism are rectangles.

triangular pyramid	The base and faces are triangles.	

triangular prism	The two bases are triangles.	

rectangular pyramid	The base is a rectangle.	

rectangular prism	All faces are rectangles.	

Classify the solid figure. Write *prism, pyramid, cylinder,* or *sphere*.

The solid figure has one base.

The rest of its faces are triangles.

So, the solid figure is a ___pyramid___.

Classify each solid figure. Write *prism, pyramid, cylinder,* or *sphere*.

1.	2.	3.	4.

_____ _____ _____ _____

Classify the solid figure. Write *prism*, *pyramid*, *cylinder*, or *sphere*.

5.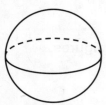

There are no bases.
There is 1 curved surface.

_____sphere_____

6.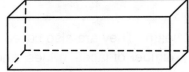

_____

7.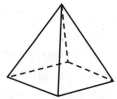

_____

Name the solid figure.

8.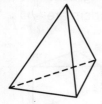

_____

9.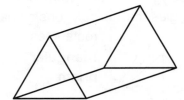

_____

10.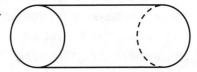

_____

11.

_____

12.

_____

13.

_____

Problem Solving REAL WORLD

14. Darrien is making a solid figure out of folded paper. His solid figure has six faces that are all rectangles. What solid figure does Darrien make?

_____

15. Nanako said she drew a square pyramid and that all of the faces are triangles. Is this possible? **Explain.**

_____

Name _____

Lesson **12.2**

Lesson Objective: Name, classify, compare, and contrast three-dimensional figures.

Compare and Contrast Three-Dimensional Figures

Three-dimensional figures have length, width, and height.

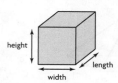

Look at the table. Which solid figure has 0 faces, 0 edges, and 0 vertices?

Solid Figure	Number of		
	Faces	Edges	Vertices
Cube	6	12	8
Cylinder	2	0	0
rectangular prism	6	12	8
rectangular pyramid	5	8	5
sphere	0	0	0

So, the ___sphere___ has 0 faces, 0 edges, and 0 vertices.

Name the solid figure that the object is shaped like.

1.

2.

3.

_____ _____ _____

Name the solid figure. Then write the number of faces, edges, and vertices.

4.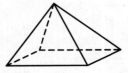

<u>rectangular pyramid</u>

<u>5 faces, 8 edges, 5</u>

<u>vertices</u>

5.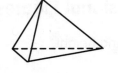

_____

_____

_____

6.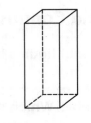

_____

_____

_____

Describe how the figures are alike and how they are different.

7. cube and rectangular prism

8. rectangular prism and rectangular pyramid

_____   _____

Use the Venn Diagram to compare and contrast solid figures. Write the names of the figures in the correct sections.

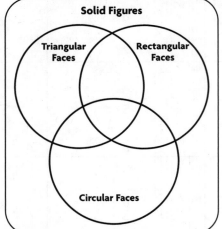

Problem Solving REAL WORLD

11. Sara has two wooden blocks. One block has 4 triangular faces and 1 rectangular face. The other has six square faces. What are the shapes of the wooden blocks?

_____

_____

12. Kyle's aquarium is shaped like a rectangular prism. The prism is longer than it is tall. Draw an example of what the aquarium might look like.

_____

_____

270

Lesson 12.3

Lesson Objective: Understand unit cubes and how they can be used to build a solid figure.

Unit Cubes and Solid Figures

A **unit cube** is a cube that has a length, width, and height of 1 unit. You can use unit cubes to build a rectangular prism.

1 unit
1 unit
1 unit

Count the number of cubes used to build the rectangular prism.

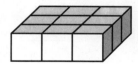

The length of the prism is made up of __8__ unit cubes.

The width of the prism is made up of __2__ unit cubes.

The height of the prism is made up of __1__ unit cube.

The number of unit cubes used to build the rectangular prism is __16__.

Count the number of unit cubes used to build each solid figure.

1.

_____ unit cubes

2.

_____ unit cubes

3.

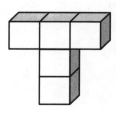

_____ unit cubes

4.

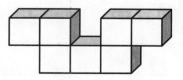

_____ unit cubes

Count the number of cubes used to build each solid figure.

5.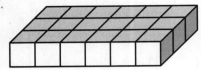

_____18_____ unit cubes

6.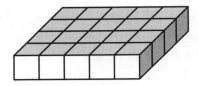

_____ unit cubes

7.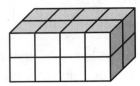

_____ unit cubes

8.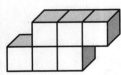

_____ unit cubes

9.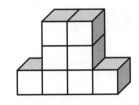

_____ unit cubes

10.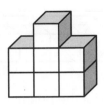

_____ unit cubes

Compare the number of unit cubes in each solid figure. Use <, >, or =.

11.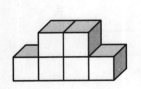

_____ unit cubes ◯ _____ unit cubes

12.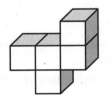

_____ unit cubes ◯ _____ unit cubes

Problem Solving REAL WORLD

13. A carton can hold 1,000 unit cubes that measure 1 inch by 1 inch by 1 inch. Describe the dimensions of the carton using unit cubes.

_____

_____

_____

_____

14. Peter uses unit cubes to build a figure in the shape of the letter X. What is the fewest unit cubes that Peter can use to build the figure?

_____

272

Find Volume of Prisms

Lesson **12.4**

Lesson Objective: Count unit cubes that fill a solid figure to find volume.

The **volume** of a rectangular prism is equal to the number of unit cubes that make up the prism. Each unit cube has a volume of 1 cubic unit.

Find the volume of the prism. 1 unit cube = 1 cubic inch

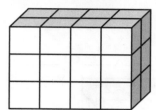

Step 1 Count the number of unit cubes in the bottom layer of the prism.

There are ____4____ unit cubes that make up the length of the first layer.

There are ____2____ unit cubes that make up the width of the first layer.

There is ____1____ unit cube that makes up the height of the first layer.

So, altogether, there are ____8____ unit cubes that make up the bottom layer of the prism.

Step 2 Count the number of layers of cubes that make up the prism.

The prism is made up of ____3____ layers of unit cubes.

Step 3 Find the total number of cubes that fill the prism.

Add the number of cubes per layer, or multiply the number of layers by the number of cubes in each layer.

8 + 8 + 8 ___24___ unit cubes or 3 × 8 = ___24___ unit cubes

Each unit cube has a volume of 1 cubic inch.

So, the volume of the prism is 24 × 1, or ___24___ cubic inches.

Use the unit given. Find the volume.

1.

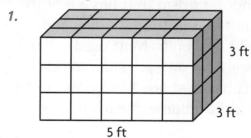

3 ft

3 ft

5 ft

Each cube = 1 cu ft

Volume = _____ cu _____

2.

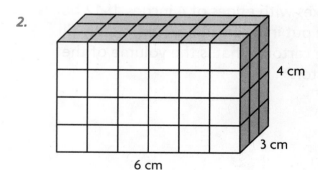

4 cm

3 cm

6 cm

Each cube = 1 cu cm

Volume = _____ cu _____

Use the unit given. Find the volume.

3.

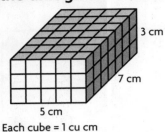

3 cm
7 cm
5 cm
Each cube = 1 cu cm

Volume = ___105___ cu ___cm___

4.

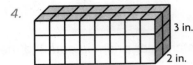

3 in.
2 in.
8 in.
Each cube = 1 cu in.

Volume = _____ cu _____

5.

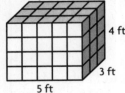

2 ft
4 ft
7 ft
Each cube = 1 cu ft

Volume = _____ cu _____

6.

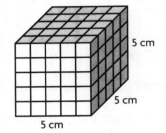

5 cm
5 cm
5 cm
Each cube = 1 cu cm

Volume = _____ cu _____

7. Compare the volumes. Write <, >, or =.

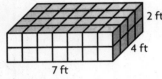

4 ft
3 ft
5 ft
Each cube = 1 cu ft

_____ cu ft ◯ _____ cu ft

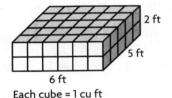

2 ft
5 ft
6 ft
Each cube = 1 cu ft

Problem Solving REAL WORLD

8. A manufacturer ships its product in boxes with edges of 4 inches. If 12 boxes are put in a carton and completely fill the carton, what is the volume of the carton?

_____

9. Matt and Mindy each built a rectangular prism that has a length of 5 units, a width of 2 units, and a height of 4 units. Matt used cubes that are 1 cm on each side. Mindy used cubes that are 1 in. on each side. What is the volume of each prism?

_____

_____

Name _____

Building Facts Fluency

Review Multiplication and Division Facts

Write the set of related facts for each of the arrays.

1.
• • • • • • • •
• • • • • • • •
• • • • • • • •
• • • • • • • •

_____ × _____ = _____

_____ × _____ = _____

_____ ÷ _____ = _____

_____ ÷ _____ = _____

2.
• • • • • • • •
• • • • • • • •
• • • • • • • •

_____ × _____ = _____

_____ × _____ = _____

_____ ÷ _____ = _____

_____ ÷ _____ = _____

Multiply.

3.

×	7
8	56
3	
9	
6	
7	

4.

×	9
3	
	63
	54
	45
9	

5. 9
  × 3

6. 4
  × 9

7. 8
  × 9

8. 5
  × 9

9. 9
  × 9

© Houghton Mifflin Harcourt Publishing Company

Building Facts Fluency

275

Name _____

Review Multiplication and Division Facts

Write four number sentences for each set of related facts.

1. 5, 7, 35 _____ _____ _____ _____

2. 6, 8, 48 _____ _____ _____ _____

Complete.

3. $4 \times 8 =$ _____ $32 \div 8 =$ _____

   $8 \times 4 =$ _____ $32 \div 4 =$ _____

4. $6 \times 7 =$ _____ $42 \div 7 =$ _____

   $7 \times 6 =$ _____ $42 \div 6 =$ _____

5. $8 \times 5 =$ _____ $40 \div 5 =$ _____

   $5 \times 8 =$ _____ $40 \div 8 =$ _____

6. $4 \times 9 =$ _____ $36 \div 9 =$ _____

   $9 \times 4 =$ _____ $36 \div 4 =$ _____

Divide.

7. $9 \overline{)45}$ 8. $5 \overline{)40}$ 9. $6 \overline{)54}$ 10. $7 \overline{)28}$

Read each question and choose the best answer.

1. Kennedy draws a solid figure with a triangle base. The solid figure has 4 faces, 6 edges, and 4 vertices. What solid figure did Kennedy draw?

   A cube

   B rectangular prism

   C triangular pyramid

   D square pyramid

2. Brian built a solid figure with unit cubes.

   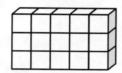

   How many unit cubes did he use for his figure?

   A 3   **B** 5

   C 15   **D** 23

3. Which of the following best classifies this three-dimensional figure?

   A triangular pyramid

   B rectangular pyramid

   C triangular prism

   D rectangular prism

4. Tristan sees a box of butter at the grocery store.

   What solid figure is the box of butter shaped like?

   A triangular pyramid

   B triangular prism

   C rectangular pyramid

   D rectangular prism

5. Erin filled a box with 1-centimeter cubes.

   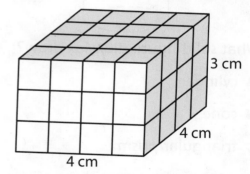

   What is the volume of the box?

   A 16 cubic centimeters

   B 32 cubic centimeters

   C 48 cubic centimeters

   D 64 cubic centimeters

GO ON

6. Gracie placed some unit cubes on the floor as shown below.

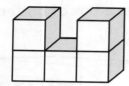

How many unit cubes did Gracie use?

A 4

B 5

C 6

D 11

7. Max drew this solid figure on his paper.

What solid figure did Max draw?

A cylinder

B cone

C triangular prism

D rectangular pyramid

8. Ashton stacked these unit cubes.

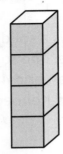

How many unit cubes did Ashton stack?

A 9

B 4

C 3

D 1

9. Amelia sees this solid figure.

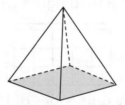

Which describes the solid figure?

A The solid figure has 4 faces, 6 edges, 4 vertices.

B The solid figure has 5 faces, 8 edges, 5 vertices.

C The solid figure has 6 faces, 12 edges, 8 vertices.

D The solid figure has 2 faces, 5 edges, 4 vertices.

10. A packing company makes boxes with edges each measuring 4 feet. What is the volume of the boxes?

A 16 square feet

B 64 square feet

C 16 cubic feet

D 64 cubic feet

11. Kelli is making a sculpture. She carves two bases with four sides each. She then carves four rectangular faces that connect the two bases. What three-dimensional figure did Kelli make?

   A triangular pyramid

   B triangular prism

   C rectangular prism

   D cylinder

12. Derek compares a cube and a square pyramid. Which statement is *not* true?

   A Both objects have a square base.

   B The 6 faces of the cube are squares.

   C The 4 faces of the pyramid are triangles.

   D Both objects have the same number of edges.

13. Which of the following best classifies this three-dimensional figure?

   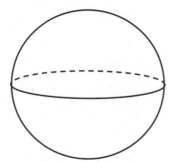

   A sphere

   B cylinder

   C rectangular prism

   D triangular pyramid

14. Alejandro built a rectangular prism with 1-inch cubes.

   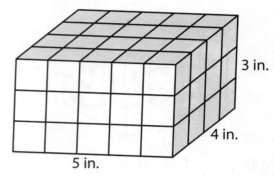

   What is the volume of the rectangular prism?

   A 100 cubic inches

   B 60 cubic inches

   C 40 cubic inches

   D 20 cubic inches

15. Amanda stacked these unit cubes.

   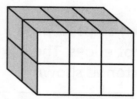

   How many unit cubes did Amanda stack?

A 6	**B** 12
C 14	**D** 15

16. Huy is playing with a toy.

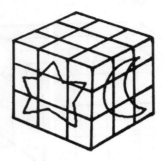

Which describes Huy's toy?

A The toy has 4 faces, 6 edges, 4 vertices.

B The toy has 5 faces, 8 edges, 5 vertices.

C The toy has 6 faces, 12 edges, 8 vertices.

D The toy has 3 faces, 9 edges, 7 vertices.

18. Nathaniel drew this solid figure on a poster.

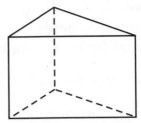

What solid figure did Nathaniel draw?

A triangular prism

B triangular pyramid

C cylinder

D rectangular prism

17. A company ships its products in boxes with 1-foot edges. The boxes are put into a carton as shown.

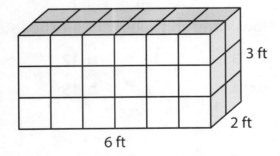

3 ft

2 ft

6 ft

What is the volume of the carton?

A 12 square feet

B 36 square feet

C 12 cubic feet

D 36 cubic feet

STOP

Chapter 13

Divide by 1-Digit Numbers

Math in the Real World

Four teachers bought 10 origami books and 100 packs of origami paper for their classrooms. They will share the cost of the items equally. How much should each teacher pay?

The Craft Store	
Item	Price
Origami Book	$24 each
Origami Paper	$6 per pack
Origami Kit	$8 each

What skills do I know that will help me solve this problem?

_____

_____

_____

What do I need to know that can help me solve this problem?

_____

_____

_____

_____

My solution to the problem:

Building Your Math Abilities

Before you begin to explore dividing by 1-digit numbers, fill in the chart with what you know about dividing by 1-digit numbers, and then, what you would like to learn. As you go through the chapter, add to the chart the things you have learned.

What I know . . .	What I want to know . . .	What I have learned . . .

Go Deeper

What additional questions do you have about dividing by 1-digit numbers? Write your questions in the space below.

_____

_____

_____

_____

Estimate Quotients Using Multiples

Find two numbers the quotient of 142 ÷ 5 is between. Then estimate the quotient.

You can use multiples to estimate. A **multiple** of a number is the product of a number and a counting number.

Step 1 Think: What number multiplied by 5 is about 142?
Since 142 is greater than 10 × 5, or 50, use counting numbers 10, 20, 30, and so on to find multiples of 5.

Step 2 Multiply 5 by multiples of 10 and make a table.

Counting Number	10	20	30	40
Multiple of 5	50	100	150	200

Step 3 Use the table to find multiples of 5 closest to 142.

$20 \times 5 = $ __100__

$30 \times 5 = $ __150__   ⟵ 142 is between __100__ and __150__.

142 is closest to __150__, so 142 ÷ 5 is about __30__.

Find two numbers the quotient is between. Then estimate the quotient.

1. 136 ÷ 6

   between _____ and _____

   about _____

2. 95 ÷ 3

   between _____ and _____

   about _____

3. 124 ÷ 9

   between _____ and _____

   about _____

4. 238 ÷ 7

   between _____ and _____

   about _____

Find two numbers the quotient is between. Then estimate the quotient.

5. $175 \div 6$

   between 20 and 30

   about 30

Think: $6 \times 20 = 120$ and $6 \times 30 = 180$.
So, $175 \div 6$ is between 20 and 30. Since 175 is closer to 180 than to 120, the quotient is about 30.

6. $53 \div 3$

7. $75 \div 4$

8. $215 \div 9$

9. $284 \div 5$

10. $191 \div 3$

11. $100 \div 7$

12. $438 \div 7$

13. $103 \div 8$

14. $255 \div 9$

Problem Solving REAL WORLD

15. Joy collected 287 aluminum cans in 6 hours. About how many cans did she collect per hour?

16. Paul sold 162 cups of lemonade in 5 hours. About how many cups of lemonade did he sell each hour?

284

Lesson 13.2

Lesson Objective: Use models to divide whole numbers that do not divide evenly.

Investigate • Remainders

Use counters to find the quotient and remainder.

$$9\overline{)26}$$

- Use 26 counters to represent the dividend, 26.

- Since you are dividing 26 by 9, draw 9 circles.
  Divide the 26 counters into 9 equal-sized groups.

- There are 2 counters in each circle, so the quotient is **2**.
  There are 8 counters left over, so the remainder is **8**.

$$\overset{2\ r8}{9\overline{)26}}$$

Divide. Draw a quick picture to help.

$$7\overline{)66}$$

- Use 66 counters to represent the dividend, 66.

- Since you are dividing 66 by 7, draw 7 circles.
  Divide 66 counters into 7 equal-sized groups.

- There are 9 counters in each circle, so the quotient is **9**.
  There are 3 counters left over, so the remainder is **3**.

$$\overset{9\ r3}{7\overline{)66}}$$

Use counters to find the quotient and remainder.

1. $6\overline{)19}$

2. $3\overline{)14}$

Divide. Draw a quick picture to help.

3. $39 \div 4$
_____

4. $29 \div 3$
_____

Use counters to find the quotient and remainder.

5. 13 ÷ 4

    _____3 r1_____

6. 24 ÷ 7

    _____

7. 39 ÷ 5

    _____

8. 36 ÷ 8

    _____

9. 6)‾27‾

    _____

10. 25 ÷ 9

    _____

11. 3)‾17‾

    _____

12. 26 ÷ 4

    _____

Divide. Draw a quick picture to help.

13. 14 ÷ 3

14. 5)‾29‾

Problem Solving  REAL WORLD

15. What is the quotient and remainder in the division problem modeled below?

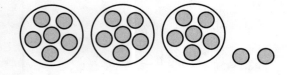

_____

16. Mark drew the following model and said it represented the problem 21 ÷ 4. Is Mark's model correct? If so, what is the quotient and remainder? If not, what is the correct quotient and remainder?

_____

_____

_____

_____

Lesson **13.3**

Lesson Objective: Divide tens, hundreds, and thousands by whole numbers through 10.

Divide Tens, Hundreds, and Thousands

You can use base-ten blocks, place value, and basic facts to divide.

Divide. 240 ÷ 3

Use base-ten blocks.	Use place value.
Step 1 Draw a quick picture to show 240.	**Step 1** Identify the basic fact to use. Use <u>24 ÷ 3</u>.
Step 2 You cannot divide 2 hundreds into 3 equal groups. Rename 2 hundreds as tens. 240 = <u>24</u> tens	**Step 2** Use place value to rewrite 240 as tens. 240 = <u>24</u> tens
Step 3 Separate the tens into 3 equal groups to divide. There are 3 groups of <u>8</u> tens. Write the answer. 240 ÷ 3 = <u>80</u>	**Step 3** Divide. 24 tens ÷ 3 = <u>8</u> tens = <u>80</u> Write the answer. 240 ÷ 3 = <u>80</u>

Use basic facts and place value to find the quotient.

1. 280 ÷ 4

   What division fact can you use?

   _____

   280 = _____ tens

   28 tens ÷ 4 = _____ tens

   280 ÷ 4 = _____

2. 1,800 ÷ 9

   What division fact can you use?

   _____

   1,800 = _____ hundreds

   18 hundreds ÷ 9 = _____ hundreds

   1,800 ÷ 9 = _____

3. 560 ÷ 7 = _____

4. 180 ÷ 6 = _____

5. 1,500 ÷ 5 = _____

6. 3,200 ÷ 4 = _____

Use basic facts and place value to find the quotient.

7. $3,600 \div 4 =$ ___900___

Think: 3,600 is 36 hundreds.

Use the basic fact $36 \div 4 = 9$.

So, 36 hundreds $\div 4 = 9$ hundreds, or 900.

8. $240 \div 6 =$ _____

9. $5,400 \div 9 =$ _____

10. $300 \div 5 =$ _____

11. $4,800 \div 6 =$ _____

12. $420 \div 7 =$ _____

13. $150 \div 3 =$ _____

14. $6,300 \div 7 =$ _____

15. $1,200 \div 4 =$ _____

16. $360 \div 6 =$ _____

Find the quotient.

17. $28 \div 4 =$ _____

18. $18 \div 3 =$ _____

19. $45 \div 9 =$ _____

$280 \div 4 =$ _____

$180 \div 3 =$ _____

$450 \div 9 =$ _____

$2,800 \div 4 =$ _____

$1,800 \div 3 =$ _____

$4,500 \div 9 =$ _____

Problem Solving REAL WORLD

20. At an assembly, 180 students sit in 9 equal rows. How many students sit in each row? Make a model to solve.

_____

21. Hilary can read 560 words in 7 minutes. How many words can Hilary read in 1 minute?

_____

22. A company produces 7,200 gallons of bottled water each day. The company puts 8 one-gallon bottles in each carton. How many cartons are needed to hold all the one-gallon bottles produced in one day?

_____

23. An airplane flew 2,400 miles in 4 hours. If the plane flew the same number of miles each hour, how many miles did it fly in 1 hour?

_____

Estimate Quotients Using Compatible Numbers

Compatible numbers are numbers that are easy to compute mentally. In division, one compatible number divides evenly into the other. Think of the multiples of a number to help you find compatible numbers.

Estimate. 6)216

Step 1 Think of these multiples of 6:

6   12   18   24   30   36   42   48   54

Find multiples that are close to the first 2 digits of the dividend.
__18__ tens and __24__ tens are both close to __21__ tens. You can use either or both numbers to estimate the quotient.

Step 2 Estimate using compatible numbers.

216 ÷ 6   216 ÷ 6
↓   ↓
180 ÷ 6 = 30   240 ÷ 6 = 40

So, 216 ÷ 6 is between __30__ and __40__.

Step 3 Decide whether the estimate is closer to 30 or 40.

216 − 180 = 36   240 − 216 = 24

216 is closer to 240, so use __40__ as the estimate.

Use compatible numbers to estimate the quotient.

1. 3)25

2. 6)546

3. 4)254

_____   _____   _____

4. 5)314

5. 2)157

6. 8)28

_____   _____   _____

Use compatible numbers to estimate the quotient.

7. $389 \div 4$
8. $35 \div 3$
9. $784 \div 8$
10. $179 \div 9$

$400 \div 4 = 100$

11. $315 \div 8$
12. $16 \div 7$
13. $415 \div 7$
14. $474 \div 9$

Use compatible numbers to find two estimates that the quotient is between.

15. $162 \div 3$
16. $259 \div 6$
17. $113 \div 2$
18. $175 \div 9$

19. $23 \div 8$
20. $164 \div 5$
21. $55 \div 7$
22. $364 \div 6$

Problem Solving REAL WORLD

23. A CD store sold 346 CDs in 7 days. About the same number of CDs were sold each day. About how many CDs did the store sell each day?

24. Marcus has 731 books. He puts about the same number of books on each of 9 shelves in his bookcase. About how many books are on each shelf?

Investigate • Division and the Distributive Property

Divide. 678 ÷ 6

Use the Distributive Property and quick pictures to break apart numbers to make them easier to divide.

Step 1 Draw a quick picture to show 678.

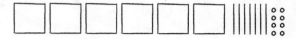

Step 2 Think about how to break apart 678.
Break apart 600. You know 6 hundreds ÷ 6 = 100.
Break apart 78.
You know 6 tens ÷ 6 = 10, so use 78 = **60 + 18**.
Draw a quick picture to show 6 hundreds, 6 tens, and 18 ones.

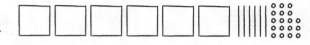

Step 3 Draw circles to show
6 hundreds ÷ 6, 6 tens ÷ 6, and
18 ones ÷ 6. Your drawing shows
the use of the Distributive Property.

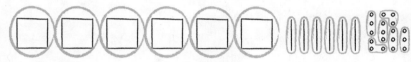

$678 ÷ 6 = \underline{(600 ÷ 6)} + \underline{(60 ÷ 6)} + \underline{(18 ÷ 6)}$

Step 4 Add the quotients to find 678 ÷ 6.

$$678 ÷ 6 = (600 ÷ 6) + (60 ÷ 6) + (18 ÷ 6)$$
$$= \underline{\quad 100 \quad} + \underline{\quad 10 \quad} + \underline{\quad 3 \quad}$$
$$= \underline{\quad 113 \quad}$$

Use quick pictures to model the quotient.

1. 84 ÷ 4 = _____

2. 654 ÷ 3 = _____

3. 68 ÷ 2 = _____

4. 165 ÷ 5 = _____

5. 96 ÷ 8 = _____

6. 90 ÷ 6 = _____

Find the quotient.

7. $54 \div 3 = ($ ___30___ $\div\ 3) + ($ ___24___ $\div\ 3)$

    $=$ ___10___ $+$ ___8___

    $=$ ___18___

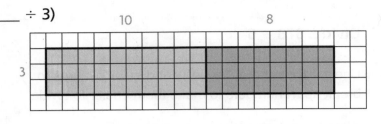

8. $81 \div 3 =$ _____

9. $232 \div 4 =$ _____

10. $305 \div 5 =$ _____

11. $246 \div 6 =$ _____

12. $69 \div 3 =$ _____

13. $477 \div 9 =$ _____

14. $224 \div 7 =$ _____

15. $72 \div 4 =$ _____

16. $315 \div 3 =$ _____

Problem Solving REAL WORLD

17. Cecily picked 219 apples. She divided the apples equally into 3 baskets. How many apples are in each basket?

_____

18. Jordan has 260 basketball cards. He divides them into 4 equal groups. How many cards are in each group?

_____

19. The Wilsons drove 324 miles in 6 hours. If they drove the same number of miles each hour, how many miles did they drive in 1 hour?

_____

20. Phil has 189 stamps to put into his stamp album. He puts the same number of stamps on each of 9 pages. How many stamps does Phil put on each page?

_____

1. Look at the model.

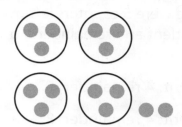

   What division does the model show?

   A 4 ÷ 3

   B 12 ÷ 3

   C 12 ÷ 4

   D 14 ÷ 4

2. Brooke and two friends share 1,509 pennies equally. About how many pennies did each girl receive?

   A about 400

   B about 500

   C about 600

   D about 750

3. The bakery made 105 apple muffins. They will put the muffins into boxes of 6. About how many boxes will there be?

   A about 18

   B about 16

   C about 14

   D about 12

4. Jackie is using the Distributive Property to divide 96 by 8. Which does **not** show an effective way to break apart the dividend?

   A 96 ÷ 8 = (80 ÷ 8) + (16 ÷ 8)

   B 96 ÷ 8 = (72 ÷ 8) + (24 ÷ 8)

   C 96 ÷ 8 = (64 ÷ 8) + (32 ÷ 8)

   D 96 ÷ 8 = (90 ÷ 8) + (6 ÷ 8)

5. Badri put 700 pennies in 7 equal rolls. How many pennies were in each roll?

   A 1

   B 10

   C 100

   D 1,000

6. Between which two numbers is the quotient of 90 ÷ 7?

   A between 10 and 11

   B between 12 and 13

   C between 13 and 14

   D between 14 and 15

GO ON

7. Which number sentence is **not** true?

   A $200 \div 5 = 4$

   B $350 \div 7 = 50$

   C $4,800 \div 6 = 800$

   D $8,100 \div 9 = 900$

8. Claire arranged 37 counters into 4 groups of 8. There were 5 counters left over. What quotient and remainder did she model?

   A   quotient: 4 remainder: 5

   B   quotient: 4 remainder: 8

   C   quotient: 8 remainder: 5

   D   quotient: 8 remainder: 4

9. Paige has 54 books. She wants to place the same number of books on each of 2 shelves. Explain a way to use the Distributive Property to find the number of books she will place on each shelf.

   _____

   _____

   _____

   _____

10. Luke has 214 baseball cards. He is putting them into stacks of 7 cards. About how many stacks of cards will Luke have? Explain how to use compatible numbers to solve.

   _____

   _____

   _____

   _____

(STOP)

        Apply Your Understanding

Name _____

Lesson Objective: Use repeated subtraction and multiples to find quotients.

Investigate. Divide Using Repeated Subtraction

You can use repeated subtraction to divide. Use repeated subtraction to solve the problem.

Nestor has 108 shells to make bracelets. He needs 9 shells for each bracelet. How many bracelets can he make?

Divide. 108 ÷ 9

Write $9\overline{)108}$

Step 1

Subtract the divisor until the remainder is less than the divisor. Record a 1 each time you subtract.

So, Nestor can make 12 bracelets. He will have 0 shells left.

```
  108
 -  9    1
 ───
   99
 -  9    1
 ───
   90
 -  9    1
 ───
   81
 -  9    1
 ───
   72
 -  9    1
 ───
   63
 -  9    1
 ───
   54
 -  9    1
 ───
   45
 -  9    1
 ───
   36
 -  9    1
 ───
   27
 -  9    1
 ───
   18
 -  9    1
 ───
    9
 -  9  +  1
 ───   ───
    0     12
```

Step 2

Count the number of times you subtracted the divisor, 9.

9 is subtracted 12 times with 0 left.

$$108 \div 9$$
$$\underline{12}$$

Use repeated subtraction to divide.

1. 30 ÷ 4

2. 324 ÷ 5

3. 247 ÷ 7

Use repeated subtraction to divide.

4. $42 \div 7 = \underline{\quad 6 \quad}$

$$
\begin{array}{rr}
42 & \\
-\ 7 & 1 \\
\hline
35 & \\
-\ 7 & 1 \\
\hline
28 & \\
-\ 7 & 1 \\
\hline
21 & \\
-\ 7 & 1 \\
\hline
14 & \\
-\ 7 & 1 \\
\hline
7 & \\
-\ 7 & +\ 1 \\
\hline
0 & 6
\end{array}
$$

5. $372 \div 4 = \underline{\qquad\qquad}$

6. $693 \div 3 = \underline{\qquad\qquad}$

7. $35 \div 4 \ \underline{\qquad\qquad}$

8. $593 \div 10 \ \underline{\qquad\qquad}$

Draw a number line to divide.

9. $70 \div 5 = \underline{\qquad\qquad}$

Problem Solving REAL WORLD

10. Gretchen has 348 small shells. She uses 6 shells to make one pair of earrings. How many pairs of earrings can she make?

11. Mr. Chase has 463 pencils to share with 5 classrooms. How many pencils will each class be given?

Divide Using Partial Quotients

You can use partial quotients to divide.

Divide. $492 \div 4$

Step 1 Subtract greater multiples of the divisor. Repeat if needed.

Step 2 Subtract lesser multiples of the divisor. Repeat until the remaining number is less than the divisor.

Step 3 Add the partial quotients.

Partial quotients

```
  4)492
   -400      100 × 4      100
    92
   - 80       20 × 4       20
    12
   - 12        3 × 4      + 3
     0                    ___
                          123
```

Use rectangular models to record partial quotients.

```
        100                         492
  4  |  400      | 80 | 12 |      - 400
                                    92

        100        20               92
  4  |  400      | 80 | 12 |      - 80
                                    12

        100        20   3           12
  4  |  400      | 80 | 12 |      - 12
                                     0
```

$$\frac{100}{\quad} + \frac{20}{\quad} + \frac{3}{\quad} = \frac{123}{\quad}$$

Divide. Use partial quotients.

1.
```
  3)6 5 7
  _____    100 × __     100
  _____    100 × __    _____
  _____    __ × __     _____
  _____    __ × __   + _____
```

Divide. Use rectangular models to record the partial quotients.

2. $852 \div 6 =$ _____

Divide. Use partial quotients.

3.
```
        23
   8)184
   - 80   10 × 8    10
    104
   - 80   10 × 8    10
     24
   - 24    3 × 8    +3
      0              23
```

4. 6)258

5. 5)634

Divide. Use rectangular models to record the partial quotients.

6. $246 \div 3 =$ _____

7. $126 \div 2 =$ _____

8. $605 \div 5 =$ _____

Divide. Use either way to record the partial quotients.

9. $492 \div 3 =$ _____

10. $224 \div 7 =$ _____

11. $695 \div 4 =$ _____

Problem Solving REAL WORLD

12. Allison took 112 photos on vacation. She wants to put them in a photo album that holds 4 photos on each page. How many pages can she fill?

13. Hector bought 350 bottles of water. He drinks 6 bottles of water each day. How many days worth of water did Hector buy?

Lesson 13.8

Lesson Objective: Use base-ten blocks to model division with regrouping.

Investigate. Model Division with Regrouping

You can use base-ten blocks to model division with regrouping.
Marissa has 565 pennies. She placed the same number
of pennies in 4 piles. How many pennies are in each pile?

Use base-ten blocks to find the quotient 565 ÷ 4.

Step 1 Show 565 with base-ten blocks.

Step 2 Draw 4 circles to represent dividing
565 into 4 equal groups. Share the hundreds
equally among the 4 groups.

Step 3 Regroup leftover hundreds as tens.

Step 4 Share the tens and ones equally among
the 4 groups.

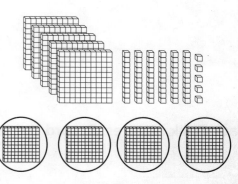

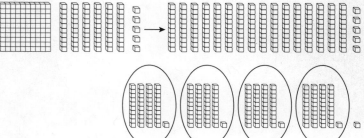

There are __1__ hundred(s), __4__ ten(s), and
__1__ one(s) in each group with __1__ left over.

So, Marissa placed ___141___ pennies in each pile and has __1__ penny left over.

Divide. Use base-ten blocks.

1. 89 ÷ 2

   _____

2. 374 ÷ 3

   _____

3. 168 ÷ 5

   _____

Divide. Use base-ten blocks.

4. 63 ÷ 4 __15 r3__

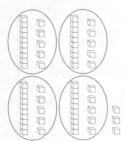

5. 413 ÷ 3 _____

Divide. Draw quick pictures. Record the steps.

6. 385 ÷ 5 _____

7. 597 ÷ 4 _____

Problem Solving REAL WORLD

8. Tamara sold 192 cold drinks during her 4-hour shift at a festival food stand. If she sold the same number of drinks each hour, how many cold drinks did she sell each hour?

_____

_____

9. Dane has 357 comic books. He is packing them into 5 boxes. He packs the same number of comic books in each box. How many comic books are in each box?

_____

_____

Lesson Objective: Use place value to determine where to place the first digit of a quotient.

Place the First Digit

Divide. 763 × 3 = ▪

Step 1 Estimate. Then divide the hundreds.

Think: 3 × 1 hundred = 3 hundreds
       3 × 2 hundreds = 6 hundreds
       3 × 3 hundreds = 9 hundreds

3 × 3 hundreds is too large.
Use 2 hundreds as an estimate.

$$\begin{array}{r} 2 \\ 3\overline{)763} \\ -\,6 \\ \hline 1 \end{array}$$

← Divide 7 hundreds by 3.
← Multiply. 3 × 2 hundreds
← Subtract.

Step 2 Bring down the tens digit. Then divide the tens.

$$\begin{array}{r} 2 \\ 3\overline{)763} \\ -\,6\downarrow \\ \hline 16 \end{array}$$

← Bring down the 6.

$$\begin{array}{r} 25 \\ 3\overline{)763} \\ -\,6 \\ \hline 16 \\ -\,15 \\ \hline 1 \end{array}$$

← Divide 16 tens by 3.

← Multiply. 3 × 5 tens
← Subtract.

Step 3 Bring down the ones digit. Then divide the ones.

$$\begin{array}{r} 25 \\ 3\overline{)763} \\ -\,6 \\ \hline 16 \\ -\,15 \\ \hline 13 \end{array}$$

← Bring down the 3.

$$\begin{array}{r} 254 \\ 3\overline{)763} \\ -\,6 \\ \hline 16 \\ -\,15 \\ \hline 13 \\ -\,12 \\ \hline 1 \end{array}$$

← Divide 13 ones by 3.

← Multiply. 3 × 4 ones
← Subtract.

Step 4 Check to make sure that the remainder is less than the divisor. Write the answer.

$$\begin{array}{r} 254 \text{ r1} \\ 3\overline{)763} \end{array}$$ 1 < 3

Divide.

1. 2$\overline{)531}$

2. 4$\overline{)628}$

3. 9$\overline{)349}$

4. 7$\overline{)794}$

Divide.

5. $\quad\begin{array}{r}62\\3\overline{)186}\\-18\!\!\downarrow\\\hline06\\-6\\\hline0\end{array}$

6. $4\overline{)298}$

7. $3\overline{)461}$

8. $9\overline{)315}$

9. $2\overline{)766}$

10. $4\overline{)604}$

11. $6\overline{)796}$

12. $5\overline{)449}$

13. $6\overline{)756}$

14. $7\overline{)521}$

15. $5\overline{)675}$

16. $8\overline{)933}$

Problem Solving REAL WORLD

17. There are 132 projects in the science fair. If 8 projects can fit in a row, how many full rows of projects can be made? How many projects are in the row that is not full?

18. There are 798 calories in six 10-ounce bottles of apple juice. How many calories are there in one 10-ounce bottle of apple juice?

302

Lesson Objective: Divide multidigit numbers by 1-digit divisors.

Divide by 1-Digit Numbers

Divide. 766 ÷ 6 = ▇

Step 1 Use place value to place the first digit.
Think: 7 hundreds can be shared among 6 groups without regrouping.

Step 2 Bring down the tens digit. Then divide the tens.

```
      1
6)766
   - 6↓
     16
```
← Bring down the 6.

```
     12
6)766
   - 6
     16
   -12
      4
```
← Divide 16 tens by 6.
← Multiply. 6 × 2 tens
← Subtract.

Step 3 Bring down the ones digit. Then divide the ones.

```
     12
6)766
   - 6
     16
   -12↓
     46
```
← Bring down the 6.

```
    127
6)766
   - 6
     16
   -12
     46
   - 42
      4
```
← Divide 46 ones by 6.
← Multiply. 6 × 7 ones
← Subtract.

Step 4 Check to make sure that the remainder is less than the divisor. Write the answer.

```
   127 r4      4 < 6
6)766
```

Step 5 Use multiplication and addition to check your answer.

```
    127
  ×   6
    762
  +   4
    766
```

Divide and check.

1. 4)868

2. 2)657

3. 7)849

4.
$$
\begin{array}{r}
318 \\
2)\overline{636} \\
-6\downarrow \\
\hline
03 \\
-2\downarrow \\
\hline
16 \\
-16 \\
\hline
0
\end{array}
\qquad
\begin{array}{r}
318 \\
\times\ 2 \\
\hline
636
\end{array}
$$

5. $4)\overline{631}$

6. $8)\overline{906}$

7. $6)\overline{679}$

8. $4)\overline{984}$

9. $5)\overline{754}$

Problem Solving REAL WORLD

Use the table for 10 and 11.

10. The Briggs rented a car for 5 weeks. What was the cost of their rental car per week?

_____

11. The Lees split the cost of their rental car evenly between 4 family members. How much did each person pay. Explain what your answer means.

Rental Car Costs	
Family	**Total Cost**
Lee	$626
Brigg	$985
Santo	$328

Algebra · Patterns in Division

You can use basic facts and patterns to find quotients.

Use basic fact patterns to find the quotient of 36,000 ÷ 60**.**

Step 1 Find the basic fact.

36,000 ÷ 60

The basic fact is 36 ÷ 6 = 6.

Step 2 Look at patterns of zeros in division.

36 ÷ 6 = 6	36 ÷ 6 = 6	**Think:** The total number of zeros in the divisor and the quotient is equal to the number of zeros in the dividend.
360 ÷ 6 = 60	360 ÷ 60 = 6	
3,600 ÷ 6 = 600	3,600 ÷ 600 = 6	

Step 3 Use the pattern of zeros to find the quotient.

36,000 ÷ 60

There are 3 zeros in the dividend and 1 zero in the divisor, so there should be
3 − 1 = 2 zeros in the quotient.

36,000 ÷ 60 = 600

So, 36,000 ÷ 60 = **600**.

Use basic facts and patterns to find the quotient.

1. 40 ÷ 2

2. 160 ÷ 8

3. $270 ÷ 90

4. 42,000 ÷ 7,000

_____   _____   _____   _____

5. 500 ÷ 50

6. 120 ÷ 40

7. 480 ÷ 6

8. 560 ÷ 70

_____   _____   _____   _____

9. 6,300 ÷ 7

10. 60,000 ÷ 2,000

11. 3,000 ÷ 30

12. $4,500 ÷ 50

_____   _____   _____   _____

Use basic facts and patterns to find the quotient.

13. $60 \div 10$

       6
    ‾‾‾‾‾‾‾‾‾‾‾

14. $140 \div 7$

_____

15. $\$18,000 \div 9,000$

_____

16. $480 \div 6$

_____

17. $40,000 \div 5,000$

_____

18. $160 \div 40$

_____

19. $360 \div 6$

_____

20. $560 \div 80$

_____

21. $2,400 \div 3$

_____

22. $\$2,000 \div 10$

_____

23. $6,300 \div 70$

_____

24. $4,200 \div 60$

_____

25. $81,000 \div 90$

_____

26. $80,000 \div 2,000$

_____

27. $90,000 \div 30$

_____

28. $\$35,000 \div 50$

_____

Problem Solving  REAL WORLD

29. A warehouse stored 10 crates of paper. The paper weighed a total of 7,000 pounds. How much did one crate of paper weigh?

_____

30. An office bought 8 office chairs for a total of $720. Each chair came with a $15 mail-in rebate. After the rebate, how much money did each chair cost?

_____

Name _____

Dividing by 1-Digit Divisors

Decide whether the first number in the pair is divisible by the second.
Write *divisible* or *not divisible*.

1. 17; 4

   _____

2. 35; 3

   _____

3. 200; 5

   _____

4. 70; 10

   _____

5. 95; 5

   _____

6. 29; 3

   _____

7. 65; 10

   _____

8. 12; 6

   _____

9. 120; 4

   _____

Circle the best estimate.

10. $85 \div 9$
    a. 7
    b. 8
    c. 9

11. $49 \div 5$
    a. 8
    b. 9
    c. 10

12. $19 \div 5$
    a. 3
    b. 4
    c. 5

Estimate. Decide if the quotient will be greater than 10. Write *yes* or *no*.

13. $2\overline{)35}$

14. $5\overline{)62}$

15. $9\overline{)75}$

16. $6\overline{)52}$

17. $8\overline{)84}$

18. $7\overline{)52}$

Name _____

Dividing by 1-Digit Divisors

Divide. Check your answers by multiplying.

1. $3\overline{)67}$ 2. $4\overline{)46}$ 3. $2\overline{)85}$ 4. $5\overline{)58}$ 5. $2\overline{)49}$

6. $4\overline{)85}$ 7. $3\overline{)94}$ 8. $2\overline{)65}$ 9. $3\overline{)38}$ 10. $7\overline{)89}$

Divide.

11. $2\overline{)462}$ 12. $3\overline{)669}$ 13. $7\overline{)924}$ 14. $5\overline{)585}$

15. $4\overline{)952}$ 16. $3\overline{)474}$ 17. $6\overline{)426}$ 18. $4\overline{)732}$

19. $8\overline{)9,842}$ 20. $9\overline{)5,581}$ 21. $5\overline{)9,250}$ 22. $7\overline{)8,123}$

Find the dividend or divisor.

23. $\boxed{} \div 5 = 5$ 24. $56 \div \boxed{} = 7$ 25. $46 \div \boxed{}$ 5 r1

26. $26 \div \boxed{}$ 4 r2   27. $50 \div \boxed{}$ 8 r2   28. $66 \div \boxed{}$ 8 r2

Read each question and choose the best answer.

1. John is putting apples into bags. He is placing 4 apples into each bag. How many bags can John fill with 120 apples?

   A 3

   B 4

   C 30

   D 40

2. Chase needs to divide these base-ten blocks into 4 equal groups.

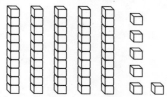

   Which model shows how many should be in each group?

   A

   B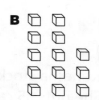

   C 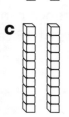   **D**

3. Look at the model.

   What division does the model show?

   A 6 ÷ 3   **B** 6 ÷ 4

   C 18 ÷ 3   **D** 19 ÷ 3

4. Drew writes a division problem to find out how many stamps he should put on each page of the 9 pages in his album. He has 288 stamps. In what place is the first digit of the quotient?

   A ones

   B tens

   C hundreds

   D thousands

5. Blake is using bricks to build a planter. He has 72 bricks in his truck. He can carry 12 bricks at a time. Which number sentence can be used to find the number of trips Blake will have to take from his truck to the building site?

   A 72 − 12 − 12 − 12 − 12 − 12 − 12 = 0

   B 72 − 12 = 60

   C 72 + 12 = 84

   D 72 − 24 − 24 − 12 = 12

GO ON

6. A restaurant has 77 chairs total. There are 8 chairs at each table. About how many tables are in the restaurant?

   A about 7

   B about 8

   C about 9

   D about 10

7. Ivy rode her bike 2,100 meters in 7 minutes. How many meters does she bike in 1 minute?

   A   3 meters

   B   30 meters

   C   300 meters

   D 3,000 meters

8. Jade draws this model to find 198 ÷ 9.

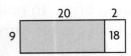

   What partial dividend is missing from the model?

   A 18

   B 29

   C 180

   D 1,800

9. There are 763 people signed up for a race. There are 7 volunteers working at the registration desk. Each volunteer helps the same number of people. How many people does each volunteer help?

   A 18

   B 19

   C 108

   D 109

10. A landscaper plants 207 bushes in 9 equal rows at a new park. How many bushes does the landscaper plant in each row?

    A 20

    B 21

    C 23

    D 25

11. Kenesha stocks shelves at a grocery store. She puts 65 cans of green beans onto the shelves. Which number sentence can be used to find how many rows of 15 cans of green beans there are?

    A $65 - 15 = 50$

    B $65 + 15 = 80$

    C $65 - 30 - 15 = 20$

    D $65 - 15 - 15 - 15 - 15 = 5$

GO ON

12. The Distributive Property can help you divide. Which is not an effective way to break apart the dividend to find the quotient of 477 ÷ 9?

   A (450 ÷ 9) + (27 ÷ 9)

   B (400 ÷ 9) + (77 ÷ 9)

   C (360 ÷ 9) + (117 ÷ 9)

   D (270 ÷ 9) + (207 ÷ 9)

13. Kate needs to divide these base-ten blocks into 5 equal groups.

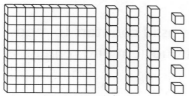

Which model shows how many should be in each group?

   A
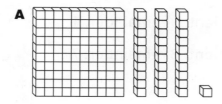

   B
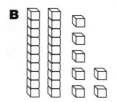

   C
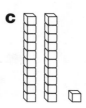

   D
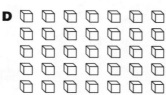

14. Faith is planting seeds for a greenhouse. She plants 9 seeds in each container. If Faith has 391 seeds, about how many containers will she use?

   A about 30

   B about 40

   C about 300

   D about 400

15. Between which two numbers is the quotient of 49 ÷ 3?

   A between 15 and 16

   B between 16 and 17

   C between 17 and 18

   D between 18 and 19

16. Ms. Baker pays $798 for 7 nights at a hotel. She uses division to find out how much she paid per night. In what place is the first digit of the quotient?

   A thousands

   B hundreds

   C tens

   D ones

GO ON

17. Which number sentence is **not** true?

    A $240 \div 8 = 40$

    B $560 \div 8 = 70$

    C $3,500 \div 7 = 500$

    D $9,000 \div 3 = 3,000$

18. A school bought 5 projectors for a total of $2,000. How much did each project cost?

    A $4

    B $40

    C $400

    D $4,000

19. Students in the third, fourth, and fifth grades made 510 balloon animals. Each grade made the same number of animals. How many balloon animals did each grade make?

    A 180

    B 170

    C 18

    D 17

20. James used counters to model $5\overline{)47}$. What quotient and remainder did he find?

    A quotient: 10 remainder: 3

    B quotient: 9 remainder: 2

    C quotient: 9 remainder: 1

    D quotient: 8 remainder: 7

STOP